ENGLISH PLAYS OF THE
NINETEENTH CENTURY

ENGLISH PLAYS

OF THE

NINETEENTH CENTURY

===

I. *Dramas 1800–1850*

===

EDITED BY MICHAEL R. BOOTH

OXFORD

AT THE CLARENDON PRESS

1969

Oxford University Press, Ely House, London W. 1

GLASGOW NEW YORK TORONTO MELBOURNE WELLINGTON
CAPE TOWN SALISBURY IBADAN NAIROBI LUSAKA ADDIS ABABA
BOMBAY CALCUTTA MADRAS KARACHI LAHORE DACCA
KUALA LUMPUR HONG KONG SINGAPORE TOKYO

PRINTED IN GREAT BRITAIN

FOREWORD

In recent years both the theatre and its historians have been more concerned than they used to be with the plays and theatre of nineteenth-century England. The stage has discovered that audiences actually enjoy revivals of nineteenth-century plays. The actor can find interest in a century where his highly individual ancestor was free from the tyranny of the producer and where acting styles, in tragedy and strong drama especially, were marked by a colour, a rhetoric, and a larger-than-life passion too often absent in the theatre of today. The historian wishes to show that what has long been considered the Dark Ages of the drama is worth the attention of anyone studying the continuity of theatrical growth and the background of modern theatre, as well as being in its own right a period of the most absorbing interest.

Thus no apology is needed for a collection of this kind, its chief justification being the necessity of making available at least a reasonable selection of nineteenth-century plays for the purposes of knowledge and evaluation. The first two volumes, under the general heading of Dramas, contain examples of tragedy, melodrama, and the 'drama'; further volumes will illustrate comedy, farce, extravaganza, and burlesque. The terminal date of 1900 is arbitrary; perhaps a more natural one would be 1914. Yet the theatrical years between 1900 and 1914 are better known than those before 1900, and to represent adequately the drama of the Edwardian period would have meant significantly weakening representation of nineteenth-century drama itself. In another sense 1900 is a satisfactory terminus: by then the major changes which had been going on all century in acting, costuming, lighting, stage management, commercial organization, and styles of drama had been completed; there remained for this theatre a few years until 1914 in which a widening in choice of theme and the increasing acceptability of new subject matter were important, but were developments begun some years before the turn of the century.

Primarily musical entertainment, almost meaningless on the printed page, has been excluded from selection, and so have plays by Wilde and Shaw, who, important though they are in the drama of the 1890s, are easily found in all sorts of modern collections and editions. In selecting a play, I have tried to achieve a rough balance between four criteria: merit, significance (including value as an example of a particular trend), contemporary popularity, and readability. Only plays that saw life on the stage have been chosen, and the emphasis of the collection is theatrical rather than literary, in so far as this is possible when one is dealing with texts rather than drama in performance. The act of recreating the theatrical life and contemporary times of a nineteenth-century play by reading it is a difficult one, and to this end I have related the plays to their theatrical and social contexts in general introductions and individual prefaces, as well as supplying the occasional appendix relevant to a play's stage existence or critical reception.

The texts themselves are my own conflation of acting editions such as *Cumberland, Duncombe, Lacy, Dicks'*, and *French*, ordinary editions (where these exist), prompt books (in one or two instances), and manuscripts submitted to the Examiner of Plays in the Lord Chamberlain's collection. Where there are grounds for basing a text primarily on a single edition which seems authoritative, I have indicated this in the brief textual note in each preface. I have thought it neither necessary nor desirable to treat nineteenth-century plays in the same way that modern editors deal with the texts of Elizabethan drama. Accordingly there is neither exegesis nor textual annotation; the textual work has been done, so to speak, behind the scenes. The authority of acting editions has been generally preferred to that of ordinary editions, but to facilitate reading I have mostly discarded stage directions relating to particular entrance and exit positions and to exact places characters take up on stage. All other directions and scene descriptions have been left virtually intact. Misprints have been corrected and punctuation improved, a task necessary in the often badly printed acting editions.

The text of *The Corsican Brothers* appears by permission of the Harvard College Library; and acknowledgements are due to Samuel French for permission to print *The Second Mrs.*

Tanqueray, to Mrs. Dorinda Maxse for *Mrs. Dane's Defence*, and to the Victoria and Albert Museum for the illustrations in both volumes. I also wish to express my personal gratitude to the Canada Council for the generous financial assistance that made this work possible.

MICHAEL R. BOOTH

University of Guelph
Guelph, Ontario

CONTENTS

List of Illustrations   xi

Introduction   1

The Miller and His Men   29

Virginius   73

Black-Eyed Susan   151

The Factory Lad   201

Richelieu   235

Appendix: Macready's Richelieu   308

ILLUSTRATIONS

1. *The Miller and His Men*, Act I, Scene 5   *facing page* 52

2. *The Miller and his Men*, Act II, Scene 5   ,,   70

3. *Virginius*, Act I, Scene 1   ,,   86

4. *Virginius*, Act I, Scene 2   ,,   93

5. *Virginius*, Act IV, Scene 1   ,,   134

6. *Black-Eyed Susan*, Mr. Cooke as WILLIAM   ,,   184

7. *Richelieu*, Act III, Scene 1   ,,   276

8. *Richelieu*, Act V, Scene 2   ,,   304

INTRODUCTION TO VOLUME ONE

There has been no period, for the last two centuries, in which invention and activity have been more conspicuous in the dramatic field than during the thirty or forty years which include the epoch of such dramatists as Miss Mitford, Sheridan Knowles, Bulwer Lytton, James White, Jerrold, Browning, G. Darley, Searle, Marston, Horne, Lovell, Troughton, Bell, Mrs. Gore, Sullivan, Peake, Poole, Hook, Planche, Charles and George Dance, the Mortons, Mark Lemon, Buckstone, Selby, Fitzball . . . Bernard, Coyne, Oxenford, Shirley Brooks, Watts Phillips, and those peculiar products of our own time, the burlesque writers, like the Brothers Brough, and Messrs. Byron and Burnand.[1]

THE modern reader interested in the history of English drama can only gaze in amazement at a list resembling a catalogue of obscure warriors in a long-forgotten minor epic. He would be more inclined to agree with William Harness, who in 1825 declared in an open letter to Charles Kemble and William Elliston, managers respectively of Covent Garden and Drury Lane, 'Your stages have fallen into the hands of the most contemptible of the literary tribe; and your admirers, both in number and in consequence, have been worthy your play-writers. Who are your successful authors? Planche and Arnold, Poole and Kenney; names so ignoble in the world of literature that they have no circulation beyond the green-room.'[2]

So ignoble has the drama of the nineteenth century been considered that only now is it emerging from that arid waste-land of indifference and contempt to which opinion has con-signed it, but its steps are slow and painful. Generally, historians and critics who have bothered with the subject at all have said that the drama of about 1800 to 1890 is a formless mass of mediocrity, dull and repetitive, lacking literary quality and

---

[1] Tom Taylor, Introduction to *The Ticket-of-Leave Man*, 1863.
[2] 'A Letter . . . on the Present State of the Stage', *Blackwood's Magazine*, xvii (June 1825), 730.

thematic significance, a vast sea of theatrical trivia and downright badness, a drama that slumbered fitfully for a hundred years while the glorious dawn of Shaw and Oscar Wilde waited in an East pregnant with momentous art.[1] This is still the common view, and the student of drama usually takes a colossal leap over the dark abyss yawning dangerously between Sheridan and Shaw, and lands thankfully on the other side.

No one can claim that the nineteenth century was an age of dramatic excellence; it was the opposite. Yet one cannot ignore a century of development in which the theatre abandoned traditional modes of expression and came haltingly into modernity. In 1800 the English theatre was a theatre of illusion still. Staging was symbolic rather than realistic. Scenery with conventional designs of wood, castle, chamber, palace, and street, painted on the flat surfaces of wings and shutters that changed in grooves, moved on and off stage in full view of the audience, as it had since 1660. Players entered and exited through proscenium doors opening and shutting upon library and forest alike, and they made their most effective 'points' downstage dead centre. Acting, whether in tragedy, comedy, farce, or melodrama, was considerably larger than life: stylized, energetic, and highly emphatic. Costume was sometimes vaguely suggestive of period, sometimes traditional, sometimes exaggerated for comic effect, sometimes contemporary even in classical drama. Both stage and auditorium were lit throughout the performance by candles and oil lamps, and pit and gallery audiences were, in the event of a full house, desperately overcrowded on hard, backless, unreserved benches.

By 1900, for better or worse, the theatre was a theatre of realism: realism in staging, acting, costuming, and all aspects of production. The box set, built-up scenery, and elaborate imitation of the settings of modern and ancient life replaced the simple wing, shutter, and groove system. The art of stage management had developed enormously, and styles of performance had become steadily more restrained and natural; for

[1] The authors of special studies of nineteenth-century theatre have, of course, been much more careful and detailed in their judgements. Notable among these studies are Ernest B. Watson, *Sheridan to Robertson* (1926); George Rowell, *The Victorian Theatre* (1956); and Allardyce Nicoll, *A History of English Drama*, iv-v, 2nd edn. (1955–9). To Nicoll's work in particular all historians of the nineteenth-century stage are greatly in debt.

perhaps the first time in theatre criticism underplaying and not overplaying was complained of. Costume and furnishings were exactly appropriate for a play with a contemporary setting, archaeologically correct for a play set in the past. Well-behaved middle-class audiences sat comfortably on reserved seats in darkened auditoriums, watching stages illuminated by the latest electric lighting.

Thus traditionalism slowly broke down under the impact of changes in a theatre anything but stagnant and backward. The nineteenth century has not generally been regarded as a period of theatrical experiment and innovation, but it was, and struggling underneath the apparent tyranny of conformity and convention was the rebellious spirit of reform. It is not my purpose here to examine the many changes in theatrical practice briefly summarized above—they are fully described by Watson, Nicoll, and Rowell—but it is important to remember that in the nineteenth century theatrical change preceded, and had to precede, changes in the content of drama, that dramatic reforms would not have occurred without theatrical reforms preparing the way. The work of Madame Vestris at the Olympic (1831–8), of Macready at Covent Garden (1837–9) and Drury Lane (1841–3), of Samuel Phelps at Sadler's Wells (1844–62), of Charles Kean at the Princess's (1850–9), and of the Bancrofts at the Prince of Wales's (1865–79), was collectively responsible for much improvement in standards of acting and production, as well as providing the theatre with considerable impetus to travel further along its already chosen road to realism. The end of this road was reached before the twentieth century began, and the climax and perfection of earlier developments was attained by the managements of Henry Irving at the Lyceum (1878–1902), John Hare at the Garrick (1889–95), George Alexander at the St. James's (1891–1918), and Herbert Beerbohm Tree at the Haymarket and Her Majesty's (1887–1915).

Where the theatre went the drama followed. A drama realistic in characterization, theme, and dialogue became possible only when acting, staging, and costuming had themselves become more realistic, and a good deal of theatrical spadework had to be done before a quality drama in the realistic mode could emerge in the 1890s and the pre-war years of the next century. The return of Society and the more intellectual playgoer to the theatre was of the greatest importance, for it changed the drama and was responsible for the upper-middle-class settings and themes of Jones, Pinero, Wilde, and Shaw. Thus the theatrical legacy of the nineteenth century seems more significant than the dramatic. Yet the realistic stage observation of the daily life of ordinary people is nineteenth century in origin. The domestic conflict and suffering that mark the work of many modern British playwrights goes back to the agonies of domestic melodrama. Prose drama with working- and middle-class settings, and dialogue with regional working-class dialects and accents, are nineteenth- and not twentieth-century creations. The vigorous and varied creativity that bridged the vast gulf of conception and style between *Virginius* in 1820 and *Mrs. Dane's Defence* in 1900 can only be fully understood in relation to its theatrical and social context, but it cannot be understood at all without a reading of the plays themselves. The personality and taste of an age can be studied in the drama of that age as well as in its fiction, painting, poetry, music, and architecture. There is no doubt that on the whole the nineteenth century got from its dramatists the plays it wanted and refused the plays it did not want; and that what it got suited it admirably.

Whatever their opinion of the merit of nineteenth-century drama, critics have been unanimous in pronouncing it lower than ever before. 'Why has the drama declined?' was a perennial question, a question discussed endlessly in the press, in theatrical memoirs, and even posed to witnesses before Select Parliamentary Committees. Nobody could agree on the causes of this decline; they are still argued over, and when added together make a list of formidable length. It was said that theatres were in a bad way because of too much competition (and because of too little); that star actors received immense salaries and authors not nearly enough; that actors and managers treated authors abominably; that the later dinner hour kept fashionable people away; that such people did not attend theatres because the lower classes were too noisily in evidence; that anyway they preferred exhibiting themselves at the opera and at the visits of French companies; that the solid middle class did not come because of increased evangelical hostility to the theatre and because of the presence of their inferiors who corrupted the drama because they *did* come and liked mere entertainment and vulgar show; that Drury Lane and Covent Garden were too big to see and hear in properly; that these two theatres were overburdened with the expense of providing virtually separate companies for tragedy, comedy, opera, and pantomime; that good authors were not to be found; that too many new amusements were competing for public attention; that people preferred reading novels to going to plays. Poets did not choose, or were unable, to write well for the stage. Managers were incompetent and tyrannical, stars jealous and selfish. Times were hard. The drama was separate from literature. As to the plays themselves, if they were comedies or farces they were frivolous and inane, if tragedies dull or extravagant, if melodramas crude and sensational. Whatever they were they might well be French in origin and thus unworthy of the consideration of a true Englishman.

Whether such allegations, all made before 1840 and all supportable by facts or a body of contemporary opinion, or both, name factors actually or substantially contributory to 'the decline of the drama', ascertainable conditions—apart from the constantly iterated complaints of managers, dramatists, actors, and critics—testify to one fact of decline. From the financial viewpoint alone, Drury Lane and Covent Garden suffered as badly before the abolition of their monopoly on the legitimate drama in 1843 as after it. By 1818 Drury Lane's debts amounted to £80,000, and the receipts of the new theatre had fallen from £75,584 in its first season of operation, 1812–13, to £41,066 in 1817–18, or from a nightly average of £370 to one of £205.[1] The sensational attraction of Edmund Kean, who first appeared at Drury Lane in 1814, could do nothing in the long run to increase dwindling receipts. In the 1820s and 1830s Elliston, Price, Lee, Polhill, Bunn, and Hammond tried to make a success of management but were driven into retreat and bankruptcy. Macready's management of 1841–3 also proved a financial failure, and the theatre reverted once more to the indefatigable Bunn. During a similar period Covent Garden had as many managers—Charles Kemble, Laporte, Bunn, Osbaldiston, Macready, Vestris—and fared as badly as its rival. By 1832, when Charles Kemble testified that theatres were on the

[1] *The Theatrical Inquisitor*, xiii (November 1818), 366–7.

average 'never above one half full',[1] Covent Garden's debts amounted to £160,000, and receipts had dropped from a seasonal average of £79,000 during 1809–20 to one of £55,000 during 1820–32. In 1810–11 £98,000 was taken in, in 1828–9 £41,000.[2] Drury Lane did not become a successful financial venture until after Augustus Harris took it over in 1879. Covent Garden never recovered, and became an opera house in 1847. Their competitors the minor theatres, where before 1843 only the 'illegitimate' drama containing songs and music could be staged, did not do much better. Theatrical hard times prevailed almost everywhere in the first half of the century, and the long-awaited abolition of the patent monopoly in 1843 brought relief to neither major nor minor theatres. In such conditions it is difficult to see how any kind of drama could have flourished.

To investigate all the non-financial aspects of the so-called decline of drama during this period would require much more space than this Introduction can provide, but the picture is not so black as it is often painted: it would be fairer to say that drama did not so much 'decline' as, within new social and cultural contexts, radically change its nature. If the quality of the old tragedy was low, there was compensation in the bustling high spirits and rough energy of the new melodrama, and the compromise between the 'legitimate' and 'illegitimate' determines the nature of the best serious drama after 1850.

What determined the nature of all drama was public taste as it operated in the theatre. In the first three decades of the century the Romantic spirit dominated fiction, poetry, and the theatre; audiences sated themselves on Gothic tragedy, Gothic melodrama, and dramatizations of Scott. When Romanticism exhausted itself on the stage, the most popular drama became (and remained until the end of the century) that with a strong domestic flavour. The artistic pleasures of the working and lower middle classes, who comprised the bulk of the new audiences, were entirely 'popular' and what we would term crude and vulgar, but those of the more educated classes

[1] *Report from the Select Committee on Dramatic Literature* (1832), p. 52. Poor attendance was in spite of rapidly increasing population. London grew from about a million in 1800 to nearly three million in 1850. Of course the number of theatres increased too, from nine in 1800 to twenty-two in 1851.

[2] Ibid. pp. 101, 249.

inclined also to the simple and unsophisticated; this lack of sophistication marks fiction as well as drama. What both the reading and play-going public looked for was a great deal of sentiment and strong pathos, domestic suffering and domestic bliss, a good story line, sensation and violence, a stern morality, much positive virtue and its reward in the almost inevitable happy ending, eccentric humour, and native English jollity and spirit. This pattern of taste established itself before the accession of Victoria as a powerful shaping force in the theatre, and dramatists had to follow the pattern if they wished their work to remain acceptable to an innately conservative public. The boundaries of this taste were clearly marked and cosily restrictive. They were made even more restrictive by the Lord Chamberlain and his subordinate the Examiner of Plays, who presided despotically over the moral and political health of the stage. The main reason why the vigorous political life of the century is not reflected in the drama, thus robbing it of much contemporary significance, is that the Examiner of Plays would not allow it; neither would he allow any serious experimentation with sexual themes. One must not conclude, however, that these officials were reactionaries damming up the tide of dramatic progress, fuddy-duddy autocrats in an age longing for bold and daring plays. Nothing of the sort: until late in the century dramatists, managers, and audiences were as conservative as the Lord Chamberlain and his Examiner, whose edicts were quite in accord with the taste of the times.

The tragedy performed in the theatres of the first fifty years of the century was *not* in accord with the new public taste, and it failed. Most of it is very bad. If the reader looks askance at the choice of *Virginius* as the sole representative of the tragedies of the time, he should read the rest of them. The complaint that nineteenth-century drama was bad because it was divorced from literature was heard then and is repeated now, but the trouble with nineteenth-century tragedy is that its authors were concerned to produce 'literature' when they wrote it. Abetted by a circle of intellectual and literary critics, they scorned the base earth of the world around them and loftily fixed their gaze on the bright stars of Shakespeare and the Elizabethan drama. James Cooke typified the judgements of a score like him when he declared that the degradation of the drama was owing to the 'neglect of the great models of stage literature';[1] to repair such neglect he urged that by the publication of Elizabethan plays 'the public mind be instructed to the knowledge of what a rich mine of pure dramatic gold we have amongst us'.[2] Richard Hengist Horne objected that 'the propensity of modern times to reduce everything as much as possible to a tangible reality . . . has done incalculable mischief in its sweeping application to the ideal arts'.[3] To him drama was an ideal art, with no significant relation to contemporary society; 'whether the circumstances of modern society and civilization are eventful enough to give new incidents to the Drama, may be doubted. If not, it must and will, in future, take a more imaginative and philosophical tone.'[4] The public did not, of course, object to 'literary' tragedies, since the most popular tragic writer on the stage was Shakespeare. What they refused to see were literary tragedies with a lack of external action, or with entirely mental action substituted for stirring outward events, tragedies written without stagecraft, tragedies with introspective characters philosophizing statically in pseudo-Elizabethan blank verse.

For writers seeking dramatic models to emulate, as too many did, the fatal error of trying to write like the Elizabethans was compounded by the example of the great Romantics. Again, it has been said that because the Romantic poets could not or would not participate fully in the theatre the drama suffered and lost potentially great leaders. This argument is tenuous; it is closer to the truth to argue that the early nineteenth-century theatre would have been much better off it if had never heard of Byron and Coleridge. The Romantics modelled their plays on a dead Elizabethan mode and were prone to the faults enumerated above. They knew little about the theatre and cared less; they were primarily interested in drama for the exploration of character and ignored plot and action; they were fascinated by psychology, motive, theory, and abstraction; they tried to make their verse as Shakespearean as possible. Their genius was poetic, not dramatic, and when their tragedies succeeded on the stage—a most rare event—it was either because of spectacular production, as in the case of Coleridge's *Remorse* (1813),

---

[1] *The Stage* (1840), p. 5.   [2] Ibid. p. 12.
[3] 'An Essay on Tragic Influence', Preface to *Gregory VII* (1840), xvi.
[4] *A New Spirit of the Age* (1844), ii. 123.

or fine acting, such as Macready's in Byron's *Werner* (1830). Yet the fact that they were unsuccessful and often unacted did not prevent them from being admired and imitated. The imitation of an imitation did not go far to strengthen drama.

The Romantic influence on drama was, as I have said, strongest in the first three decades of the century, when the passion for Gothic engulfed tragedy and melodrama alike. Because of its extravagance of setting and characterization, Gothic tragedy sometimes possesses a vigour and manic excitement lacking in later tragedy. The tormented hero, the gloomy castle and dungeon, the monk and the hermit's cell, the dark forest, the persecuted heroine, and the robber band, were already familiar from earlier plays like Horace Walpole's unacted *The Mysterious Mother* (1768), Robert Jephson's *The Count of Narbonne* (1781), an adaptation of *The Castle of Otranto*, Richard Cumberland's *The Carmelite* (1784), Andrew McDonald's *Vimonda* (1787), and *The Regent* (1788) by Bertie Greatheed. In the 1790s the novels of Ann Radcliffe began their stage career and were immediately influential. There are at least ten dramatizations of her books, among them James Boaden's *Fontainville Forest* (1794), from *The Romance of the Forest*, and Henry Siddons's *The Sicilian Romance, or The Apparition of the Cliffs* (1794), from *A Sicilian Romance*.

The Gothic vogue continued unabated. Joanna Baillie's *De Montfort* (1800), written—typically of the Romantic approach to drama—to embody in dramatic form the passion of Hatred, contains a melancholy and tortured central character who hates his enemy so powerfully that finally he murders him in a forest. The directions indicate well-established acting and staging conventions for this kind of play. De Montfort *'comes forward to the front of the stage and makes a long pause, expressive of great agony of mind'*. He enters *'with a disordered air, and his hand pressed against his forehead'*, and later *'gives loose to all the fury of gesture, and walks up and down in great agitation'*. The last scene of Act IV and most of Act V takes place where monks and nuns huddle together, terrified by sounds of murder in the storm outside the convent: *'The inside of a Convent Chapel, of old Gothick architecture, almost dark: two torches only are seen at a distance, burning over a new-made grave. The noise of loud wind, beating upon the windows and roof, is heard.'* The author was so fond of this setting that she used it again in *Henriquez* (1836), with the addition of *'a solemn Requiem for the Dead'*, which *'is heard at a distance, sounding from above'*. Henriquez enters and delivers a meditative speech of forty-five lines; it is characteristic of this school of tragic writing that the verse should either blaze with impossible passion or, more frequently, slacken listlessly into decorative and protracted description. Joanna Baillie wrote far better verse than most of her contemporaries and successors, yet such a speech as this, by the King of Castile in *Henriquez*, illustrates the common tendency to engage in leisurely poetry for its own sake:

> But finding
> From wrecks of mountain torrents, or neglect,
> The straight road to Zamora was impassable,
> I took the wider compass, and proceeding
> Through these domains by favour of the night,
> Yon castle from its woods looked temptingly
> And beckoned me afar to turn aside.
> The light from every lattice gaily streamed,
> Lamps starred each dusky corridor, and torches
> Did from the courts beneath cast up the glare
> Of glowing flame upon the buttress'd walls
> And battlements, whilst the high towers aloft
> Show'd their jagged pinnacles in icy coldness
> Cloth'd with the moon's pale beam.

Hazlitt's objection is relevant here:

The modern romantic tragedy is a mixture of fanciful exaggeration and indolent sensibility . . . [it] courts distress, affects horror, indulges in all the luxury of woe, and nurses its languid thoughts and dainty sympathies, to fill up the void of action. . . . The unexpected stroke of true calamity, the biting edge of true passion, is blunted, sheathed, and lost, amidst the flowers of poetry strewed over unreal, unfelt distress, and the flimsy topics of artificial humanity prepared beforehand for all occasions.[1]

Fifty years after *De Montfort* tragic dramatists were still composing in well-worn Gothic conventions. F. G. Tomlins's *Garcia* (1849), set in Spain in 1488, tells the story of Count

---

[1] *A View of the English Stage* (1818), pp. 288–9.

Garcia, who at the instigation of the villain murders a Moorish refugee on his way to testify to the Inquisition that he received illicit shelter for a few hours at the mountain castle of the Garcia family. After the murder Garcia is seized with remorse and horror, and the Inquisition arrests villain and hero for the crime. Although Tomlins was a leader of the movement asserting the dramatic and literary superiority of the 'unacted drama', and although he and his cohorts heaped scorn on the acted drama, his sole stage play is lamentable, yet fully representative of a class of drama which the authors believed would save the stage and restore it to pristine glory if only their work was performed. This movement was especially strong about 1840, but we can only conclude from examining its plays that managers were wise to reject them.

The climax of Gothic tragedy was reached in Charles Maturin's *Bertram, or the Castle of St. Aldobrand* (1816), the most extreme example of its kind. Maturin, the author of a noted Gothic novel, *Melmoth the Wanderer* (1820), also wrote *Manuel* (1817) and *Fredolfo* (1819), the former set in medieval Switzerland on Mount St. Gothard and the latter in feudal Spain; neither had the success of *Bertram*. The exiled Bertram, shipwrecked under the cliffs of the priory of St. Anselm, finds his beloved Imogine married to his enemy Aldobrand. Bitter and tormented, he leads a desperate band of outlaws and at their head murders the good Aldobrand. Imogine runs mad and dies; Bertram stabs himself. A summary conveys no idea of the intense ferocity of Bertram's passions and Imogine's despair, or of the wild extravagance of Maturin's tragic conception. *Bertram* is a bad play, but it is sensationally bad, and audiences were swept into rapture for twenty-two nights by Kean's Bertram. The acting was thoroughly melodramatic, as a look at the stage directions will show. At different times Bertram '*meditates in gloomy reflection*', and '*looking round ghastlily*', '*bursting into ferocity*', expressing himself '*with frantic violence*', is the complete Gothic hero-villain. The first scene of Act IV is '*a dark night under the Castle Walls*'; BERTRAM *appears in a state of the utmost agitation; he extends his arms towards a spot where the Moon has disappeared*' and speaks. We find Imogine '*throwing herself vehemently on her knees*', '*sinking down*', '*recoiling*', '*shrieking*', and rushing in '*with her child, her hair dishevelled, her dress stained with blood'*. Over thirty years later one writer still vividly remembered the acting:

> Who can forget the terrific effect produced by Kean: the agonised glare he threw on the dead Imogen [*sic*], the rapidly-changing features, fiercely agitated by the storm of passion within, and finally the desperate energy with which he plunged the fatal weapon, to the very hilt, into his bosom, caused a thrill of horror, and almost awakened a transient emotion of pity.[1]

It was Kean, too, who raged and suffered as Brutus and drew crowded houses to J. H. Payne's indifferent *Brutus, or The Fall of Tarquin* (1818), delivering speeches like the following denouncing Sextus Tarquin:

> [*With a burst of frenzy.*] The furies curse you then! Lash you
>   with snakes!
> When forth you walk may the red flaming sun
> Strike you with livid plagues!
> Vipers that die not, slowly gnaw your heart! *etc.*

The Gothic past, ancient Rome, the Italian Renaissance, medieval Spain, sometimes the England of history or feudal Scotland—these were the commonly employed settings of tragic dramatists. Occasionally a play of this sort achieves a certain distinctive quality. One such is Douglas Jerrold's *Thomas à Becket* (1829), in vigorous rhetorical prose rather than verse, an unusual choice of form, but then Jerrold was writing for the melodrama-loving audience of a minor theatre, the Surrey. It was not a success, and William Moncrieff commented in the preface to Richardson's acting edition that 'it wants the domestic charm that appeals to men's business and bosoms: the struggles of church and state are "caviare to the million" '. Another better-than-average tragedy is *Feudal Times* (1847), by James White, set in Scotland in the reign of James III and depicting a fatal enmity between the Earl of Mar and the Douglas. The plot is simple, not overburdened with history, and the verse, though often over-poetic, is relatively natural and easy. For instance, the Douglas dismisses a bishop's hint that Mar should be assassinated:

> I know the sort of slaying pleases best
> Our holy mother Church; a quiet stab

---

[1] An Old Playgoer, *Desultory Thoughts on the National Drama* (1850), p. 48.

> Where no one sees; a sleeping draught too strong;
> An eyeless dungeon in some hidden tower:
> I'll have no deed like this to please the Church.
> This Cochrane is a Man, and as a man,
> And by a man, he shall be slain.

Nevertheless, *Feudal Times* suffers badly from the general nineteenth-century tendency to idealize innocence and goodness and love to the point of incredibility; Mar is such a noble, good-hearted man, with no discernible faults, that he is quite unfit for the role of tragic hero. The same tendency enervates *Virginius* and *Richelieu*, especially in their portrayal of womanhood, and imparts an essential lifelessness to the serious drama of the day.

All the faults of contemporary tragic practice are present in one of the most admired tragedies of its time, Thomas Noon Talfourd's *Ion* (1836). Set in classical Greece, it shows an Argos instructed by the oracle of Apollo that the curse of pestilence upon it will not end until the tyrant Adrastes and his race are eliminated. A gentle, noble-spirited foundling, Ion, goes to kill Adrastes, but discovers that the latter is his father. Another conspirator murders the king; Ion assumes the throne in a public ceremony and then kills himself; the pestilence ends. Prolonged love scenes between Clemanthe and Ion weaken the dramatic structure, and the verse is characterized by a speech of Ion's when he asks Adrastes if he has ever loved:

> Think upon the time
> When the clear depths of thy yet lucid soul
> Were ruffled with the troublings of strange joy,
> As if some unseen visitant from heaven
> Touch'd the calm lake and wreath'd its images
> In sparkling waves; recall the dallying hope
> That on the margin of assurance trembled,
> As loth to lose in certainty too bless'd
> Its happy being; taste in thought again
> Of the stolen sweetness of those evening walks,
> When pansied turf was air to winged feet,
> And circling forests by etherial touch
> Enchanted, wore the livery of the sky
> As if about to melt in golden light
> Shapes of one heavenly vision; and thy heart
> Enlarged by its new sympathy with one,
> Grew bountiful to all!

Ion is a recitation rather than a play; an icy coldness deadens verse, character, and situation alike, and it would seem that only the skill of Macready and later of Ellen Tree in the part of Ion ensured success. In his preface to the fourth edition (1837) Talfourd admitted as much in praising Macready:

> By the graces of beautiful elocution, he beguiled the audience to receive the Drama as belonging to a range of associations which are no longer linked with the living world, but which retain an undying interest of a gentler cast. . . . The consequence of this extraordinary power of vivifying the frigid, and familiarising the remote, was to dissipate the fears of my friends; to render the play an object of attraction during the short remainder of the season.

The more acute contemporaries of the tragic dramatists well knew where the weaknesses lay. Blaming the intellectual milieu, the *London Magazine* said that 'if a bias to abstraction is evidently, then, the reigning spirit of the age, dramatic poetry must be allowed to be most irreconcilable with this spirit; it is essentially individual and concrete both in form and in power'.[1] John Lacy condemned the love of poetry for its own sake:

> All our modern tragedists indulge in a similar liberal effusion of the talking-principle within them: the same indolent dicacity, the same proneness to disburse copious harangues and monotonous dissertations, characterize the poetic school of the drama in general. A verbal diarrhoea is the epidemic disease which afflicts the whole tribe. . . . It seems to be forgotten . . . that the end of tragedy is not to tranquillise, but to rouse.[2]

In another article, referring to *Bertram*, Lacy thought that 'if we are to choose between Tom o'Bedlam and Sir Velvet-lungs, give us the madman rather than the poet. It requires no great depth of penetration to see which will best succeed upon the stage.'[3] He was not therefore surprised at the popular failure of modern tragedy, an instance of which he graphically described:

> Another tragedy is produced: three acts are suffered to pass over in noiseless tranquillity; no sound whatever, but the drawing of an occasional cork, or the blowing of a solitary nose: but at the close of

---

[1] *The London Magazine*, i (April 1820), 433.

[2] 'A Letter to the Dramatists of the Day', *The London Magazine*, viii (September 1823), 281.   [3] Ibid. ix (January 1824), 62-3.

the fourth, the audience begins to yawn, gape, sneeze, cough, and throw orange-peel at the musicians: in the fifth some fall fast asleep, others retire to the lobbies, the pit begins to squabble, the boxes to chatter, and the galleries grow noisy, boozy, and amorous: nothing like interest, attention, or enjoyment—till the horses or the dancing-girls enter! Why? Why because the people (blockheads and bar-barians as they are!) cannot perceive the excellence of the piece.[1]

Writing in 1850, George Henry Lewes generalized usefully on the principal defect in the dramatists of the past fifty years, from which other defects arose:

If they had never known this Old Drama, they must perforce have created a new form, and instead of the thousand-and-one imitations of the old dramatists . . . we might have had some sterling plays. Who are the successful dramatists of our day? Precisely those who do *not* imitate the Elizabethan form! . . . We do wish that the dramatist should not be an archeologist, that he should not strive to revive defunct forms, but produce a nineteenth century drama: something that will appeal to a wider audience than that of a few critics and black-letter students.[2]

Preferring historical settings and themes of rebellion, conspiracy, and love, dramatists turned their backs on their own century and tried to bring history and ancient tragic subject matter to life. Sometimes it appears that their main concern was history rather than drama. Charles Kean's declaration in 1859 that he had never permitted historical truth to be sacrificed to theatrical effect might be removed from its context of his management of the Princess's and applied to the composition of historical tragedies and dramas. In his preface to *The Earl of Gowrie*, published in 1845 and acted at Sadler's Wells in 1852, James White remarked that 'whether this is a fit subject for dramatic treatment I am no judge, but it will be seen that I have followed the historical narrative with very little alteration'. Browning, in the preface to the unsuccessful *Strafford*, done by Macready at Covent Garden in 1837, admitted the Romantic weakness of 'Action in Character rather than Character in Action. To remedy this, in some degree, considerable curtail-ment will be necessary.' However, he was proud of his history.

---

[1] 'Theatricals of the Day', *The London Magazine*, x (December 1824), 641. These articles under John Lacy's name are attributed by Nicoll to George Darley.
[2] *The Leader*, 3 August 1850.

'The portraits are, I think, faithful; and I am exceedingly
fortunate in being able, in proof of this, to refer to the subtle
and eloquent exposition of the characters of Eliot and Strafford,
in the Lives of the Eminent British Statesmen, now in the
course of publication in Lardner's Cyclopaedia.' Yet faithfulness
to the 1630s clogs *Strafford* with events obscure to a nineteenth-
century audience, and tragedy suffocates in the airlessness of
historical reference.[1]

Only a few attempts were made to construct tragedy out of
the materials of modern life, and these are failures because their
traditionally minded authors could not satisfactorily adapt new
subject matter to antique methods of treatment. *A Blot in the
Scutcheon* (1843), written by Browning for Macready's Drury
Lane management, was a worse failure than *Strafford*. Although
he set it in the eighteenth century Browning did try to shape his
material according to the melodramatic and increasingly domestic taste of the times. Lord Mertoun obtains Lord Tresham's
permission to ask for the hand of his sister, Mildred. But
Mertoun and Mildred are already lovers, and he climbs nightly
to her window. Tresham discovers all, kills Mertoun in a duel,
and abuses his sister. She dies of a broken heart and the remorseful Tresham takes poison. The play is obscured, not by history,
but by 'Action in Character' and a style of verse-writing the
opposite of the 'indolent sensibility' Hazlitt complained of.
Tresham asks for an opinion about Mertoun:

> How seems he?—seems he not—come, faith, give fraud
> The mercy-stroke whenever they engage!
> Down with fraud, up with faith! How seems the Earl?
> A name! a blazon! if you knew their worth,
> As you will never! come—the Earl?

Guendolen speaks to Mildred of Mertoun:

> Ask and have!
> Demand, be answered! Lack I ears and eyes?
> Am I perplexed which side of the rock-table

---

[1] 'In all the historical plays of Shakespeare, the great poet has only introduced
such events as act on the individuals concerned, and of which they are themselves
a part; the persons are all in direct relation to each other, and the facts are present
to the audience. But in Browning's play we have a long scene of passion—upon
what? A plan destroyed, by whom or for what we know not. . . .' (*The Diaries of
William Charles Macready*, ed. William Toynbee (1912), i. 390.)

> The Conqueror dined on when he landed first,
> Lord Mertoun's ancestor was bidden take—
> The bow-hand or the arrow-hand's great meed?
> Mildred, the Earl has soft blue eyes!

Actors must have found such lines difficult, but one pities audiences more.

A dramatist who made a deliberate effort to use modern life for tragic purposes was Westland Marston. In the preface to *The Patrician's Daughter* (1842), Marston writes:

> The following pages originated in the desire of the Author to write a Tragedy indebted for its incident, and passion, to the habits and spirit of the age. It is well that an attempt of this kind should be made. . . . The elevated and gifted Spirit sees the sublime in The Present, recognizes the Hero *in undress*, and discovers greatness, though it be divested of pomp. . . . To limit to the past, the dramatic exhibitions of our nature, is virtually to declare our nature itself radically altered.

The theory is excellent, but the practice falls somewhat short. Mordaunt, a radical politician, is invited to stay in the country with his chief political opponent, the Earl of Lynterne, a cabinet minister, and falls in love with Lynterne's daughter Mabel. Fooled by her proud aunt into believing that the true-hearted Mabel scorns him because of his humble birth, Mordaunt seeks revenge by betrothing himself to Mabel and then publicly denouncing her on the eve of the marriage. Some months later the grief-stricken Mabel expires in the arms of the now un-deceived and repentant Mordaunt. At first sight it seems that the political overtones of *The Patrician's Daughter* might make the play a genuine modern tragedy of political life and satisfy Bulwer-Lytton's complaint of some years earlier:

> We banish the Political from the stage, and we therefore deprive the stage of the most vivid of its actual sources of interest. At present the English, instead of finding politics on the stage, find their stage in politics. . . . In these times the public mind is absorbed in politics, and yet the stage, which should represent the times, especially banishes appeal to the most general feelings. To see our modern plays, you would imagine there were no politicians among us.[1]

---

[1] *England and the English*, 2nd edn. (1833), ii. 141–2. Bulwer-Lytton was, however, forgetting the Lord Chamberlain, and perhaps Marston was not.

In reality, *The Patrician's Daughter* has nothing whatever to do with politics (the political reference is extremely vague), and its only claim to modernity is the theme of class enmity between the low-born radical and the conservative aristocratic family, a theme only made relevant to the plot by an extraneous piece of trickery. Furthermore, Marston's experiment did not extend to the use of a medium other than blank verse, which he wrote as badly as his contemporaries.[1] After reverting to a conventional historical background for *Strathmore* (1849), a tragedy set in Scotland in 1679, Marston essayed the contemporary once again with the verse drama *Anne Blake* (1852), specifically located *'near the middle of the nineteenth century'*. Anne Blake, embittered by dependence on her heartless and snobbish uncle and aunt, Sir Joshua and Lady Toppington, loves the poor artist Thorold, although uncle and aunt try to force her by threats and subterfuge into a match with the heir to a peerage and a fortune. The play is mostly taken up by misunderstandings caused by superficial tricks of plot. Finally Thorold, suddenly rich from a fortune in newly prosperous Indian mines, wins Anne, also enriched by her dead father's share in the same mines. Here again, except for a general sense of class hostility, *Anne Blake* draws nothing from the life of the mid nineteenth century.

When one examines the stage career of tragedy and the serious legitimate drama in the last century, one is surprised— bearing in mind their too common failure to please—that they lingered so long and that many plays passed into the standard repertory for fifty years or more. However, such plays were often first-class acting vehicles, and in any consideration of nineteenth-century drama we must never forget the skill of the great actors in transforming what today seem pages of lifeless and unreadable text into *tours de force* which electrified audiences and stirred memories years after the event. I have already instanced Kean's Bertram and Macready's Ion; Marston's

---

[1] *The Patrician's Daughter* was also done by Macready, who is extolled by historians for his exacting standards of production and his courage in making a stand, against hopeless financial odds, in defence of the legitimate drama. This is true, but it must also be realized that because of his abhorrence of the popular and domestically melodramatic—the true taste of the age—Macready, in his otherwise admirable search for new serious authors, would accept only the 'legitimate' work of writers like Talfourd, Browning, and Marston, and rejected, for instance, *Oliver Twist* when Dickens offered it to him for the stage. In this respect Macready was a reactionary figure.

description of Macready's Richelieu is also relevant,[1] but perhaps the point can be made more fully—and it is an important one—by contemporary impressions of actors at work on seemingly intractable material.

Henry Hart Milman's tragedy *Fazio* (1816) has a setting of Renaissance Florence and presents Fazio's theft of the miser Bartolo's gold after Bartolo has been stabbed by robbers, Fazio's betrayal, out of jealousy, by his wife Bianca, and Bianca's remorseful and unavailing efforts to save him from execution for Bartolo's murder. Milman said in a note to the play, which was published before it was acted, that *Fazio* was 'written with some view to the stage', but speeches are verbose and scenes follow each other without a change in speaker: for example in Act I Fazio utters four consecutive speeches totalling ninety lines in four scenes, and in Acts IV and V Bianca speaks a despairing soliloquy of over seventy lines extending through three scenes. However, *Fazio* contains two fine acting parts, especially that of Bianca. About 1847 John Coleman saw Charlotte Cushman as Bianca in Edinburgh. From the time Bianca came on to denounce her husband to the Duke,

I had eyes and ears only for the poor demented creature whose face was transformed into the mask of Medusa, and whose eyes . . . glittered with infernal fire; whose hair, like a mantle of flame, streamed over her fair shoulders, while from the simple tunic of white muslin, which fell from head to heel, gleamed forth a pair of statuesque arms and a superbly moulded bust which rose and sank tumultuously as though about to burst with the agonies of a tortured, despairing heart.[2]

Later in the play Bianca, pleading to the Duke for her husband's life when Fazio is about to be executed, says,

> Ha! ye've been dancing, dancing—so have I:
> But mine was heavy music, slow and solemn—
> A bell, a bell: my thick blood roll'd to it. . . .

Coleman recalled the delivery of these lines:

The words are commonplace enough, but the tone, the look, the action, as she clutched at the great tumbling masses of hair as if about

---

[1] See the Appendix on Macready's Richelieu.
[2] *Fifty Years of an Actor's Life* (1904), i. 294.

to tear them up by the roots, were awe-inspiring! Then, pausing, she
rubbed her temples, rubbed, and rubbed again, as if trying to expunge
some damned spot, to exorcise the remorse, the agony of the demented
brain. A mist arose before my eyes; a thrill, half-pleasure, half-pain,
passed through the spinal column; a lump arose in my throat; and I
sat shivering and shuddering till the fatal bell, which heralded the
death of Fazio, sounded the death-knell of his hapless wife, and she,
collapsing, fell an inert and helpless thing, dead ere she reached the
earth.[1]

Charlotte Cushman's most famous part was Meg Merrilies
in an adaptation of Scott's *Guy Mannering*. In the text of the
adaptation, Meg seems merely a stock melodramatic creation of
the 'weird woman'; Cushman turned her into a figure of terror
and tragic pity. From the wings, Coleman watched her initial
entrance the first time she played Meg in Edinburgh:

There swept on like a whirlwind a great, gaunt, spectral thing, clad
from head to heel in one, and only one, loose flowing garment, com-
pact of shreds and patches in neutral colours. Its elf-locks were of iron
grey; its face, arms and neck were those of a mummy new risen from
the sepulchre, while its eyes, aflame with living fire, were riveted on the
lost heir of Ellangowan, who gasped and remained speechless. . . .
The audience were breathless and dumbfounded. . . . The creature
spoke, or rather croaked, in a low guttural voice; then she crooned
forth in a voice of infinite tenderness the sweet old melody, 'Rest
thee, babe, rest thee', and tears, despite myself, rolled down my cheeks.[2]

In 1847 Fanny Kemble reappeared on the English stage and
Coleman saw her play Julia in Knowles's drama *The Hunchback*,
a part she created in 1832. In Act V Julia implores the mysterious
Master Walter, her seeming-guardian, to break off her coming
nuptials with a man she does not love. The speech does not
inspire when read; it concludes:

> Thou canst save me.
> Thou ought'st! thou must! I tell thee at his feet
> I'll fall a corse—ere mount his bridal bed!
> So choose between my rescue and my grave:—
> And quickly too! The hour of sacrifice
> Is near! Anon the immolating priest

---

[1] *Fifty Years of an Actors' Life*, i. 295.   [2] Ibid. i. 302–3.

Will summon me! Devise some speedy means
To cheat the altar of its victim. Do it!
Nor leave the task to me!

This is how Coleman saw Fanny Kemble play it:

Tortured, despairing, maddened, she sprang to her feet erect and terrible. With fiery eyes and dilated form she turned at bay, even as a wounded hind might turn upon the hunter's spear, then with quivering lips she commenced the famous speech, extending over some thirty lines. As it proceeded her voice gained strength, changing from the flute to the bell—from the bell to the clarion. Then upon a rising *sostenuto* of concentrated agony and defiance, she smote and stabbed Walter with that awful 'Do it! Nor leave the task to me!' Even as the last word left her lips, she strode down to the right hand corner, returned to the centre, and then came to anchor, her right hand clutched on the back of the great oaken chair, her left thrown out towards Walter, her blazing eyes fixed on him in an attitude of denunciation and defiance. Then it was, and not till then, that the breathless and enthralled auditors rose in such an outburst of wild enthusiasm as I have never heard equalled before or since.[1]

In such ways the great figures of the nineteenth-century stage overwhelmed audiences with a rhetoric and passion that made many an indifferent tragedy and melodrama acceptable and even popular.

It may appear that too much time has been spent investigating the nature and decline of a dramatic type represented in this volume by only one play, *Virginius*. Yet the fall of the mighty is never without significance and fascination for the spectator. The Victorian theatre witnessed the death of English classical tragedy, a form exhausted and in ill health all through the eighteenth century, but whose conventions and styles had persisted on the stage for over two hundred and fifty years. As has been suggested, its demise occurred largely because its authors looked back to a former age and were cut off from the mainsprings of modern English life and thought; no purely imitative drama or one so detached from its society and culture has been successful or significant. However, the causes of this failure are philosophically and socially interesting. The larger-than-life world, the metaphysical matrix and values of classical

---

[1] 'Fanny Kemble', *The Theatre* (March 1893), p. 143.

tragedy, were no longer within reach of playwrights living in a growingly materialistic, non-metaphysical England of bustling progress and rapidly changing values. No matter how much they kept this world out of their tragedies, they still lived in it themselves, and were no longer capable of a meaningful expression of the ideal in dramatic terms. As yet no new tragic ideas could find their way into the vacuum; dramatists were through no fault of their own suspended between two realms of tragedy, ancient and modern. The ancient, respectable and 'literary', was dead to them, no matter how hard they struggled to keep it alive, but the modern had not yet been born. Before 1850 it was too early for tragedies of environmental and psychological determinism, too early for tragedies about the war of sex, the failure of religion, and the hopelessness, futility, and emptiness of life.

In one respect tragedy came to terms with its age and evolved: it took on a strongly melodramatic emphasis and a happy ending and became the 'drama', that peculiarly Victorian form compounded of intrigue, sensation, idealism, and domestic sentiment. The period after 1850 is dominated by this form, but it developed in the first half of the century. In its purer, more 'legitimate' aspect it is represented by the dramas of Knowles and Bulwer-Lytton's *The Lady of Lyons* (1838) and *Richelieu*, but even here there is a definite compromise between the older literary drama and the popular 'illegitimate' types, between tragedy and melodrama. *The Lady of Lyons*, with themes of class pride, ideal and ennobling love, the perfect bliss of Home (whether real or illusory), and the merited climb to fame, social distinction, and wealth, is modern in spirit and essentially domestic in feeling, despite historical trappings. A father–daughter relationship and young, innocent love were part of the appeal of *Richelieu* to audiences; precisely the same appeal was made in *Virginius*. The replacement of a metaphysical with a domestic ideal and the trend toward domestic themes and domestic realism are features of early Victorian plays that operate strongly in the more popular 'drama' and melodrama. Even in tragedy there are the same signs. In Mary Mitford's *Rienzi* (1828), a story of intrigue, conspiracy, rebellion, and young love in fourteenth-century Rome, the following speech by Rienzi's beautiful and loving daughter might—except for the

verse—come straight from any domestic melodrama of the
next forty years:

> Father, I love not this new state, these halls
> Where comfort dies in vastness; these trim maids
> Whose service wearies me. Oh! mine old home!
> My quiet and pleasant chamber, with the myrtle
> Woven round the casement; and the cedar by
> Shading the sun; my garden overgrown
> With flowers and herbs, thick-set as grass in fields;
> My pretty snow-white doves; my kindest nurse;
> And old Camille. Ah! mine own dear home!

Before *Rienzi*, the village heroine in J. H. Payne's operatic
melodrama *Clari, the Maid of Milan* (1823) was uttering the
same lament in the Duke's palace, mourning her lost cottage
home and singing the song written for the play, 'Home, Sweet
Home'. Horne might have deplored the tendency of the stage
to 'shadow forth the smaller peculiarities of an actual and every-
day life domesticity',[1] but this sort of domesticity and the
presentation of a domestic ideal were to become the dominant
subject matter of the Victorian stage for the rest of the century.

The drama dealing with the household and family relationships, refining itself as time passed and culminating in the 1890s
in the work of Henry Arthur Jones, Pinero, Wilde, and Shaw,
did not grow up independently, but evolved as part of a melodrama which by 1825 had developed three closely related but
distinctive branches: the Romantic, encompassing Gothic and
Eastern melodrama; the nautical (partly Romantic and partly
domestic), and the domestic itself, roughly in that chrono-
logical order.[2] The third kind, the domestic, became the back-
bone of Victorian drama. When Bulwer-Lytton called on
intellectual dramatists to be modern and use 'tales of a household nature, that find their echo in the heart of the people—the
materials of the village tragedy, awakening an interest common
to us all; intense yet homely, actual—earnest—the pathos and
passion of every-day life',[3] he was describing a drama that
already existed on a popular level. In melodrama lies the

---

[1] *A New Spirit of the Age*, ii. 99.

[2] For brief discussions of these individual types, see the prefaces to *The Miller
and His Men*, *Black-Eyed Susan*, and *The Factory Lad*.

[3] *England and the English*, ii. 145.

fulfilment of Bulwer-Lytton's desire that 'among the people, then, must the tragic author invoke the genius of Modern Tragedy, and learn its springs',[1] and the truth of his statement, 'I doubt if the drama will become thoroughly popular until it is permitted to embody the most popular emotions'.[2] Crude, healthy, vulgar, energetic, colourful, and popular, melodrama was everything that legitimate tragedy was not, and because of these qualities and the fact that it was in touch with its age it bloomed where tragedy withered and died.

What gave melodrama impetus were Gothic novels of terror and the supernatural, and Gothic tragedies, some of them adaptations of the novels performed both before and after 1790. Melodrama's rigid moral pattern, character types, and much of its machinery were derived from eighteenth-century senti-mental tragedy and comedy with their excess of moral senti-ment, exaltation of virtue, exhaustive exploitation of pathos and distress, generous but erring heroes, suffering heroines, comic servants, surprising revelations, mistaken identities, long-lost orphans, and missing documents. The English sentimental drama and novel in turn influenced the French comédie larmoyante and drame bourgeois; indeed, there was con-siderable interaction between these forms and current English drama on the one hand and English Gothic, German Gothic, and French boulevard melodrama of the post-Revolutionary period on the other. This Parisian melodrama, supplied in vast quantities to an avid public by Guilbert de Pixérécourt and his followers, possessed the same ingredients of violence, show, moral simplicity, emotional distress, rhetoric, and music as early English melodrama, which of course it strongly influenced. Yet Parisian melodrama was in turn derived from English Gothic, and it would be wrong to say that English melodrama was a French product. By 1800 the pattern of melodrama was set, and the rest of the century made additions and variations only. French plays continued to supply plots for melodramatists, and the novel proved fruitful for the adapter. The tendency of much nineteenth-century fiction is to the same extremes of vice, virtue, sensationalism, and pathos that one finds in melo-drama. Scott's romantic Gothicism and Dickens's domestic sentiment were enormously popular on the stage, and from *The*

---

[1] *England and the English*, ii. 150.   [2] Ibid. ii. 142.

Castle of Otranto to *East Lynne* and *Trilby* the melodrama of the novel provided melodrama for the theatre.

The main features of melodrama are familiar: the concentration on externals, the emphasis on situation at the expense of motivation and characterization, the firm moral distinctions, the unchanging character stereotypes of hero, heroine, villain, comic man, comic woman, and good old man, physical sensation, spectacular effects (made possible by improvements in stage technology), marked musical accompaniment, the rewarding of virtue and punishing of vice, the rapid alternation between extremes of violence, pathos, and low comedy. Melodrama appears to represent a complete breakdown of dramatic forms in its variety of content; yet paradoxically it is an extremely rigid form that especially in its most popular manifestations in the working-class theatres remained fixed for a hundred years.

The needs of spectators primarily determined melodrama's content and style. Music and wordless physical incident were at first dictated by the Lord Chamberlain, who originally permitted only unspoken drama outside the patent theatres and later allowed the spoken word accompanied by music. But in any case these features admirably suited the taste of audiences who were indifferent to the static poetic tragedy, genteel comic wit, and delicate sentimentality. They were the new uneducated and largely illiterate urban masses who lived in bleak and depressing circumstances; what they wanted from the stage was thrilling action, stirring emotion, spectacle, jolly farce, and an ideal image of themselves and their own lives. All this they obtained from melodrama, which simultaneously satisfied their desires for escapist entertainment, for a better world where such as they received the happiness and rewards proper to the virtuous poor, and for a quasi-realistic presentation of the every-day occurrences of their own domestic existence. For the first time in English dramatic history, they themselves were the heroes of a drama written especially for them in a language and with a simplicity they could understand, a drama concerned with their own lives and dreams. Even if the melodramatist offered them history or pure romance he did it sensationally and colourfully; not for him blank verse, long speeches, and action in character. Audiences liked to see, in William Dimond's adaptation of Byron, *The Bride of Abydos* (1818), the features of the heroine

Zulieka *'express the terror of her sex'* and those of the tyrant pasha Giaffier *'ghastly with a deeper fear'*. They liked such a climax as the *'Towers of Abydos in flames—grand tableau'*, a *'desperate conflict'* between the hero Selim and Giaffier, a rescue of Zulieka by Selim, who *'breaks with overwhelming frenzy through all opposition and springs into the ruin'*, rushes through the flames up the staircase of a tower, pursued by a dagger-wielding villain about to strike him when *'a third explosion is heard and the entire floor of the apartment gives way and sinks with* MURTEZA *into the flames below.* ZULIEKA *by clinging to the stone pillar is preserved'*; Selim returns triumphantly with her *'over the perilous ruin'*. These audiences equally liked to hear such speeches as Ben's in T. E. Wilks's *Ben the Boatswain* (1839), which tells the world what an excellent fellow the common man is:

> My father was jolly young waterman on the Thames and rowed folks from Wapping to Rotherhithe for a penny a head; and as to my mother, why—bless her kind old heart! my mother keeps a mangle, and takes in a little bit of washing. And now what of all that there? Can't I hand, reef, and steer as well as any man in the fleet? Did any one ever see me show the white feather in an engagement, or a gale? . . . Ain't I got as pretty a sweetheart as your lordship any day? . . . Werry well, says I—then if that there be the case, what the devil does it matter who my father was, or whether my mother keeps a mangle, and takes in a bit of washing?

If the legitimate drama was as good as that they might go to see it, or something like it; otherwise they had plenty of their own kind of theatre to satisfy them. Sometimes the legitimate drama would come to them; Shakespeare was melodramatized within the law for the Surrey; Kean acted at the Coburg and the City Theatre. Thomas Dibdin described the staging at the Surrey in 1819 of Home's eminently literary *Douglas*:

> Which tragedy, without omitting a single line of the author, made a very splendid melo-drama, with the additions of Lord Randolph's magnificent banquet, a martial Scotch dance, and a glee . . . exquisitely set by Sanderson, and delightfully sung, together with an expensive processional representation of the landing of the Danes: besides all this, as a Surrey Theatre gallery audience always expects some *ultra* incident, I had a representative of Lady Randolph in the person of a very clever boy, by whose good acting and fearless

agility, the northern dame, at the conclusion of the tragedy, was seen to throw herself from a distant precipice into a boiling ocean, in a style which literally brought down the house.[1]

Although melodrama began its career in Drury Lane and Covent Garden as well as in the transpontine Royal Circus and Astley's, it soon became the staple fare of working-class theatres like the Surrey, the Coburg (later the Victoria), the Britannia, the Pavilion, the City of London, the Standard, the Effingham, and the Grecian—all of these in operation before 1850 and the six last-named in the East End. Of course melodrama was performed everywhere (its main West End stronghold was the Adelphi), but in the first half of the century it was mainly popular and proletarian in theme and treatment. Thus it was radical in tone; its heroes were peasants, workmen, and common sailors, its villains landlords, squires, peers, and factory owners. Much melodrama, particularly the domestic, is permeated with class hatred and darkened by a grim vision of a wealthy, authoritarian, repressive upper class tyrannizing over a poor suffering proletariat. Its attitudes were inherited from the democratic idealism of the romantic dramas of Goethe and Schiller, such as *Götz von Berlichingen* and *Die Räuber*, and more directly from the political sentiments of the French Revolution embodied in the fervent anti-tyrannical melodramas of Pixérécourt and his school. Naturally these sentiments could not be bluntly stated on a stage subject to control by government and magistrate, and anyway the English theatre vulgarized and played down foreign idealism. However, melodrama provides the richest material in English dramatic literature for the study of a rebellious class spirit in action, and an illuminatingly different insight into nineteenth-century social history.

Because melodrama reflected popular and radical feeling, it frequently expressed, no matter how crudely and fantastically, the social problems of the day; of all the nineteenth-century dramatic forms it has the most relevance to contemporary life and is the only one to treat of serious issues. By 1850 the subject matter of melodrama included slavery, the urban environment and a nostalgia for a lost rural heritage, temperance and the

---

[1] *The Reminiscences of Thomas Dibdin* (1827), ii. 270. At Drury Lane and Covent Garden the chances were that the more melodramatic and spectacular the legitimate tragedy, the greater the success.

problems of drink, industrialism and the life of the factory worker, the game laws, the homeless poor, and class relationships. Melodrama had always been patriotic and militantly nationalistic, and for the whole century proclaimed the superiority of England to any other country on earth, as well as depicting in violent physical action English triumphs in battles on land and sea, and idealizing English military heroes. Even Horne was forced to admit that popular melodrama, farce, and light comedy, although simple, was closest to life:

> The most simple is that which reflects the tone and temperament of the age. This kind of Drama must not now be looked for amongst what is sometimes absurdly called the 'legitimate'. That phrase is foolishly applied to a form—the five-act form; and to that kind of Drama which includes philosophical exposition of human character and philosophical and rhetorical dissertation upon it. But the most legitimate, because the genuine offspring of the age, is that Drama which catches the manners as they rise and embodies the characteristics of the time. This, then, has forsaken the five-act form, and taken shelter at what have been named 'Minor Theatres'. . . . Whatever the amount of their ability, the truly dramatic, as far as it exists on the modern stage at all, will be found in those comparatively neglected writers of the minor drama.[1]

Growing upward from the sturdy root of popular melodrama was the Victorian 'drama'; in fact one can trace a direct line of descent from *The Miller and His Men* and *The Factory Lad* to *The Second Mrs. Tanqueray*, *An Ideal Husband*, and *Widowers' Houses*. All late Victorian and Edwardian serious drama was fathered by the earlier melodrama. As sometimes happens in life, the intellectual middle-class son despised his humble working-class parents, but his parents they were all the same. The melodrama, farce, and pantomime of the nineteenth century, especially of the first fifty years, represented the last time that the English theatre was in touch with the mass of the population and popular sentiment, and the only time since the Middle Ages that it has been dominated by neither the aristocracy nor the middle class.

[1] *A New Spirit of the Age*, ii. 90–4.

THE MILLER AND HIS MEN

A MELODRAMA IN TWO ACTS

BY

ISAAC POCOCK (1782–1835)

═══════

First performed at Covent Garden Theatre
21 October 1813

═══════

CAST

GRINDOFF, the miller	Mr. Farley
COUNT FREDERICK FRIBERG	Mr. Vining
KARL, his servant	Mr. Liston
LOTHAIR, a young peasant	Mr. Abbott
KELMAR, an old cottager	Mr. Chapman
KRUITZ, his son	Master Gladstanes
RIBER ⎫	Mr. Jefferies
GOLOTZ ⎬ Banditti	Mr. King
ZINGRA ⎭	Mr. Sladen
CLAUDINE ⎫ Kelmar's daughters	Miss Booth
LAURETTE ⎭	Miss Carew
RAVINA	Mrs. Egerton

The Miller's Men, Banditti, Officers of Count Friberg

═══════

SCENE

The Banks of a River on the Borders of a Forest
in Bohemia

PREFACE TO
THE MILLER AND HIS MEN

A SIGNIFICANT context for melodrama is the Romantic movement. The unbounded expression of emotion, the heroic individualism, the sweep of rhetoric, the richness of setting, the despondency and wild flights of joy that mark Romantic poetry also mark melodrama—to some extent all melodrama, but especially Gothic and Eastern melodrama, which flourished from the 1790s until about 1830. This kind of melodrama represented Romanticism in the popular theatre, and historians of the Romantic movement could profitably add melodrama to their field of study, for in the staging and subject matter of Gothic and Eastern drama the expression of Romanticism was far more extravagant than in any other contemporary art form.

The Miller and His Men is more typical of the second variety of Gothic melodrama than the first, which had already been on the stage for twenty years, and included in its sterner material the gloom-ridden tyrant dwelling in a forbidding castle full of dark passageways and dank dungeons, and the spectre of his past victim giving dreadful warning to the frightened heroine.[1] Much of this material was already familiar in the Gothic novel; melodramatists, to whom subtlety of effect was useless, intensified emotions, added sensations, and emphasized the supernatural. The leading writer of this type of Gothic melodrama was Matthew Gregory Lewis, author of the most notorious of Gothic novels, *The Monk*. Lewis produced ten such plays, among them *The Castle Spectre* (1797), whose usurping tyrant meets his death in his own dungeons at the hands of the heroine and the ghost of her murdered mother; *Adelmorn, the Outlaw* (1801), in which the blood-stained spectre of the usurper Osric's victim rises slowly with a flaming dagger in his hand and terrifies Osric into a confession; and *One O'Clock* (1811), with a fearful tyrant in Hardyknute, who sacrifices a

[1] The first half of the nineteenth century was the Indian summer of the English stage ghost. Melodrama, particularly the Gothic but also the other kinds, is peopled by spectres.

child every year to the Wood Demon and is finally dragged
down by the Demon and assistant fiends into the earth of a
cavern in which blue fire flickers from the tongues of writhing
snakes. All these plays are full of spectacular visions, invisible
choruses, and low comic relief. Of all Gothic melodramatists
Lewis excelled in sensations of the horrible and supernatural.

Naturally the first variety of Gothic overlaps the second,
chiefly distinguished from the former by the absence of the
supernatural, the replacement of the usurping tyrant by the
bandit chief, the grim castle by the peasant's cottage, and a
greater domesticity of characterization and sentiment. Sensational effects still occurred, however. In Samuel Arnold's
The Woodman's Hut (1814), the hero and heroine escape on a
raging river lit by flashes of lightning, and the pursuing villains
are trapped in a climactic forest fire. The use of chivalric matter
in spectacular settings was also common, as in William Barrymore's *The Blood-Red Knight* (1810), with equestrian show,
processions of knights, and the attack on the tyrant's castle,
which goes up in flames. Barrymore's *Wallace, the Hero of
Scotland* (1817) has a grand procession of Scottish soldiers and
chiefs, battle scenes, and the rescue of Wallace from the
enemy's castle battlements. Both plays were performed in the
circus ring at Astley's, and their superfluity of dumbshow,
music, and the noise of battle is a reminder that not only did
legal restrictions necessitate wordless display, but also that the
origins of melodrama were as much popular as literary. The
pageantry, physical business, supernaturalism, and extreme
Romanticism of Scott made him ideal material for the Gothic
melodramatist, and adaptations of almost all Scott's novels and
narrative poems flooded the stage: from 1819 to 1821 there
were nineteen versions of *Ivanhoe, The Heart of Midlothian*, and
Kenilworth. Blasted heaths, wild moors, and abbey ruins from
Scott were added to conventional Gothic settings of forest,
castle, and convent, and Scottish comic men recruited to the
ranks of Gothic comic relief.

A form of Romantic melodrama even more exotic and spectacular in staging than the Gothic was the Eastern, in which
local colour was lavishly applied. One of the first was George
Colman's *Blue-Beard* (1798), with all the familiar Gothic
elements in a Turkish setting, a Blue Chamber streaming with

blood, and a skeleton that impales Bluebeard with its dart and sinks with him into the earth. Several Eastern melodramas were adapted from Romantic poetry, notably H. M. Milner's *Mazeppa* (1823) and William Dimond's *The Bride of Abydos* (1818), from Byron, and Edward Fitzball's *Thalaba, the Destroyer* (1823), from Southey. The most sumptuous of Eastern productions was Moncrieff's *The Cataract of the Ganges* (1823) at Drury Lane. The curtain rises on a moonlit battlefield littered with arms, cannon, horses, Mohammedan and Hindu dead and dying; the ruins of a city burn in the background. There are processions of Brahmin priests and the Rajah's warriors, a temple full of huge golden images, and a Pavilion of Pleasures. The play concludes with the hero's horseback rescue of the heroine from a forest fire; he rides right up the great cataract itself, running with satisfyingly real water.

Highly romantic and thoroughly escapist, Gothic and Eastern melodrama bloomed with the Romantic movement and slowly withered as it died. The Gothic could still be found at East End theatres in the 1860s and 1870s, but its heyday was long over. *The Miller and His Men* appeared at the height of the vogue and contains features familiar in melodrama for the rest of the century: aged and lamenting parent, brave and virtuous young hero, menacing villain, threatened heroine, low comedy, last-minute rescue, a sensational physical effect, and the overthrow of vice and triumph of righteousness. In respect of its Gothic nature the play is interesting because it possesses not only the conventional Gothic material of forest, robber chief, and secret cavern, but also basically domestic matter—such as the humble cottage home and its virtuous occupants, the peasant hero— that becomes enlarged in nautical melodrama and finally comes into its own in domestic melodrama proper.

Isaac Pocock himself was the son of a Bristol marine painter and took up the career of artist, studying under Romney and exhibiting at the Royal Academy. He turned to the stage in 1808, and by his death in 1835 had written forty-two plays, most of them melodramas. These included eight adaptations of Scott, the best known—and a repertory piece in Scotland for a hundred years—being *Rob Roy Macgregor* (1818). *The Miller and His Men* was the best loved of all plays for the toy theatres, passing through thirty-six editions from the publishers of juvenile drama sheets.[1] At Covent Garden, which gave Pocock £100 for the play, it was set to music by Sir Henry Bishop, acted fifty-one times in its first season, and frequently revived thereafter. Its last West End revival was at the Haymarket in 1861.

The Miller and His Men was published in 1813, but underwent slight changes in performance as it continued to appear at Covent Garden. This text is therefore based primarily on the earliest acting edition, in *Cumberland's British Theatre*, v. 26, supplemented by the 1813 second edition. The acting copy in *Lacy* supplementary v. 1 is that of the Haymarket revival of 1861, but is useful for correcting misprints in *Cumberland*. The still later acting edition in *Dicks'* no. 28 is identical with *Cumberland*.

[1] George Speaight, *Juvenile Drama* (1946), p. 241.

ACT I

SCENE I. *The Banks of a River in Bohemia. On the right, in the distance, a rocky eminence, on which is a windmill at work—a cottage in front, R. Sunset.*

Music. The MILLER'S MEN *are seen in perspective, descending the eminence—they cross the river in boats, and land near the cottage, with their sacks, singing the following round:*

> When the wind blows,
>   When the mill goes,
> Our hearts are all light and merry;
>   When the wind drops,
>   When the mill stops,
> We drink and sing, hey down derry.
>
> > [*Exeunt.*

Enter KELMAR *from the cottage.*

KELMAR. What! more sacks, more grist to the mill! Early and late the miller thrives: he that was my tenant is now my landlord; this hovel, that once sheltered him, is now the only dwelling of bankrupt broken-hearted Kelmar—well, I strove my best against misfortune, and thanks be to heaven have fallen respected, even by my enemies.

Enter CLAUDINE *with a basket.*

So, Claudine, you are returned. Where stayed you so long?

CLAUDINE. I was obliged to wait ere I could cross the ferry—there were other passengers.

KELMAR. Amongst whom I suppose was one in whose company time flew so fast—the sun had set before you had observed it.

CLAUDINE. No, indeed, father: since you desired me not to meet Lothair—and I told him what you had desired—I have never seen him but in the cottage here, when you were present.

KELMAR. You are a good girl—a dutiful child, and I believe you—you never yet deceived me.

CLAUDINE. Nor ever will, dear father—but—

KELMAR. But what?

CLAUDINE. I—I find it very lonely passing the borders of the forest without—without—

KELMAR. Without Lothair.

CLAUDINE. You know 'tis dangerous, father.

KELMAR. Not half so dangerous as love—subdue it, child, in time.

CLAUDINE. But the robbers?

KELMAR. Robbers! what then? They cannot injure thee or thy father—alas! we have no more to lose—yet thou hast one treasure left, innocence! Guard well thy heart, for should the fatal passion there take root, 'twill rob thee of thy peace.

CLAUDINE. You told me once, love's impulse could not be resisted.

KELMAR. When the object is worthless, it should not be indulged.

CLAUDINE. Is Lothair worthless?

KELMAR. No; but he is poor, almost as you are.

CLAUDINE. Do riches without love give happiness?

KELMAR. Never.

CLAUDINE. Then I must be unhappy if I wed the miller Grindoff.

KELMAR. Not so—not so; independence gives comfort, but love without competence is endless misery. You can never wed Lothair.

CLAUDINE [sighing]. I can never love the miller.

KELMAR. Then you shall never marry him—though to see you Grindoff's wife be the last wish of your old father's heart. Go in, child; go in, Claudine. [CLAUDINE kisses his hand, and exit into cottage.] 'Tis plain her heart is riveted to Lothair, and honest Grindoff yet must sue in vain.

Enter LOTHAIR, *hastily.*

LOTHAIR. Ah! Kelmar, and alone! Where is Claudine?

KELMAR. At home, in her father's house—where should she be?

LOTHAIR. Then she has escaped—she is safe, and I am happy—
I did not accompany her in vain.

KELMAR. Accompany! Accompany! Has she then told me a
falsehood? Were you with her, Lothair?

LOTHAIR. No—ye—yes. [*Aside.*] I must not alarm him.

KELMAR. What mean these contradictions?

LOTHAIR. She knew not I was near her—you have denied our
meeting, but you cannot prevent my loving her—I have
watched her daily through the village and along the borders
of the forest.

KELMAR. I thank you, but she needs no guard; her poverty will
protect her from a thief.

LOTHAIR. Will her beauty protect her from a libertine?

KELMAR. Her virtue will.

LOTHAIR. I doubt it: what can her resistance avail against the
powerful arm of villainy?

KELMAR. Is there such a wretch?

LOTHAIR. There is.

KELMAR. Lothair, Lothair! I fear you glance at the miller Grindoff. This is not well; this is not just.

LOTHAIR. Kelmar, you wrong me; 'tis true, he is my enemy, for
he bars my road to happiness. Yet I respect his character;
the riches that industry has gained him he employs in assisting the unfortunate—he has protected you and your child,
and I honour him.

KELMAR. If not to Grindoff, to whom did you allude?

LOTHAIR. Listen: as I crossed the hollow way in the forest, I
heard a rustling in the copse. Claudine had reached the bank
above. As I was following, voices, subdued and whispering,
struck my ear. Her name was distinctly pronounced: 'She
comes,' said one: 'Now! now we may secure her,' cried the
second; and instantly two men advanced. A sudden exclamation burst from my lips, and arrested their intent; they
turned to seek me, and with dreadful imprecations vowed
death to the intruder. Stretched beneath a bush of holly, I lay
concealed; they passed within my reach. I scarcely breathed,

while I observed them to be ruffians, uncouth and savage—they were banditti.

KELMAR. Banditti! Are they not yet content? All that I had—all that the hand of Providence had spared, they have deprived me of; and would they take my child?

LOTHAIR. 'Tis plain they would. Now, Kelmar, hear the last proposal of him you have rejected. Without Claudine my life is but a blank—useless to others and wretched to myself; it shall be risked to avenge the wrongs you have suffered. I'll seek these robbers! If I should fall, your daughter will more readily obey your wish, and become the wife of Grindoff. If I should succeed, promise her to me. The reward I shall receive will secure our future comfort, and thus your fears and your objections both are satisfied.

KELMAR [*affected*]. Lothair, thou art a good lad, a noble lad, and worthy my daughter's love; she had been freely thine, but that by sad experience I know how keen the pangs of penury are to a parent's heart. My sorrows may descend to her when I am gone, but I have nothing to bequeath her else.

LOTHAIR. Then you consent?

KELMAR. I do, I do; but pray be careful. I fear 'tis a rash attempt; you must have help.

LOTHAIR. Then, indeed, I fail as others have before me. No, Kelmar, I must go alone, pennyless, unarmed, and secretly. None but yourself must know my purpose, or my person.

KELMAR. Be it as you will; but pray be careful. Come, thou shalt see her. [*The mill stops.*]

LOTHAIR. I'll follow; it may be my last farewell.

KELMAR. Come in—I see the mill has stopped. Grindoff will be here anon; he always visits me at nightfall, when labour ceases. Come.

[*Exit* KELMAR *into the cottage.*

LOTHAIR. Yes, at the peril of my life, I'll seek them. With the juice of herbs my face shall be discoloured, and in the garb of misery I'll throw myself within their power—the rest I leave to Providence. [*Music.*] But the miller comes.

[*Exit to the cottage. The* MILLER *appears in perspective coming from the crag in the rock—the boat disappears on the opposite side.*

Enter the two ROBBERS, RIBER *and* GOLOTZ, *hastily—they rush up to the cottage and peep in at the window.*

RIBER [*retiring from the window*]. We are too late—she has reached the cottage.

GOLOTZ. Curse on the interruption that detained us; we shall be rated for this failure.

RIBER. Hush! not so loud. [*Goes again cautiously to the window of the cottage.*] Ha! Lothair.

GOLOTZ. Lothair! 'twas he, then, that marred our purpose; he shall smart for't.

RIBER. Back! back! he comes. On his return he dies; he cannot pass us both.

[*Music. They retire behind a tree—a boat passes in the distance from the mouth of the cavern in the rock beneath the mill; then draws up to the bank.*

Enter GRINDOFF, *the* MILLER, *in the boat, who jumps ashore. Re-enter* LOTHAIR, *at the same moment, from the cottage.*

GRINDOFF [*disconcerted*]. Lothair!

LOTHAIR. Ay, my visit here displeases you, no doubt.

GRINDOFF. Nay, we are rivals, but not enemies, I trust. We love the same girl; we strive the best we can to gain her. If you are fortunate, I'll wish you joy with all my heart; if I should have the luck on't, you'll do the same by me, I hope.

LOTHAIR. You have little fear; I am poor, you are rich. He needn't look far that would see the end on't.

GRINDOFF. But you are young and likely. I am honest and rough; the chances are as much yours as mine.

LOTHAIR. Well, time will show. I bear you no enmity. Farewell!

GRINDOFF [*aside*]. He must not pass the forest. [*To* LOTHAIR.] Whither go you?

LOTHAIR. To the village; I must haste, or 'twill be late ere I reach the ferry. [*It begins to grow dark.*]

RIBER [*who with* GOLOTZ *is watching them*]. He will escape us yet.

GRINDOFF. Stay, my boat shall put you across the river. Besides, the evening looks stormy—come, it will save your journey half a league.

RIBER [*aside*]. It will save his life.

LOTHAIR. Well, I accept your offer, and I thank you.

GRINDOFF. Your hand.

LOTHAIR. Farewell! [*He goes into the boat, and pushes off.*]

GRINDOFF. So, I am rid of him. If he had met Claudine! But she is safe—now then for Kelmar.

[*Exit into the cottage.*

Re-enter RIBER *and* GOLOTZ.

RIBER. Curse on this chance! We have lost him!

GOLOTZ. But a time may come.

RIBER. A time shall come, and shortly, too.

[*Exeunt.*

SCENE II. *The Forest—distant thunder—stage dark.*

Enter KARL, *dragging after him a portmanteau.*

KARL. Here's a pretty mess! here's a precious spot of work! Pleasant upon my soul—lost in a labyrinth, without love or liquor—the sun gone down, a storm got up, and no getting out of this vile forest, turn which way you will.

COUNT [*calling without*]. Halloo! Karl! Karl!

KARL. Ah, you may call and bawl, master of mine; you'll not disturb anything here but a wild boar or two, and a wolf, perhaps.

Enter COUNT FREDERICK FRIBERG.

COUNT. Karl, where are you?

KARL. Where am I! that's what I want to know—this cursed wood has a thousand turnings, and not one that turns right.

COUNT. Careless coxcomb! said you not you could remember the track?

KARL. So I should, sir, if I could find the path—but trees will grow, and since I was here last, the place has got so bushy and briery that—that I have lost my way.

COUNT. You have lost your senses.

KARL. No, sir, I wish I had; unfortunately my senses are all in the highest state of perfection.

COUNT. Why not use them to more effect?

KARL. I wish I'd the opportunity; my poor stomach can testify that I taste—

COUNT. What?

KARL. Nothing; it's as empty as my head; but I see danger, smell a tempest, hear the cry of wild beasts, and feel—

COUNT. How?

KARL. Particularly unpleasant. [*Thunder and rain.*] Oh, we are in for it; do you hear, sir?

COUNT. We must be near the river; could we but reach the ferry 'tis but a short league to the Château Friberg.

KARL. Ah, sir, I wish we were there, and I seated in the old arm-chair in the servant's hall, taking of—holloa!

COUNT. What now?

KARL. I felt a spot of rain on my nose as big as a bullet. [*Thunder and rain.*] There, there, it's coming on again—seek some shelter, sir; some hollow tree, whilst I, for my sins, endeavour once more to find the way, and endure another curry-combing among these cursed brambles. Come sir. [*The storm increases.*] Lor', how it rumbles—this way, sir—this way.

[*Exeunt.*

SCENE III. *A Room in the Cottage—a door,* R. *flat—a window,* L. *flat—a fire,* R.—*tables,* R. *and* L.—*chairs, etc.*

GRINDOFF *and* KELMAR *discovered sitting at the table—thunder and rain.*

KELMAR. 'Tis a rough night, miller: the thunder roars, and, by the murmuring of the flood, the mountain torrents have descended. Poor Lothair! he'll scarcely have crossed the ferry.

GRINDOFF. Lothair by this is safe at home, old friend; before the storm commenced I passed him in my boat across the river. [*Aside.*] He seems less anxious for his daughter than for this bold stripling.

KELMAR. Worthy man! you'll be rewarded for all such deeds hereafter. Thank heaven, Claudine is safe! Hark!

[*Thunder heard.*

GRINDOFF [*aside*]. She is safe by this time, or I am much mistaken.

KELMAR. She will be here anon.

GRINDOFF [*aside*]. I doubt that. [*To* KELMAR.] Come, here's to her health, old Kelmar—would I could call you father!

KELMAR. You may do soon; but even your protection would now, I fear, be insufficient to—

GRINDOFF. What mean you? Insufficient!

KELMAR. The robbers—this evening in the forest—

GRINDOFF [*rising*]. Ha!

KELMAR [*rising*]. Did not Lothair, then, tell you?

GRINDOFF. Lothair?

KELMAR. Yes; but all's well; be not alarmed—see, she is here.

GRINDOFF. Here!

Enter CLAUDINE. GRINDOFF *endeavours to suppress his surprise.*

GRINDOFF. Claudine! Curse on them both!

KELMAR. Both! how knew you there were two?

GRINDOFF. 'Sdeath! you—you said robbers, did you not? They never have appeared singly; therefore, I thought you meant two.

KELMAR. You are right. But for Lothair they had deprived me of my child.

GRINDOFF. How! Did Lothair—humph! he's a courageous youth.

CLAUDINE, That he is; but he's gentle, too. What has happened?

KELMAR. Nothing, child, nothing. [*Aside to* GRINDOFF.] Do not speak on't, 'twill terrify her. Come, Claudine, now for supper. What have you brought us?

CLAUDINE. Thanks to the miller's bounty, plenty.

KELMAR. The storm increases!

KARL [*calling without*]. Holloa! holloa!

KELMAR. And hark! I hear a voice—listen!

KARL [*calling again without*]. Holloa!

CLAUDINE. The cry of some bewildered traveller.

[*The cry repeated, and a violent knock at the door.*

KELMAR. Open the door.

GRINDOFF. Not so; it may be dangerous.

KELMAR. Danger comes in silence and in secret; my door was never shut against the wretched while I knew prosperity, nor shall it be closed now to my fellows in misfortune. [*To* CLAUDINE.] Open the door, I say.

[*The knock is repeated, and* CLAUDINE *opens the door.*

Enter KARL *with a portmanteau.*

KARL. Why, in the name of dark nights and tempests, didn't you open the door at first? Have you no charity?

KELMAR. In our hearts plenty, in our gift but little; yet all we have is yours.

KARL. Then I'll share all you have with my master. Thank you, old gentleman; you won't fare the worse for sheltering honest Karl and Count Frederick Friberg.

GRINDOFF. Friberg!

KARL. Ay, I'll soon fetch him; he's waiting now, looking as melancholy as a mourning coach in a snow-storm, at the foot of a tree, wet as a drowned rat; so stir up the fire, bless you! clap on the kettle, give us the best eatables and drinkables you have, a clean table-cloth, a couple of warm beds, and don't stand upon ceremony. We'll accept every civility and comfort you can bestow upon us without scruple.

[*Throws down the portmanteau and exit.*

GRINDOFF. Friberg, did he say?

CLAUDINE. 'Tis the young count, so long expected.

KELMAR. Can it be possible? Without attendants, and at such a time, too?

GRINDOFF [*looking at the portmanteau, on which is the name in brass nails*]. It must be the same! Kelmar, good night.

KELMAR. Nay, not yet—the storm rages.

GRINDOFF. I fear it may increase; besides, your visitors may not like my company; good night.

Enter COUNT FREDERICK FRIBERG, *followed by* KARL—*he stops suddenly, and eyes the* MILLER, *as if recollecting him.* GRINDOFF *appears to avoid his scrutiny.*

COUNT. Your kindness is well timed; we might have perished. Accept my thanks. [*Aside.*] I should know that face.

GRINDOFF. To me your thanks are not due.

COUNT. That voice, too!

GRINDOFF. This house is Kelmar's.

[KARL *places the portmanteau on the table.*]
COUNT. Kelmar's!

KELMAR. Ay, my dear master; my fortunes have deserted me, but my attachment to your family still remains.

COUNT. Worthy old man. How happens this: the richest tenant of my late father's land—the honest, the faithful Kelmar, in a hovel?

KELMAR. It will chill your hearts to hear.

KARL [*at the fire, drying and warming himself*]. Then don't tell us, pray, for our bodies are cramped with cold already.

KELMAR. 'Tis a terrible tale.

KARL [*advancing*]. Then, for the love of a good appetite and a dry skin, don't tell it, for I've been terrified enough in the forest tonight to last me my life.

COUNT. Be silent, Karl. [*Retires to fire with* KELMAR.]

GRINDOFF. In—in the forest?

KARL. Ay.

GRINDOFF. What should alarm you there?

KARL. What should alarm me there? come, that's a good one. Why, first I lost my way; trying to find that, I lost the horses; then I tumbled into a quagmire, and nearly lost my life.

GRINDOFF. Psha! this is of no consequence.

KARL. Isn't it? I have endured more hardships since morning than a knight-errant. My head's broken; my body's bruised, and my joints are dislocated. I haven't three square inches about me but what are scarified with briers and brambles; and, above all, I have not tasted a morsel of food since sunrise. Egad! instead of my making a meal of anything, I've been in constant expectation of the wolves making a meal of me.

GRINDOFF. Is this all?

KARL. All! No, it's not all; pretty well, too, I think. When I recovered the path, I met two polite gentlemen with long knives in their hands.

GRINDOFF. Hey!

KARL. And because I refused a kind invitation of theirs, they were affronted, and were just on the point of ending all my troubles when up came my master.

GRINDOFF. Well!

KARL. Well! yes, it was well indeed, for after a struggle they made off. One of them left his sting behind, though; look, here's a poker to stir up a man's courage with! [*Showing a poniard.*]

GRINDOFF. A poniard!

KARL. Ay.

GRINDOFF [*snatching at it*]. Give it me.

KARL [*refusing the dagger*]. For what? It's lawful spoil—didn't I win it in battle? No! I'll keep it as a trophy of my victory.

[*During this time*, KELMAR *and* CLAUDINE *have taken and hung up the* COUNT'S *cloak, handed him a chair, and are conversing.*

GRINDOFF. It will be safer in my possession: it may lead to a discovery of him who wore it—and—

KARL. It may—you are right—therefore I'll deliver it into the hands of Count Frederick: he'll soon ferret the rascals out; set a reward on their heads—five thousand crowns, dead or alive! that's the way to manoeuvre 'em. [*Poking* GRINDOFF *in the ribs.*]

GRINDOFF. Indeed! humph!

KARL. Humph! don't half like that chap—never saw such a ferocious black muzzle in my life—that miller's a rogue in grain.

COUNT [*advancing*]. Nay, nay, speak of it no more. I will not take an old man's bed to ease my youthful limbs; I have slept soundly on a ruder couch—and that chair shall be my resting-place.

CLAUDINE. The miller's man, Riber, perhaps can entertain his excellency better—he keeps the Flask here, on the hill, sir.

GRINDOFF. His house contains but one bed.

KARL. Only one?

GRINDOFF. And that is occupied.

KARL. The devil it is!

COUNT. It matters not; I am contented here.

KARL. That's more than I am.

GRINDOFF. But stay; perchance his guest has left it; if so, 'tis at Count Frederick's service. I'll go directly and bring you word. [*Aside.*] I may now prevent surprise—the storm has ceased; I will return immediately.

[*Unseen he drops the sheath of a dagger and exit.*

COUNT [*eagerly*]. Kelmar, tell me, who is that man?

KELMAR. The richest tenant, sir, you have; what Kelmar was when you departed from Bohemia, Grindoff now is.

COUNT. Grindoff! I remember in my youth a favoured servant of my father's, who resembled him in countenance and voice —the recollection is strong upon my memory but I hope deceives me, for he was a villain who betrayed his trust.

KELMAR. I have heard the circumstance; it happened just before I entered your good father's service—his name was Wolf.

COUNT. The same.

KARL. And if this is not the same, I suspect he is a very near relation.

KELMAR [*angrily*]. Nay, sir, you mistake—Grindoff is my friend. Come, Claudine, is all ready?

KARL. Oh, it's a sore subject is it?

[Exeunt KELMAR and CLAUDINE.

Your friend, is he, old gentleman? Sir—sir—

COUNT [<i>who has become thoughtful</i>]. Well! what say you?

KARL. I don't like our quarters, sir; we are in a bad neighbour-hood.

COUNT. I fear we are; Kelmar's extreme poverty may have tempted him to league with—yet his daughter?

KARL. His daughter—a decoy! nothing but a trap; don't believe her, sir; we are betrayed, murdered, if we stay here. I'll endure anything, everything, if you will but depart, sir. Dark nights, bad roads, hail, rain, assassins, and—hey! what's this? [<i>Sees and picks up the scabbard dropped by</i> GRINDOFF.] Oh, Lord, what's the matter with me? My mind misgives me; and here—[<i>He sheaths the dagger in it and finds it fits.</i>] fits to a hair—we are in the lion's den!

COUNT. 'Tis evident we are snared, caught.

KARL. Oh, lord! don't say so.

Re-enter KELMAR and CLAUDINE, followed by LAURETTE and KRUITZ with supper things, etc.

KELMAR. Come, come, youngsters, bestir—spread the cloth, and—

COUNT. Kelmar, I have bethought me; at every peril, I must on tonight.

KELMAR. Tonight!

CLAUDINE. Not tonight, I beseech you; you know not half your danger. [<i>Goes to the table and places her hand carelessly on the portmanteau.</i>]

KARL. Danger! [<i>Aside.</i>] Cockatrice! [<i>To</i> CLAUDINE.] I'll thank you for that portmanteau.

COUNT. Let it remain—it may be an object to them, 'tis none to me—it will be safer here with honest Kelmar.

KELMAR. But why so sudden?

KARL. My master has recollected something that must be done tonight—or tomorrow it may be out of his power.

CLAUDINE. Stay till the miller returns.

KARL. Till he returns! [*Aside.*] Ah, the fellow's gone to get assistance, and if he comes before we escape, we shall be cut and hashed to mincemeat.

COUNT. Away! [*Advancing to the door.*]

Enter GRINDOFF, *suddenly.*

KARL. It's all over with us.

KELMAR. Well, friend, what success?

GRINDOFF. Bad enough—the count must remain here.

COUNT. Must remain!

GRINDOFF. There is no resource.

KARL. I thought so.

GRINDOFF. Tomorrow Riber can dispose of you both.

KARL. Dispose of us! [*Aside.*] Ay, put us to bed with a spade— that fellow's a gravedigger.

COUNT. Then I must cross the ford tonight.

GRINDOFF. Impossible; the torrent has swept the ferry barge from the shore, and driven it down the stream.

COUNT. Perhaps your boat—

GRINDOFF. Mine! 'twould be madness to resist the current now —and in the dark, too.

COUNT. What reward may tempt you?

GRINDOFF. Not all you are worth, sir, until tomorrow.

KARL. Tomorrow! [*Aside.*] Ah! we are crow's meat to a certainty.

GRINDOFF [*aside, looking askance around the room*]. All is right: they have got the scabbard, and their suspicions now must fall on Kelmar.

[*Exit* GRINDOFF, *bidding them all good night.*

COUNT. Well, we must submit to circumstances. [*Aside to* KARL.] Do not appear alarmed; when all is still, we may escape.

KARL. Why not now? There are only two of 'em.

COUNT. There may be others near.

Sestette.

CLAUDINE. Stay, prithee, stay—the night is dark,
            The cold wind whistles—hark! hark! hark!

COUNT. ⎫   ⎧ We must away.
KARL. ⎭ [*Together.*] ⎨ Pray, come away.

CLAUDINE.   The night is dark,
            The cold wind whistles.

ALL.   Hark! hark! hark!

CLAUDINE. Stay, prithee, stay—the way is lone,
            The ford is deep—the boat is gone.

KELMAR.   And mountain torrents swell the flood,
            And robbers lurk within the wood.

ALL.   Here ⎧ you ⎫ must stay till morning bright
                ⎩ we ⎭
            Breaks through the dark and dismal night,
            And merry sings the rising lark,
            And hush'd the night bird—hark! hark! hark!

[CLAUDINE *tenderly detains the* COUNT—KELMAR *detains* KARL, *and the scene closes.*

SCENE IV. *The Depth of the Forest—stage dark.*

Enter LOTHAIR, *with his dress and complexion entirely changed; his appearance is extremely wretched.*

LOTHAIR. This way, this—in the moaning of the blast, at inter-
    vals, I heard the tread of feet—and as the moon's light burst
    from the stormy clouds, I saw two figures glide like departed
    spirits to this deep glen. Now heaven prosper me, for my
    attempt is desperate! [*Looking off.*] Ah, they come! [*Retires.*]

    [*Music. Enter* RIBER, GOLOTZ *follows; they look around
    cautiously, then advance to a particular rock,* L. C., *which is
    nearly concealed by underwood and roots of trees.*

811494   E

LOTHAIR [*advancing*]. Hold! [*The* ROBBERS *start, and eye him with ferocious surprise.*] So, my purpose is accomplished—at last I have discovered you.

RIBER. Indeed! it will cost you dear.

LOTHAIR. It has already—I have been hunted through the country, but now my life is safe.

RIBER. Safe!

LOTHAIR. Ay, is it not? Would you destroy a comrade? Look at me, search me—I am unarmed, defenceless!

GOLOTZ. Why come you hither?

LOTHAIR. To join your brave band—the terror of Bohemia.

RIBER. How knew you our retreat?

LOTHAIR. No matter. In the service of Count Friberg I have been disgraced—and fly from punishment to seek revenge.

GOLOTZ [*to* RIBER]. How say you?

LOTHAIR [*aside*]. They hesitate—the young Count is far from home, and his name I may use without danger. [*To the* ROBBERS.] Lead me to your chief.

RIBER. We will—not so fast; your sight must be concealed. [*Offering to bind his forehead.*]

LOTHAIR. Ah! [*Hesitates.*] May I trust you?

GOLOTZ. Do you doubt?

RIBER. Might we not despatch you as you are?

LOTHAIR. Enough; bind me, and lead on.

> [*Music. They conceal his sight.* GOLOTZ *leads* LOTHAIR *to the rock, pushes the brushwood aside, and both exeunt, followed by* RIBER, *watching that they are not observed.*

SCENE V. *A Cavern.*

BANDITTI *discovered variously employed, chiefly sitting carousing around tables on which are flasks of wine, etc.—steps rudely cut in the rock, in the background, leading to an elevated recess,* C., *on which is inscribed* 'Powder Magazine'—*other steps leading to an opening in the cave—a grated door,* R.—*stage light.*

Chorus. BANDITTI.

Fill, boys, and drink about—
  Wine will banish sorrow;
Come, drain the goblet out,
  We'll have more tomorrow.

[*The* ROBBERS *all rise and come forward.*

Slow Movement.

We live free from fear,
  In harmony here,
Combin'd just like brother and brother;
  And this be our toast,
  The free-booter's boast,
Success and good-will to each other!

Chorus   Fill, boys, &c.

Enter RAVINA *through the grated door, as they conclude.*

RAVINA. What, carousing yet—sotting yet!

ZINGRA. How now, Ravina, why so churlish?

RAVINA. To sleep, I say—or wait upon yourselves. I'll stay no longer from my couch to please you. Is it not enough that I toil from daybreak, but you must disturb me ever with your midnight revelry?

ZINGRA. You were not wont to be so savage, woman.

RAVINA. Nor you so insolent. Look you repent it not!

FIRST ROBBER. Psha! heed her no more. Jealousy hath soured her.

ZINGRA. I forgive her railing.

RAVINA. Forgive!

ZINGRA. Ay, our leader seeks another mistress; and 'tis rather hard upon thee, I confess, after five years captivity, hard service too, and now that you are accustomed to our way of life—we pity thee.

RAVINA. Pity me! I am indeed an object of compassion: five long years a captive, hopeless still of liberty. Habit has almost made my heart cold as these rude rocks that screen me from the light of heaven. Miserable lost Ravina! by dire necessity become an agent in their wickedness: yet I pine for virtue and for freedom.

ZINGRA. Leave us to our wine. Come, boys, fill all, fill full, to our captain's bride.

ROBBERS. To our captain's bride!

> [*A single note on the bugle is heard from below.*

ZINGRA. Hark! 'tis from the lower cave. [*Bugle note repeated.*] She comes! Ravina, look you receive her as becomes the companion of our chief—remember!

RAVINA. I shall remember. So, another victim to hypocrisy and guilt. Poor wretch! she loves perhaps, as I did, the miller Grindoff; but, as I do, may live to execrate the outlaw and the robber!

> [*Music—the trap in the floor is thrown open.*

Enter RIBER *through the floor, followed by* GOLOTZ *and*
LOTHAIR.

ROBBERS. Hail to our new companion!

RAVINA. A man!

> [*LOTHAIR tears the bandage from his eyes as he arrives in the cave—the* ROBBERS *start back on perceiving a man.*

LOTHAIR. Thanks for your welcome!

ZINGRA. Who have we here? Speak!

RIBER. A recruit. Where is the captain?

ZINGRA. Where is the captain's bride?

RIBER. Of her hereafter. [*A bugle is heard above.*]

ROBBERS. Wolf! Wolf!

PLATE 1

The Miller and His Men. George Cruikshank's drawing of Farley as Grindoff.
Act One, scene five.

Enter GRINDOFF *in robber's apparel—he descends the opening, and advances.*

ZINGRA. ⎫
      ⎬ Welcome, noble captain!
ROBBERS. ⎭

GRINDOFF [*starts at seeing* LOTHAIR]. A stranger!

LOTHAIR [*aside*]. Grindoff!

[*The* ROBBERS *lay hands on their swords, etc.*

GRINDOFF. Ha, betrayed! Who has done this?

RIBER. I brought him hither to—

GRINDOFF. Riber! humph! You have executed my orders well, have you not? Where is Claudine?

LOTHAIR. Claudine! [*Aside.*] Villain! hypocrite!

GRINDOFF. Know you Claudine likewise?

RIBER. She escaped us in the forest. Some meddling fool thwarted our intent, and—

GRINDOFF. Silence; I know it all. A word with you presently. Now, stranger—but I mistake; we should be old acquaintance —my name is so familiar to you. What is your purpose here?

LOTHAIR. Revenge!

GRINDOFF. On whom?

LOTHAIR. On one whose cruelty and oppression well deserve it.

GRINDOFF. His name?

LOTHAIR [*aside*]. Would I dare mention it!

GRINDOFF. His name, I say?

RIBER. He complains of Count Friberg.

GRINDOFF. Indeed! then your purpose will soon be accomplished: he arrived this night, and shelters at old Kelmar's cottage. He shall never pass the river; should he once reach the Château Friberg, it would be fatal to our band.

LOTHAIR. Arrived! [*Aside.*] What have I done! My fatal indiscretion has destroyed him. [*To* GRINDOFF.] Let him fall by my hand.

GRINDOFF. It may tremble—it trembles now. The firmest of our band have failed. [*Looking at* RIBER.] Henceforth the enterprise shall be my own.

LOTHAIR. Let me accompany you.

GRINDOFF. Not tonight.

LOTHAIR. Tonight.

GRINDOFF. Ay, before the dawn appears, he dies! Riber!

> [LOTHAIR *clasps his hands in agony.*

RAVINA. What, more blood! must Friberg's life be added to the list?

GRINDOFF. It must; our safety claims it.

RAVINA. Short-sighted man! Will not his death doubly arouse the sluggish arm of justice? The whole country, hitherto kept in awe by dissension and selfish fear, will join; reflect in time; beware their retribution!

GRINDOFF. When I need a woman's help and counsel, I'll seek it of the compassionate Ravina. Begone! [*Exit* RAVINA.] Riber, I say!

RIBER. I wait your orders.

GRINDOFF. Look you execute them better than the last—look to't! The Count and his companion rest at Kelmar's; it must be done within an hour: arm, and attend me—at the same time I will secure Claudine—and should Kelmar's vigilance interpose to mar us, he henceforth shall be an inmate here.

LOTHAIR. Oh, villain!

GRINDOFF [*rushing towards* LOTHAIR]. How mean you?

LOTHAIR. Friberg—let me go with you.

GRINDOFF. You are too eager; I will not trust thy inexperience. Trust you! What surety have we of your faith?

LOTHAIR. My oath.

GRINDOFF. Swear, then, never to desert the object, never to betray the cause for which you sought our band—revenge on—

LOTHAIR. On him who has deeply, basely injured me, I swear it.

GRINDOFF. 'Tis well—your name?

LOTHAIR. Spiller.

GRINDOFF [*to* RIBER]. Quick! arm and attend me. [RIBER *retires.*] Are those sacks in the mill disposed of as I ordered?

ZINGRA. They are, captain.

GRINDOFF. Return with the flour tomorrow, and be careful that all assume the calmness of industry and content. With such appearance, suspicion itself is blind; 'tis the safeguard of our band. Fill me a horn, and then to business. [*A* ROBBER *hands him a horn of wine; he drinks.*] The Miller and his Men!

ROBBERS [*drinking*]. The Miller and his Men!

> [GRINDOFF *and* ROBBERS *laugh heartily.* GRINDOFF *puts on his miller's frock, hat, etc.* RIBER, *armed with pistols in his belt, advances with a dark lantern, and exeunt with* GRINDOFF *through the rocks.*

Chorus. BANDITTI.

Now to the forest we repair,
Awhile like spirits wander there;
In darkness we secure our prey,
And vanish at the dawn of day.

ACT II

SCENE I. *The Interior of* KELMAR'S *Cottage, as before.*

COUNT FREDERICK FRIBERG *discovered asleep in a chair, reclining on a table, and at the opposite side, near the fire,* KARL *is likewise seen asleep,* R. *The* COUNT'S *sword lies on the table,* L.—*the fire is nearly extinguished—stage dark—music as the curtain rises. Enter* CLAUDINE, *with a lamp, down the stairs.*

CLAUDINE. All still, all silent! The Count and his companions are undisturbed! What can it mean? My father wanders from his bed, restless as myself. Alas! the infirmities of age and sorrow afflict him sorely. Night after night I throw myself upon a sleepless couch, ready to fly to his assistance, and —hush—hush!

Enter KELMAR. CLAUDINE *extinguishes the light, and conceals herself.*

KELMAR. They sleep—sleep soundly—ere they wake I may return from my inquiry. If Grindoff's story was correct, I still may trust him—still may the Count confide in him; but his behaviour last night, unusual and mysterious, hangs like a fearful dream upon my mind—his anxiety to leave the cottage, his agitation at the appearance of Count Friberg— but above all, his assertion that the ferry-barge was lost, disturbs me. My doubts shall soon be ended. At this lone hour I may pass the borders unperceived, and the grey dawn that now glimmers in the east will direct my path.

[*Looks about him fearful of disturbing the sleepers, and exit.*

CLAUDINE [*advancing*]. My father appears unusually agitated. Ah, it may be! Sometimes he wanders on the river's brink, watching the bright orb of day bursting from the dark trees, and breathes a prayer, a blessing for his child; yet 'tis early, very early—yet it may be. Oh, father, my dear—dear father!

[*Exit.*

KARL. Yaw! [*Snoring.*] Damn the rats! Yaw, what a noise they keep up! Hey, where am I? Oh, in this infernal hovel; the night-mare has rode me into a jelly; then such horrible dreams, yaw! [*A light from the dark lantern borne by* RIBER *is seen passing the window.*] And such a swarm of rats—damn the rats! [*Lays his hand on his poniard.*] They'd better keep off, for I'm hungry enough to eat one. Bew—eu. [*Shivering.*] I wish it were morning. [*Music.*]

Enter RIBER; *he suddenly retires, observing a light occasioned by* KARL'*s stirring the fire with his dagger.*

KARL. What's that? [*Listens.*] Nothing but odd noises all night; wonder how my master can sleep for such a—yaw—aw! Damn the rats! [*Lies down.*]

[*Music. Enter* RIBER *cautiously, holding forward the lantern.* GRINDOFF *follows.* RIBER, *on seeing the* COUNT, *draws a poniard—he raises his arm,* GRINDOFF *catches it, and prevents the blow. Appropriate music.*

GRINDOFF. Not yet; first secure my prize, Claudine; these are safe.

KARL. How the varmint swarm!

GRINDOFF. Hush! he dreams.

RIBER. It shall be his last.

KARL. Rats, rats!

RIBER. What says he?

KARL. Rats! they all come from the mill.

RIBER. Do they so?

KARL. Ay, set traps for 'em, poison 'em.

[RIBER, *again attempting to advance, is detained by* GRINDOFF.

GRINDOFF. Again so rash—remember!

KARL. I shall never forget that fellow in the forest.

RIBER. Ha! do you mark?

GRINDOFF. Fear them not; be still till I return. He is sound; none sleep so hard as those that babble in their dreams. Stir not, I charge you; yet should Kelmar—ay—should you hear a noise without, instantly despatch.

[*Exit* GRINDOFF *up the stairs.*

RIBER. Enough! [KARL *wakes again—he observes* RIBER, *grasps his dagger, and, watching the motion of the* ROBBER, *acts accordingly.*] This delay is madness, but I must obey. [*Looking at the priming of his pistol, then towards the table—*KARL *drops to his position.*] Hey, a sword! [*Advancing to the table and removing the sword.*] Now all is safe. Hark! [*A noise without, as of something falling.*] 'Tis time! If this should fail, my poniard will secure him.

> [*Music.* RIBER *advances hastily, and, in the act of bringing his pistol to the level against the* COUNT, *is stabbed by* KARL, *who has arisen and closely followed his every movement; at the same moment enter* GRINDOFF. *The* COUNT, *rushing from the chair at the noise of the pistol, seizes him by the collar—the group stand amazed. Tableau.*

COUNT. Speak! What means this?

KARL. They've caught a tartar, sir, that's all. Hey, the miller!

GRINDOFF. Ay!

COUNT. How came you here?

GRINDOFF. To—to do you service.

COUNT. At such an hour!

GRINDOFF. 'Tis never too late to do good.

COUNT. Good!

GRINDOFF. Yes; you have been in danger.

KARL. Have we? Thank you for your news.

GRINDOFF. You have been watched by the banditti.

COUNT. So it appears.

KARL. But how did you know it?

GRINDOFF [*confused*]. There is my proof. [*Pointing to the body of* RIBER.]

KARL. But how the plague got you into the house? Through a rat-hole?

COUNT. Explain.

GRINDOFF. Few words will do that: on my return to the mill, I found you might repose there better than in this house; at all events, I knew you would be safer in my care.

COUNT. Safer! Proceed, what mean you?

KARL [*aside*]. Safer!

GRINDOFF. Kelmar—

COUNT. Hah!

GRINDOFF. Had you no suspicion of him—no mistrust of his wish to—to detain you?

COUNT. I confess, I—

GRINDOFF [*to* KARL]. The poniard you obtained in the forest, that you refused to give me—

KARL. This?

GRINDOFF. Is Kelmar's.

COUNT. Wretch!

KARL. I thought so; I found the sheath here.

GRINDOFF. I knew it instantly; my suspicions were aroused— now they are confirmed; Kelmar is in league with these marauders. I found the door open—you still slept. I searched the house for him; he is no where to be found—he and his daughter have absconded. Now sir, are you satisfied?

COUNT. I am.

KARL. I am not. I wish we were safe at home. I'm no coward by daylight, but I hate adventures of this kind in the dark. Lord, how a man may be deceived! I took you for a great rogue; but I now find you are a good Christian enough, though you are a very ill-looking man.

GRINDOFF. Indeed; we can't all be as handsome as you are, you know.

KARL [*pertly*]. No; nor as witty as you are, you know.

GRINDOFF. Come, sir, follow me. You can't mistake; see, 'tis day-break; at the cottage close to the narrow bridge that passes the ravine you will find repose.

COUNT. We'll follow you.

[*Exit* GRINDOFF.

KARL. I don't half like that fellow yet. [*Gets the portmanteau from table.*] Now, the sooner we are off the better, sir. As for this fellow, the rats may take care of him. [CLAUDINE'*s shrieks heard without.*]

COUNT [*drawing his sword*]. Ha, a woman's voice! Karl, follow me!

KARL. What, more adventures! [*Drawing his sword.*] I'm ready. I say, [*To the body of* RIBER.] take care of the portmanteau, will you?

[*Exit.*

SCENE II.—*The Forest. Stage partly dark.*

Music. Enter GRINDOFF, *with* CLAUDINE *in his arms.*

COUNT [*without*]. Karl! Karl! Follow, this way!

GRINDOFF [*resting*]. Ha, so closely pursued! Nay, then—

[*Going hastily, he pushes aside the leaves of the secret pass, and they disappear.*

Enter COUNT FREDERICK FRIBERG, *hastily.*

COUNT. Gone! Vanished! Can it be possible? Sure 'tis witchcraft. I was close upon him—Karl! The cries of her he dragged with him, too, have ceased, and not the faintest echo of his retiring footsteps can be heard—Karl!

Enter KARL.

KARL. Oh, Lord! Pho, that hill's a breather! Why, where is he? Didn't you overtake him?

COUNT. No! in this spot he disappeared, and sunk, as it should seem, ghost-like into the very earth. Follow!

KARL. Follow! Follow a will-o'-the-wisp!

COUNT. Quick—aid me to search!

KARL. Search out a ghost! Mercy on us! I'll follow you through the world, fight for you the best cock-giant robber of 'em all, but if you're for hunting goblins I'm off. Hey! where the devil's the woman, though? If she was a spirit, she made more noise than any lady alive.

COUNT. Perchance the villain, so closely pursued, has destroyed his victim.

KARL. No doubt on't; he's killed her to a certainty; nothing but death can stop a woman's tongue.

COUNT [*having searched in vain*]. From the miller we may gain
assistance: Grindoff, no doubt, is acquainted with every turn
and outlet of the forest; quick, attend me to the mill.

[*Exeunt.*

SCENE III. *The Cavern.*

Music. ROBBERS *discovered asleep in different parts,* R. *and* L.
  LOTHAIR *on guard, with a carbine, stands beneath the magazine—stage partly light.*

LOTHAIR. Ere this it must be daylight—yet Grindoff returns
not. Perchance their foul intent has failed—the fatal blow
designed for Friberg may have fallen upon himself. How
tedious drags the time, when fear, suspense, and doubt thus
weigh upon the heart. Oh Kelmar, beloved Claudine, you
little know my peril. [*Looks at the various groups of* BANDITTI,
*and carefully rests his carbine at the foot of the rugged steps
leading to the magazine.*] While yet this drunken stupor
makes their sleep most death-like, let me secure a terrible
but just revenge. If their infernal purpose be accomplished,
this is their reward. [*Draws a coil of fuse from his bosom.*]
These caverns, that spread beneath the mill, have various
outlets, and in the fissures of the rock the train will lie
unnoticed. Could I but reach the magazine.

  [*Music.* LOTHAIR *retires cautiously up—he places his foot over
  the body of a* ROBBER, *who is seen asleep on the steps leading to
  the magazine—by accident he touches the carbine, which slips
  down—the* ROBBER, *being disturbed, alters his position while*
  LOTHAIR *stands over him, and again reposes.* LOTHAIR
  advances up the steps—as he arrives at the magazine, WOLF'S
  signal, the bugle, is heard from above. The ROBBERS *instantly
  start up, and* LOTHAIR *at the same moment springs from the
  steps, and seizing his carbine stands in his previous attitude.*

Enter WOLF [GRINDOFF] *descending the steps of the opening, with*
  CLAUDINE *senseless in his arms.*

ROBBERS. The signal!

GOLOTZ. Wolf, we rejoice with you.

LOTHAIR. Have you been successful?

WOLF [*setting down* CLAUDINE]. So far, at least, I have.

LOTHAIR [*aside*]. Claudine—merciful powers! [*To* WOLF.] But Kelmar—

WOLF. Shall not long escape me—Kelmar once secure, his favourite, my redoubted rival, young Lothair, may next require attention—bear her in, Golotz. [GOLOTZ *bears* CLAUDINE *off*.] Where is Ravina?

Enter RAVINA.

Oh, you are come!

RAVINA. I am; what is your will?

WOLF. That you attend Claudine; treat her as you would treat me.

RAVINA. I will, be sure on't.

WOLF. Look you, fail not. I cannot wait her recovery—danger surrounds us.

ROBBERS. Danger!

WOLF. Ay, everyone must be vigilant, every heart resolved. Riber has been stabbed.

LOTHAIR. Then Friberg—

WOLF. Has escaped.

LOTHAIR. Thank heaven!

WOLF. How?

LOTHAIR. Friberg is still reserved for me.

WOLF. Be it so—your firmness shall be proved.

RAVINA. So—one act of villainy is spared you; pursue your fate no farther—desist, be warned in time.

WOLF. Fool! could woman's weakness urge me to retreat, my duty to our band would now make such repentance treachery.

ROBBERS. Noble captain!

WOLF. Mark you, my comrades: Kelmar has fled; left his house —no doubt for the Château Friberg. The suspicions of the

Count are upon *him*. All mistrust of me is banished from his mind, and I have lured him and his companion to the cottage of our lost comrade, Riber.

LOTHAIR. How came Claudine to fall into your power?

WOLF. I encountered her alone, as I left Kelmar's cottage. She had been to seek her father; I seized the opportunity, and conveyed her to the secret pass in the forest. Her cries caused me to be pursued, and one instant later I had fallen into their hands—by this time they have recovered the pathway to the mill. Spiller shall supply Riber's place—be prepared to meet them at the Flask, and prove yourself—

LOTHAIR. The man I am; I swear it.

WOLF. Enough—I am content!

RAVINA. Content! such guilt as thine can never feel content. Never will thy corroded heart have rest—years of security have made you rash, incautious—wanton in thy cruelty—and you will never rest until your mistaken policy destroys your band.

WOLF. No more of this—her discontent is dangerous. Spiller! when you are prepared to leave the cavern, make fast the door; Ravina shall remain here confined until our work above is finished.

LOTHAIR. I understand—

WOLF. Golotz and the rest—who are wont to cheer our revels with your music—be in waiting at the Flask, as travellers, wandering Savoyards, till the Count and his followers are safe within our toils; the delusion may spare us trouble. I know them resolute and fierce; and should they once suspect, though our numbers overpower them, the purchase may cost us dear. Away—time presses—Spiller—remember—

LOTHAIR. Fear me not—you soon shall know me.

[*Exit* WOLF *and* ROBBERS *up the steps.* LOTHAIR *immediately runs up the steps to the magazine, and places the fuse within, closes the door and directs it towards the trap by which he first entered the cave.*

RAVINA. Now then, hold firm, my heart and hand; one act of

vengeance, one dreadful triumph, and I meet henceforth the hatred, the contempt of Wolf, without a sigh.

[*In great agitation she advances to the table, and taking a vial from her bosom pours the contents into a cup, and goes cautiously across to where* CLAUDINE *has been conducted.*

RAVINA. As she revives—ere yet her bewildered senses proclaim her situation, she will drink—and—

[LOTHAIR, *who has watched the conduct of* RAVINA, *seizes her arm, takes away the cup, and throws it off.*

LOTHAIR. Hold, mistaken woman! Is this your pity for the unfortunate—of your own sex, too? Are you the advocate of justice and of mercy—who dare condemn the cruelty of Wolf, yet with your own hand would destroy an innocent fellow-creature, broken-hearted, helpless, and forlorn? Oh, shame, shame!

RAVINA. And who is he that dares to school me thus?

LOTHAIR. Who am I?

RAVINA. Ay! that talk of justice and of mercy, yet pant to shed the blood of Friberg!

LOTHAIR [*aside*]. Now, dared I trust her—I must, there is no resource, for they'll be left together. [*To* RAVINA.] Ravina —say what motive urged you to attempt an act that I must believe is hateful to your nature?

RAVINA. Have I not cause—ample cause?

LOTHAIR. I may remove it.

RAVINA. Can you remove the pangs of jealousy?

LOTHAIR. I can—Claudine will never be the bride of Wolf.

RAVINA. Who can prevent it?

LOTHAIR. Her husband.

RAVINA. Is it possible?

LOTHAIR. Be convinced. Claudine, Claudine! [*Music.*]

CLAUDINE [*without*]. Ha! that voice!

LOTHAIR. Claudine!

Enter CLAUDINE.

CLAUDINE. 'Tis he, 'tis he! then I am safe! Ah! who are these, and in what dreadful place am I?

LOTHAIR. Beloved Claudine, can this disguise conceal me?

CLAUDINE. Lothair! I was not deceived.

[*Falls into his arms.*

RAVINA. Lothair!

LOTHAIR. Ay, her affianced husband. Ravina, our lives are in your power; preserve them and save yourself. One act of glorious repentance, and the blessings of the surrounding country are yours. Observe!

> [*Music.* LOTHAIR *points to the magazine—shows the train to* RAVINA, *and explains his intention—then gives a phosphorous bottle, which he shows the purpose of—she comprehends him.* CLAUDINE's *action expresses astonishment and terror.* LOTHAIR *opens the trap up the stage.*

RAVINA. Enough, I understand.

LOTHAIR. Be careful, be cautious, I implore you—convey the train where I may distinctly see you from without the mill; and above all let no anxiety of mind, no fear of failure, urge you to fire the train till I give the signal. Remember, Claudine might be the victim of such fatal indiscretion.

RAVINA. But Wolf.

Re-enter WOLF, *who, hearing his name, halts at the back of the cavern.*

LOTHAIR. Wolf, with his guilty companions, shall fall despised and execrated. [*Seeing* WOLF.] Ah! [*Aside to* CLAUDINE.] Remove the train.

WOLF. Villain! [*Levels a pistol at* LOTHAIR. RAVINA *utters an exclamation of horror.* CLAUDINE *retreats, and removes the train to the foot of the steps.*]

LOTHAIR. Hold! you are deceived.

WOLF. Do you acknowledge it? But 'tis the last time. [*Seizing* LOTHAIR *by the collar.*]

LOTHAIR. One moment.

WOLF. What further deception?

LOTHAIR. I have used none—hear the facts.

WOLF. What are they?

LOTHAIR. Hatred to thee—jealousy of the fair Claudine urged this woman to attempt her life. [*Points to* CLAUDINE.]

WOLF. Indeed! for what purpose was that pass disclosed? [*Pointing to the trap.*]

LOTHAIR. I dared not leave them together.

WOLF. Vain subterfuge—your threat of destruction on me and my companions—

LOTHAIR. Was a mere trick, a forgery, a fabrication to appease her disappointed spirit—induce her to quit the cave, and leave Claudine in safety.

WOLF [*going up to, and closely observing* RAVINA]. Plausible hypocrite, Ravina has no weapon of destruction—how then? [*Crossing back to* LOTHAIR.]

LOTHAIR [*looking toward* RAVINA, *who holds up the vial, unseen by* WOLF]. Ah! [*Aside.*] We are saved. [*Crossing and snatching the vial, which she had retained in her hand.*] Behold, let conviction satisfy your utmost doubts.

WOLF [*looking on the label*]. Poison! you then are honest, Wolf unjust—I can doubt no longer. [*Seizes* RAVINA *by the arm.*] Fiend! descend instantly; in darkness and despair anticipate a dreadful punishment.

> [*Music.* RAVINA *clasps her hands in entreaty, and descends the trap, which is closed violently by* WOLF.

WOLF. Now, Spiller, follow me to the Flask. [*Music.*] Be sure, make fast yon upper door.

> [*He takes his broad miller's hat, for which he had returned— exit up steps,* LOTHAIR *following and looking back significantly at* CLAUDINE, *who then advances cautiously, opens the trap, and gives the train to* RAVINA—*appropriate music.* RAVINA *and* CLAUDINE *remain in attitude, the latter watching* LOTHAIR, *with uplifted hands.*

SCENE IV. *The cottage of Riber—The sign of the Flask at the door,* L. *in flat.*

Enter COUNT FREDERICK FRIBERG *and* KARL.

COUNT. This must be the house.

KARL. Clear as daylight; look, sir, 'The Flask!' Oh, and there stands the mill! I suppose old rough-and-tough, master Grindoff, will be here presently. Well, I'm glad we are in the right road at last; for such ins and outs, and ups and downs, and circumbendibuses in that forest, I never—

COUNT. True; we may now obtain guides and assistance to pursue that ruffian!

KARL [*aside*]. Pursue again! not to save all the she sex! Flesh and blood can't stand this.

COUNT [*abstracted*]. Yet, after so long an absence, delay is doubly irksome—could I but see her my heart doats on!

KARL. Ah! could *I* but see what my heart doats on.

COUNT. My sweet Lauretta!

KARL. A dish of saur-kraut!

COUNT. Fool!

KARL. Fool! so I mustn't enjoy a good dinner even in imagination.

COUNT. Still complaining!

KARL. How can I help it, sir? I can't live upon air, as you do.

COUNT. You had plenty last night.

KARL. So I had last Christmas, sir; and what sort of a supper was it, after all? One apple, two pears, three bunches of sour grapes, and a bowl of milk; one of your forest meals— I can't abide such a cruel cold diet—oh, for a bumper of brandy! But unfortunately my digestion keeps pace with my appetite—I'm always hungry. Oh, for a bumper of brandy!

[*Music heard within the Flask.*

COUNT. Hush!

KARL. What's that? Somebody tickling a guitar into fits; soft music always makes me doleful.

COUNT. Go into the house—stay; remember, I would be private.

KARL. Private—in a public-house. Oh, I understand, incog. But the miller knows you, sir.

COUNT. That's no reason all his people should.

KARL. I smoke—they'd be awed by our dignity and importance —poor things, I pity 'em—they are not used to polished society. Holloa! house! landlord! Mr. Flask!

Enter LOTHAIR *as landlord.*

KARL. Good entertainment here for man and beast, I'm told.

LOTHAIR. You are right.

KARL. Well, here am I, and there's my master!

LOTHAIR. You are welcome. [*Aside.*] I dare not say otherwise; Wolf is on the watch.

[WOLF *appears, watching at a window.*

KARL. Have you got anything ready? [*Smacking his lips.*]

LOTHAIR. Too much, I fear.

KARL. Not a bit, I'll warrant. I'm devilish sharp set.

LOTHAIR. Well, you are just in time.

KARL. Pudding-time, I hope! Have you got any meat?

LOTHAIR. I must ask him. [*Aside and looking round anxiously.*] Won't your master—

KARL. No, he lives upon love; but don't be alarmed, I'll make it worth your while. I'm six meals in arrear, and can swallow enough for both of us.

[*Exit* KARL, *with* LOTHAIR, *to the Flask.* WOLF *closes the window.*

COUNT. Yes, I'm resolved—the necessity for passing the river must by this time have urged the peasantry to re-establish the ferry—delay is needless. I'll away instantly to the Château Friberg, and with my own people return to redress the wrongs of my oppressed and suffering tenantry.

Enter KARL.

COUNT. Well, your news?

KARL. Glorious! The landlord, Mr. Flask, is a man after my own heart, a fellow of five meals a day.

COUNT. Psha! Who are the musicians?

KARL. Ill-looking dogs, truly; Savoyards, I take it; one plays on a thing like a frying-pan, the other turns something that sounds like a young grindstone.

COUNT. What else?

KARL. As fine an imitation of a shoulder of mutton as ever I clapp'd my eyes on.

Enter KELMAR, *exhausted by haste and fatigue.*

COUNT. Kelmar!

KELMAR. Ah, the Count and his companion! Thank heaven, I am arrived in time! my master will be saved, though Claudine, my poor unhappy child, is lost. Fly, I beseech you, fly from this spot! Do not question me; this is no time for explanations; one moment longer, and you are betrayed— your lives irrecoverably sacrificed.

COUNT. Would you again deceive us?

KELMAR. I have been myself deceived—fatally deceived! Let an old man's prayers prevail with you! Leave, oh leave this accursed place, and—

Enter WOLF, *in his miller's dress.*

KELMAR. Ah, the miller! then has hope forsaken me. Yet one ray, one effort more, and—

WOLF. Thy treachery is known. [*He seizes* KELMAR *by the collar.*]

KELMAR. One successful effort more, and death is welcome.

WOLF. Villain!

KELMAR. Thou art the villain—see—behold!

[*With a violent effort of strength, the old man suddenly turns upon* WOLF *and tears open his vest, beneath which he appears armed.* WOLF, *at the same instant, dashes* KELMAR *from him, who impelled forward is caught by the* COUNT. *The* COUNT *draws his sword—*WOLF *draws pistols in each hand from his side-pockets, and his hat falls off at the same instant— appropriate music.*]

COUNT. 'Tis he, the same! 'tis Wolf.

WOLF. Spiller! Golotz! [*Rushes out.*]

KARL. Is it Wolf? Damn his pistols! This shall reach him. [*Draws his sword, and hastens after* WOLF—*the report of a pistol is immediately heard.*

[*Exit* COUNT FRIBERG *and* KELMAR. *At the same moment,* GOLOTZ *and another* ROBBER, *disguised as minstrels, followed by* LOTHAIR, *burst from the house.*

GOLOTZ. We are called; Wolf called us! Ah, they have discovered him!

LOTHAIR. 'Tis too late to follow him; he has reached the bridge.

GOLOTZ. Then he is safe; but see, at the foot of the hill armed men in the Friberg uniform press forward to the mill.

LOTHAIR. This way we must meet them, then; in to the subterranean pass! [*Exeunt* GOLOTZ *and* ROBBER *to house.*] Now, Claudine, thy sufferings shall cease, and thy father's wrongs shall be revenged. [*Exit to house.*]

———

SCENE V. *A near View of the Mill,* C., *standing on an elevated projection—from the foreground a narrow bridge passes to the rocky promontory across the ravine.*

Music. Enter RAVINA, *ascending the ravine with the fuse, which she places carefully in the crannies of the rock.*

RAVINA. My toil is over; the train is safe. From this spot I may receive the signal from Lothair, and at one blow the hapless victims of captivity and insult are amply, dreadfully avenged. [*A pistol is fired without.*] Ah, Wolf! [*She retires.*]

Enter WOLF *pursued, and turning, fires his remaining pistol off; then hurries across the bridge, which he instantly draws up.* KARL *rushes on.*

WOLF [*with a shout of great exultation*]. Ha, ha! you strive in vain!

KARL. Cowardly rascal! you'll be caught at last. [*Shaking his sword at* WOLF.]

PLATE 2

The Miller and His Men. The blowing up of the mill in Hodgson's juvenile drama sheets. Act Two, scene five.

WOLF. By whom?

KARL. Your only friend, Beelzebub: run as fast as you will, he'll trip up your heels at last.

WOLF. Fool-hardy slave, I have sworn never to descend from this spot alive, unless with liberty.

KARL. Oh, we'll accommodate you; you shall have *liberty* to *ascend* from it; the wings of your own mill shall be the gallows, and fly with every rascal of you into the other world.

WOLF. Golotz! Golotz, I say! [*Calling toward the mill.*]

Enter COUNT FRIBERG, *with* KELMAR *and the* ATTENDANTS *from the Château Friberg, in uniform, and armed with sabres.*

COUNT. Wretch! your escape is now impossible. Surrender to the injured laws of your country.

WOLF. Never! The brave band that now await my commands within the mill double your number. Golotz!

Enter GOLOTZ *from a small door in the mill.*

WOLF. Quick! let my bride appear.

[*Exit* GOLOTZ.

Enter RAVINA—WOLF *starts.*

RAVINA. She is here! What would you?

WOLF. Ravina! Traitress!

RAVINA. Traitress! What then art thou? But I come not here to parley; ere it be too late, make one atonement for thy injuries—restore this old man's child.

KELMAR. Does she still live?

WOLF. She does; but not for thee, or for the youth Lothair.

RAVINA. Obdurate man! Then do I know my course.

Re-enter LOTHAIR, *conducting* CLAUDINE *from the mill, a cloak concealing him.*

CLAUDINE. Oh, my dear father!

KELMAR. My child—Claudine! Oh, spare, in pity spare her!

WOLF. Now mark me, Count: unless you instantly withdraw your followers and let my troop pass free, by my hand she dies!

KELMAR. Oh, mercy!

COUNT. Hold yet a moment!

WOLF. Withdraw your followers.

COUNT. Till thou art yielded up to justice, they never shall depart.

WOLF. For that threat, be this your recompense!

LOTHAIR [*throwing aside his cloak*]. And this my triumph!

[*Music.* LOTHAIR *places himself before* CLAUDINE *and receives* WOLF'S *attack—the* ROBBER *is wounded, staggers back, sounds his bugle, and the mill is crowded with* BANDITTI. LOTHAIR *throws back the bridge, and crosses it with* CLAUDINE *in his arms.*

Ravina, fire the train.

[RAVINA *instantly sets fire to the fuse, the flash of which is seen to run down the side of the rock into the gully under the bridge, and the explosion immediately takes place.* KELMAR, *rushing forward, catches* CLAUDINE *in his arms.*

CURTAIN

VIRGINIUS

A TRAGEDY IN FIVE ACTS

BY

AMES SHERIDAN KNOWLES (1784–1862)

———

*First performed at the Theatre Royal, Glasgow
in April 1820, and at
Covent Garden Theatre, 17 May 1820*

———

CAST

APPIUS CLAUDIUS	} Decemvirs	Mr. Abbott
SPURIUS OPPIUS		Mr. White
VIBULANUS		Mr. Jefferies
HONORIUS	} Patricians	Mr. Norris
VALERIUS		Mr. Vedy
CAIUS CLAUDIUS	} Clients to Appius	Mr. Connor
MARCUS		Mr. Claremont
DENTATUS, a veteran		Mr. Terry
VIRGINIUS, a centurion		Mr. Macready
NUMITORIUS, his brother-in-law		Mr. Egerton
ICILIUS, in love with Virginia		Mr. C. Kemble
LUCIUS, brother of Icilius		Mr. Comer
PUBLIUS	} Soldiers	Mr. Mears
DECIUS		Mr. Treby
SEXTUS		Mr. Crumpton
TITUS	} Citizens	Mr. Faucit
SERVIUS		Mr. Atkins
CNEIUS		Mr. King
VIRGINIA, daughter of Virginius		Miss Foote
SERVIA, her nurse		Mrs. Faucit
FEMALE SLAVE		Mrs. Chipp

Citizens, Male and Female, Soldiers, Lictors, &c.

———

SCENE

Chiefly Rome

PREFACE TO *VIRGINIUS*

Virginius made two theatrical reputations: that of Knowles, until 1820 an unknown Irish actor and schoolmaster who had had three plays performed in Ireland, and that of the twenty-seven year old Macready, who had been acting in London since 1816 in the shadow of Kean, praised for his obvious ability but languishing uncomfortably in melodramatic parts and the roles of horrible villains in legitimate drama. In 1819 he had challenged Kean in Richard III with great distinction; Virginius set the seal on his fame.

Besides *Virginius*, Knowles's most admired and successful plays—he wrote twenty-four altogether—were the dramas *William Tell* (1825), *The Hunchback* (1832), *The Wife* (1833), *Love* (1839), and a comedy, *The Love-Chase* (1837). These were composed in the most accepted conventions of the legitimate: blank verse, historical settings, and subject matter dealing in intrigues of love and state. *Virginius* was written at Kean's suggestion, but was not after all accepted because Drury Lane had taken on another tragedy on the same subject. Knowles's play was then performed for fourteen or fifteen nights at the Theatre Royal, Glasgow, with John Cooper in the title role. Macready received the manuscript of *Virginius* from a friend and immediately determined upon its production at Covent Garden. Although assigned the responsibility of stage management he was not allowed a penny for new costumes or scenery, and to be correct in his own dresses had to purchase them himself. On the eve of the first performance George IV sent for the manuscript, although it had passed the Lord Chamberlain's office, and the anxious company awaited the king's decision on stage next morning; the play came back with several lines on tyranny excised. The first night was an 'unquestionable triumph':

Its early scenes were not unattended with danger, Charles Kemble being so hoarse that not one word, spoken in the lowest whisper, could be heard, but the action of the scene told its story with sufficient distinctness to keep alive its interest. This grew as the play advanced, and in the third act, in Icilius' great scene, Kemble's voice came out in all its natural strength, and brought down thunders of applause. With the progress of the play the rapt attention of the audience gradually kindled into enthusiasm. Long-continued cheers followed the close of each succeeding act; half-stifled screams and involuntary ejaculations burst forth when the fatal blow was struck to the daughter's heart; and the curtain fell amidst the deafening applause of a highly-excited auditory.[1]

The play was acted fourteen times before the end of the season; it was revived in the following season, and Knowles received in all £400 from the manager, Harris.

In his own time Knowles's dramatic reputation was enormous. Hazlitt thought that *Virginius* was the best modern tragedy on the stage and Knowles 'the first tragic writer of the age'.[2] Charles Rice called him 'our modern Shakespeare'.[3] The legitimists praised him for qualities they found in the Elizabethan dramatists, but Knowles would not have been successful on those grounds alone; many pseudo-Elizabethan tragedies were rejected by their age. Apart from the fact that the best performers were attracted to his parts—Macready (who acted in six of Knowles's plays), Charles Kemble, Fanny Kemble, Ellen Tree, Charles Kean, Phelps, among many others—Knowles's essential domesticity was perfectly suited to the taste of the times. The central relationship of his tragedies and dramas is a family one, and the plays illustrate tenderness between husband and wife, true bonds of the heart between lovers, the love of father for child and child for father, the security of the family and threats to that security. The popular plays are all variations on this central relationship. The fond ties between father and son in *William Tell*, the paternal watchfulness of Master Walter over Julia in *The Hunchback*, the sweetly innocent idealism of the love of Virginia and Icilius, the doting affection of Virginius for his daughter and her loving trust in him—all played effectively on the domestic emotions of audiences. Horne noted the discrepancy between the setting of *Virginius* and its spirit: 'The costume, the settings, the decorations are heroic. We have Roman tunics, but a modern English heart, the scene is the Forum, but the sentiments those

---

[1] *Macready's Reminiscences*, ed. Sir Frederick Pollock (1875), i. 210.

[2] *The Spirit of the Age* (1825), p. 424.

[3] *The London Theatre in the Eighteen-Thirties* (1950), p. 9.

of the Bedford Arms.'[1] Traditional and legitimate in its
trappings, but entirely contemporary in homely domestic
appeal, *Virginius* remained for many years the most popular
tragedy of the century.

In Macready the domestic spirit of *Virginius* found its ideal
interpreter. Leigh Hunt, who believed that Macready surpassed Kean only in the expression of domestic tenderness, said
of his King John that 'he is best where he approaches domestic
passion, and has to give way to soft or overwhelming emotions',[2]
and of his Stranger in Kotzebue's play that 'in the expression of
a trembling tenderness nobody equals him'.[3] Westland Marston
remembered the delivery of Virginius's lines to his daughter,

> I never saw you look so like your mother
> In all my life!

'Here Macready's transition from overmastering wrath to
tenderness was made with such nature and force of contrast,
that many of his audience wept.'[4] Again, of Virginius's exclamation in the previous camp scene,

> I thank thee, Jupiter! I am still a father!

Marston wrote, 'Whoever has heard Macready's interruption
of convulsive joy . . . will hardly look for any more supreme
example of manly pathos.'[5] Macready played Virginius for the
next thirty years, nearly a hundred times in London alone.

The stage career of *Virginius* spanned the remainder of the
nineteenth century. Leading tragedians who appeared in London as Virginius included, besides Macready, Edmund Kean (in
1828), Young, Forrest, Phelps, G. V. Brooke, Charles Dillon,
and John McCullough. By 1872, when Ryder played the part,
'imitating now and then the favourite attitudes and gestures of
Macready, and repeating the points and pauses he had established',[6] *Virginius* was considered a slow, artificial, old-fashioned
play with some fine acting opportunities and a single great
scene, the climactic one in the Forum. (Even in its own time the
fifth act was looked on as an excrescence.) Nevertheless, there
were several more productions, the last of note in London being
Wilson Barrett's at the Lyric in 1897.

---

[1] *A New Spirit of the Age*, ii. 87.   [2] *The Tatler*, 29 Nov. 1830.
[3] Ibid., 14 Dec. 1830.   [4] *Our Recent Actors* (1888), i. 36.
[5] Ibid. ii. 125–6.   [6] Dutton Cook, *Nights at the Play* (1883), i. 209.

Together with the 1820 first edition of *Virginius*, the authoritative texts are *Dolby's British Theatre*, no. 38, and *Cumberland's British Theatre*, v. 6; these two last, being acting editions, are preferred to the 1820. *Dolby*, published in 1824, is closer to the date of original production than *Cumberland*, but there is very little difference between them. The later *Dicks'* no. 246 is the same as *Dolby*. The acting editions as well as the 1820 mark passages to be omitted on the stage by inverted commas. I have chosen to omit such passages entirely; thus what occasionally appear to be serious deficiencies in Knowles's metre are attributable to this cause.

PROLOGUE

By J. H. REYNOLDS, Esq.

Spoken by MISS BOOTH

———

[*Speaking behind.*] Nay, Mr. Fawcett, give me leave, I pray,
    The audience wait, and I must have my way. [*Enters.*]
    What, curb a woman's tongue! As I'm alive,
    The wretch would mar our old prerogative!
    Ladies! by very dint of pertinacity,
    Have I preserv'd the glory of loquacity.

      Oh! could you gaze, as I am gazing now,
    And see each man behind, with gather'd brow,
    And clenched hand (tho' nought my spirit damps)
    Beckoning with threats my presence from the lamps:
    Each, as I broke my way, declared how well
    His art could woo you—to be peaceable!
    One is well robed—a second greatly shines
    In the nice balance of *cast-iron* lines;
    A third can sing—a fourth can touch your tears—
    A fifth—'I'll see no more!'—a fifth appears,
    Who hath been once in Italy, and seen Rome;
    In short—there's quite a hubbub in the Green Room.
    But I—a very woman—careless—light—
    Fleet idly to your presence, this fair night;
    And, craving your sweet pardon, fain would say
    A kind word for the poet and his play.

      To night no idle nondescript lays waste,
    The fairy and yet placid bower of taste:
    No story piled with dark and cumbrous fate,
    And words that stagger under their own weight,
    But one of silent grandeur—simply said,
    As tho' it were awaken'd from the dead!

It is a tale—made beautiful by years—
Of pure old Roman sorrow—old in tears!
And those you shed o'er it in childhood may
Still fall—and fall—for sweet Virginia!

   Nor doth a crowned poet of the age,
Call the sweet spirits from the historic page!
No old familiar dramatist hath spun
This tragic, antique web to-night—but one,
An unknown author, in a sister land,
Waits, in young fear, the fiat of your hand.

ACT I

SCENE I. *A Street in Rome.*

Enter SERVIUS *and* CNEIUS *and* CITIZENS.

SERVIUS. Carbo denied a hearing!

CNEIUS. Ay, and Marcellus cast into prison because he sued a friend of one of the Decemvirs for a sum of money he had lent him.

SERVIUS. And Appius resisted not? Appius, that in the first Decemvirate was a god to the people?

CNEIUS. Resisted not! Nay, was most loud in favour of the decree; but hither comes Virginius, who interested himself so much in Carbo's affair. He looks a little heated. Is not that Titus he is speaking to? Stand aside, Master, and listen.

Enter VIRGINIUS *and* TITUS.

VIRGINIUS. Why did you make him Decemvir, and first Decemvir too?

TITUS. We had tried him, and found him honest.

VIRGINIUS. And could you not have remained content? Why try him again to find him dishonest? Knew ye not he was a Patrician, and of the Claudian family?

TITUS. He laid down the Consulate—

VIRGINIUS. Ha! ha! ha! to be elected into the Decemvirate, and he was so; and he laid down his office of Decemvir to be re-elected into the Decemvirate, and he is so. Ay, by Jupiter, and to the exclusion of his late colleagues! Did not Titus Genutius lay down the Consulate?

TITUS. He did.

VIRGINIUS. Was he not next to Appius in the Decemvirate?

TITUS. He was.

VIRGINIUS. Did you not find him honest?

TITUS. We did find him honest.

VIRGINIUS. As honest as Appius Claudius?

TITUS. Quite as honest.

VIRGINIUS. Quite as honest! And why not re-elect him Decemvir? Most sapient people! You re-elect Appius into the Decemvirate for his honesty, and you thrust Titus out of the Decemvirate—I suppose for his honesty also! Why, Appius was sick of the Decemvirate!

SERVIUS. I never heard him say so.

VIRGINIUS. But he did say so—say so in my hearing; in presence of the Senators, Valerius and Caius Claudius, and I don't know how many others. 'Twas known to the whole body of the Senate—not that he was sick, but that he said so. Yes, yes! He and his colleagues, he said, had done the work of the Republic for a whole year, and it was now but just to grant them a little repose, and appoint others to succeed them.

TITUS. Well, well, we can only say he chang'd his mind.

VIRGINIUS. No, no, we needn't say that neither; as he had laboured in the Decemvirate, perhaps he thought he might as well repose in the Decemvirate.

TITUS. I know not what he thought. He is Decemvir, and we made him so, and cannot help ourselves. Fare you well, Virginius. Come, let's to the Forum.

[*Exeunt* TITUS, SERVIUS, *and* CNEIUS.

VIRGINIUS [*looking after them and pointing*]. You cannot help yourselves! Indeed, you cannot;
You help'd to put your masters on your backs.
They like their seat, and make you show your paces;
They ride you—sweat you—curb you—lash you—and
You cannot throw them off with all your mettle!
But here comes one, whose share in giving you
To such unsparing riders, touches me
More nearly, for that I've an interest
In proving him a man of fair and most
Erect integrity. Good day, Icilius.

Enter ICILIUS.

ICILIUS. Worthy Virginius! 'tis an evil day
For Rome, that gives her more convincing proof

The thing she took for hope is but a base
And wretched counterfeit! Our new Decemvirs
Are any thing but friends to justice and
Their country.

VIRGINIUS. You, Icilius, had a hand
In their election. You applied to me
To aid you with my vote in the Comitia;
I told you then, and tell you now again,
I am not pleas'd when a Patrician bends
His head to a Plebeian's girdle! Mark me!
I'd rather he should stand aloof, and wear
His shoulder high—especially the nephew
Of Caius Claudius.

ICILIUS. I would have pledg'd my life—

VIRGINIUS. 'Twas a high gage, and men have stak'd a higher
On grounds as poor as yours—their honour, boy!
Icilius, I have heard it all—your plans—
The understanding 'twixt the heads of the people—
Of whom, Icilius, you are reckon'd one, and
Worthily—and Appius Claudius—all—
'Twas every jot disclos'd to me.

ICILIUS. By whom?

VIRGINIUS. Siccius Dentatus.

ICILIUS. He disclos'd it to you?
Siccius Dentatus is a crabbed man.

VIRGINIUS. Siccius Dentatus is an honest man!
There's not a worthier in Rome! How now,
Has he deceiv'd me? Do you call him liar?
My friend, my comrade, honest Siccius,
That has fought in six score battles?

ICILIUS. Good Virginius,
Siccius Dentatus is my friend—the friend
Of every honest man in Rome—a brave man—
A most brave man. Except yourself, Virginius,
I do not know a man I prize above
Siccius Dentatus—yet he's a crabbed man.

VIRGINIUS. Yes, yes; he is a crabbed man.

ICILIUS. A man
  Who loves too much to wear a jealous eye.

VIRGINIUS. No, not a whit! Where there is double dealing,
  You are the best judge of your own concerns;
  Yet, if it please you to communicate
  With me upon this subject, come and see me.
  I told you, boy, I favour'd not this stealing
  And winding into place. What he deserves,
  An honest man dares challenge 'gainst the world—
  But come and see me. [*Going.*] Appius Claudius chosen
  Decemvir, and his former colleagues, that
  Were quite as honest as himself, not chosen—
  No, not so much as nam'd by him—who nam'd
  Himself, and his new associates! Well, 'tis true,
  Dog fights with dog, but honesty is not
  A cur, doth bait his fellow—and e'en dogs,
  By habit of companionship, abide
  In terms of faith and cordiality—
  But come and see me.

                                        [*A shout.*

ICILIUS. Appius comes!
  The people still throng after him with shouts,
  Unwilling to believe their Jupiter
  Has mark'd them for his thunder. Will you stay,
  And see the homage that they render him?

VIRGINIUS. Not I! Stay you; and, as you made him, hail him;
  And shout, and wave your hand, and cry, long live
  Our first and last Decemvir, Appius Claudius!
  For he is first and last and every one!
  Rome owes you much, Icilius—Fare you well—
  I shall be glad to see you at my house.

                                        [*Exeunt.*

Enter APPIUS CLAUDIUS, CLAUDIUS, SICCIUS DENTATUS
LUCIUS, TITUS, SERVIUS, MARCUS, *and* CITIZENS *shouting*

TITUS. Long live our first Decemvir!
  Long live Appius Claudius!
  Most noble Appius! Appius and the Decemvirate for ever!

                                        [CITIZENS *shout.*

APPIUS. My countrymen and fellow citizens,
  We will deserve your favour.

TITUS. You have deserv'd it,
  And will deserve it.

APPIUS. For that end we named
  Ourself Decemvir.

TITUS. You could not have nam'd a better man.

DENTATUS [*aside*]. For his own purpose.

APPIUS. Be assur'd, we hold
  Our power but for your good. Your gift it was;
  And gifts make surest debtors. Fare you well—
  And, for your salutations, pardon me,
  If I repay you only with an echo—
  Long live the worthy citizens of Rome!

            [*Exit* APPIUS, *etc., the people shouting.*

DENTATUS. [*going*] That was a very pretty echo, a most soft
  echo. I never thought your voices were half so sweet, a most
  melodious echo! I'd have you ever after make your music
  before the Patricians' palaces; they give most exquisite
  responses—especially that of Appius Claudius! A most
  delicate echo!

TITUS. What means Dentatus?

SERVIUS. He's ever carping—nothing pleases him.

DENTATUS. O yes—you please me—please me mightily, I
  assure you. You are noble legislators, take most especial
  care of your own interests, bestow your votes most wisely
  too—on him who has the wit to get you into the humour;
  and withal, have most musical voices—most musical—if one
  may judge by their echo.

TITUS. Why, what quarrel have you with our choice? Could
  we have chosen better? I say they are ten honest Decemvirs
  we have chosen.

DENTATUS. I pray you name them me.

TITUS. There's Appius Claudius, first Decemvir.

DENTATUS. Ay, call him the head; you are right. Appius
  Claudius, the head. Go on.

TITUS. And Quintus Fabius Vibulanus.

DENTATUS. The body, that eats and drinks while the head thinks. Call him Appius's stomach. Fill him, and keep him from cold and indigestion, and he'll never give Appius the head-ache! Well? There's excellent comfort in having a good stomach! Well?

TITUS. There's Cornelius, Marcus Servilius, Minucius, and Titus Antonius.

DENTATUS. Arms, legs, and thighs!

TITUS. And Marcus Rabuleius.

DENTATUS. He'll do for a hand, and as he's a Senator, we'll call him the right hand. We couldn't do less, you know, for a Senator! Well?

LUCIUS. At least you'll say we did well in electing Quintius Petilius, Caius Duellius, and Spurius Oppius, men of our order, sound men. At least you'll say we did well in that!

DENTATUS. And who dares say otherwise? 'Well!' One might as well say 'ill' as 'well'. 'Well' is the very skirt of commendation; next neighbour to that mire and gutter, 'ill'. 'Well', indeed! you acted like yourselves! Nay, e'en yourselves could not have acted better! Why, had you not elected them, Appius would have gone without his left hand, and each of his two feet.

SERVIUS. Out! you are dishonest!

DENTATUS. Ha!

SERVIUS. What would content you?

DENTATUS. A post in a hot battle. Out, you cur! Do you talk to me?

CITIZEN [*from behind*]. Down with him, he does nothing but insult the people.

[*The* CITIZENS *approach* DENTATUS, *threateningly.*

Enter ICILIUS, *suddenly.*

ICILIUS. Stand back! Who is't that says down with Siccius Dentatus? Down with him! 'Tis what the enemy could never do, and shall we do it for them? Who uttered that dishonest word? Who uttered it, I say? Let him answer a fitter, though less worthy mate, Lucius Icilius!

PLATE 3

Virginius. Scharf's drawing of Macready's 1837 production: Dentatus threatened by the mob. Act One, scene one.

CITIZENS. Stand back, and hear Icilius!

ICILIUS. What, hav'n't I voted for the Decemvirs, and do I
snarl at his jests? Has he not a right to jest, the good, honest
Siccius Dentatus that alone at the head of the veterans
vanquished the Œqui for you? Has he not a right to jest? For
shame, get to your houses! The worthy Dentatus! Cheer for
him, if you are Romans! Cheer for him before you go! Cheer
for him, I say!

[*Exeunt* CITIZENS, *shouting.*

DENTATUS. And now what thanks do you expect from me,
Icilius?

ICILIUS. None.

DENTATUS. By Jupiter, young man, had you thus stepped
before me in the heat of battle, I would have cloven you down
—but I'm obliged to you, Icilius—and hark you! There's a
piece of furniture in the house of a friend of mine that's called
Virginius, I think you've set your heart upon—dainty enough
—yet not amiss for a young man to covet. Ne'er lose your
hopes. He may be brought into the mind to part with it. As to
these curs, I question which I value more, their fawnings, or
their snarlings—I thank you, boy. Do you walk this way? I
am glad of it! Come. 'Tis a noble Decemvirate you have
chosen for us! Come.

[*Exeunt.*

SCENE II. VIRGINIUS's *House.*

Enter VIRGINIUS *and* SERVIA, *with some of* VIRGINIA's *work
in her hand.*

VIRGINIUS. And is this all you have observ'd? I think
There's nothing strange in that. An L and an I
Twin'd with a V. Three very innocent letters
To have bred such mischief in thy brain, good Servia!
Come, read this riddle to me.

SERVIA. You may laugh
Virginius, but I'll read the riddle right.

The L doth stand for Lucius, and the I,
Icilius; which, I take it, will compose
Lucius Icilius.

VIRGINIUS. So it will, good Servia.

SERVIA. Then, for the V; why, that is plain Virginia.

VIRGINIUS. And now, what conjuration find you here?

SERVIA. What should I find but love? The maid's in love,
And it is with Icilius. Look, the wreath
Is made of roses that entwines the letters.

VIRGINIUS. And this is all?

SERVIA. And is it not enough?
You'll find this figuring where e'er you look:
There's not a piece of dainty work she does—
Embroidery or painting—not a task
She finishes, but on the skirt, or border,
In needle-work or pencil, this her secret
The silly wench betrays.

VIRGINIUS. Go, send her to me—
Stay! Have you spoken to her of it?

SERVIA. I! Not I, indeed; I left that task to you—
Tho' once I asked her what the letters meant.
She laugh'd and drew a scratch across them; but
Had scarce done so ere her fair visage fell,
For grief that she had spoiled the cyphers.
Never after
She let me note her at work again.
She had good reason!

VIRGINIUS. Send her to me Servia.   [*Exit* SERVIA.
There's something here that looks as it would bring me
Anticipation of my wish. I think
Icilius loves my daughter—nay, I know it;
And such a man I'd challenge for her husband;
And only waited, till her forward spring
Put on a little more the genial likeness
Of colouring into summer, ere I sought
To nurse a flower, which, blossoming too early,
Too early often dies.
I'll ascertain it shortly—soft, she comes. [*Sits.*]

Enter VIRGINIA.

VIRGINIA. Well, father, what's your will?

VIRGINIUS. I wish'd to see you,
    To ask you of your tasks—how they go on—
    And what your masters say of you—what last
    You did. I hope you never play
    The truant?

VIRGINIA. The truant! No, indeed, Virginius.

VIRGINIUS. I am sure you do not—kiss me.

VIRGINIA. O my father,
    I am so happy when you're kind to me!

VIRGINIUS. You are so happy when I'm kind to you!
    Am I not always kind? I never spoke
    An angry word to you in all my life,
    Virginia. You are happy when I'm kind!
    That's strange; and makes me think you have some reason,
    To fear I may be otherwise than kind—
    Is't so, my girl?

VIRGINIA. Indeed I did not know
    What I was saying to you!

VIRGINIUS. Why, that's worse
    And worse! What, when you said your father's kindness
    Made you so happy, am I to believe
    You were not thinking of him?

VIRGINIA. I—[*Greatly confused.*]

VIRGINIUS. Go, fetch me
    The latest task you did.   [*Exit* VIRGINIA.
    It is enough.
    Her artless speech, like crystal, shows the thing
    'Twould hide, but only covers. 'Tis enough!
    She loves, and fears her father may condemn.

Enter VIRGINIA *with a painting.*

VIRGINIA. Here, sir.

VIRGINIUS. What's this?

VIRGINIA. 'Tis Homer's history
    Of great Achilles parting from Briseis.

VIRGINIUS. You have done it well. The colouring is good,
The figures well design'd. 'Tis very well.
Whose face is this you've given to Achilles?

VIRGINIA. Whose face?

VIRGINIUS. I've seen this face! Tut tut! I know it
As well as I do my own, yet can't bethink me
Whose face it is.

VIRGINIA. You mean Achilles' face?

VIRGINIUS. Did I not say so! 'Tis the very face
Of—no, no! Not of him. There's too much youth
And comeliness and too much fire to suit
The face of Siccius Dentatus.

VIRGINIA. O!
You surely never took it for his face!

VIRGINIUS. Why, no; for now I look again, I'd swear
You lost the copy ere you drew the head,
And, to requite Achilles for the want
Of his own face, contriv'd to borrow one
From Lucius Icilius.

Enter DENTATUS.

My Dentatus,
I am glad to see you! [*Rises.* VIRGINIA *retires.*]

DENTATUS. 'Tis not for my news, then.

VIRGINIUS. Your news! What news?

DENTATUS. More violence and wrong from these new masters
of ours, our noble Decemvirs—these demigods of the good
people of Rome! No man's property is safe from them. Nay,
it appears we hold our wives and daughters but by the tenure
of their will. Their liking is the law. The Senators themselves,
scared at their audacious rule, withdraw themselves to their
villas and leave us to our fate. There are rumours also of new
incursions by the Sabines.

VIRGINIUS. Rome never saw such days.

DENTATUS. And she'll see worse, unless I fail in my reckoning.
Is that Virginia? I saw her not before. How does the fair
Virginia? Why, she is quite a woman. I was just now wishing
for a daughter.

VIRGINIUS. A plague you mean.

DENTATUS. I am sure you should not say so.

VIRGINIA. Indeed he should not; and he does not say so,
Dentatus—not that I am not a plague,
But that he does not think me one, for all
I do to weary him. I am sure, Dentatus,
If to be thought to do well is to do well,
There's nothing I do ill. But it is far
From that, for few things do I as I ought—
Yet everything is well done with my father,
Dentatus.

VIRGINIUS [*aside*]. That's well done, is it not, my friend?
But if you had a daughter, what would you do with her?

DENTATUS. I'd give her to Icilius. I should have been just now
torn to pieces, but for his good offices. The gentle citizens,
that are driven about by the Decemvir's lictors like a herd of
tame oxen, and with most beast-like docility only low ap-
plauses to them in return, would have done me the kindness to
knock my brains out; but the noble Icilius bearded them
singly and railed them into temper. Had I a daughter worthy
of such a husband, he should have such a wife, and a Patrician's
dower along with her.

VIRGINIUS. I wish to speak with you, Dentatus. Icilius is a
young man whom I honour, but so far only as his conduct
gives me warrant. He has had, as thou knowest, a principal
hand in helping us to our Decemvirs. It may be that he is
what I would gladly think him; but I must see him clearly,
clearly, Dentatus.

[*Exeunt* VIRGINIUS *and* DENTATUS.

VIRGINIA. How is it with my heart? I feel as one
That has lost every thing, and just before
Had nothing left to wish for! He will cast
Icilius off! I never told it yet;
But take of me, thou gentle air, the secret—
And ever after breathe more balmy sweet—
I love Icilius! I love Icilius!
He'll cast Icilius off—not if Icilius
Approve his honour. That he'll ever do;

He speaks and looks and moves a thing of honour,
Or honour never yet spoke, look'd, or mov'd,
Or was a thing of earth. O, come Icilius;
Do but appear, and thou art vindicated.

Enter ICILIUS.

ICILIUS. Virginia, sweet Virginia! sure I heard
My name pronounc'd. Was it by thee, Virginia?
Thou dost not answer? Then it was by thee—
O wouldst thou tell me why thou nam'dst Icilius!

VIRGINIA. My father is incens'd with thee. Dentatus
Has told him of the new Decemvirate,
How they abuse their office. You, he knows,
Have favoured their election, and he fears
May have some understanding of their plans.

ICILIUS. He wrongs me then!

VIRGINIA. I thank the gods!

ICILIUS. For me,
Virginia? Do you thank the gods for me?
Your eye is moist—yet that may be for pity;
Your hand doth tremble—that may be for fear;
Your cheek is cover'd o'er with blushes. What,
O what can that be for?

VIRGINIA. Icilius, leave me!

ICILIUS. Leave thee, Virginia? O a word—a word
Trembles upon my tongue, which if it match
The thought that moves thee now, and thou wilt let me
Pronounce that word, to speak that thought for thee,
I'll breathe—though I expire in the extacy
Of uttering it.

VIRGINIA. Icilius, will you leave me?

ICILIUS. Love! Love! Virginia! Love! If I have spoke
Thy thought aright, ne'er be it said again;
The heart requires more service than the tongue
Can at its best perform. My tongue hath serv'd
Two hearts—but, lest it should o'erboast itself,
Two hearts with but one thought. Virginia!
Virginia, speak—   [VIRGINIA *covers her face with her hands.*

PLATE 4

Virginius. Macready as Virginius: 'Thou seest that hand? It is a Roman's, boy.'
Act One, scene two.

O I have lov'd thee long:
So much the more extatic my delight,
To find thee mine at length.

VIRGINIA. My secret's yours.
Keep it and honour it, Icilius.

Enter VIRGINIUS *and* DENTATUS *behind.*

VIRGINIUS. Icilius here!

VIRGINIA. I ask thee now to leave me.

ICILIUS. Leave thee! Who leaves a treasure he has coveted
So long, and found so newly, ere he scans it
Again and o'er again; and asks and answers,
Repeats and answers, answers and repeats
The half-mistrustful, half-assured question—
And is it mine indeed?

VIRGINIA. Indeed, indeed!
Now leave me.

ICILIUS. I must see thy father first,
And lay my soul before him.

VIRGINIA. Not to-night.

ICILIUS. Now worse than ever, dear Virginia,
Can I endure his doubts; I'll lay my soul
Naked before him—win his friendship quite,
Or lose myself for ever!

[*Going, is met by* VIRGINIUS.

VIRGINIUS. Stop, Icilius!
Thou seest that hand? It is a Roman's, boy;
'Tis sworn to liberty. It is the friend
Of honour. Dost thou think so?

ICILIUS. Do I think
Virginius owns that hand?

VIRGINIUS. Then you'll believe
It has an oath deadly to tyranny,
And is the foe of falsehood! By the gods,
Knew it the lurking place of treason, though
It were a brother's heart, 'twould drag the caitiff
Forth. Dar'st thou take that hand?

ICILIUS. I dare, Virginius.

VIRGINIUS. Then take it! Is it weak in thy embrace?
  Returns it not thy gripe? Thou wilt not hold
  Faster by it, than it will hold by thee!
  I overheard thee say, thou was't resolv'd
  To win my friendship quite. Thou cans't not win
  What thou hast won already. You will stay
  And sup with us to-night?

DENTATUS. To be sure he will.

VIRGINIUS. And hark you, sir,
  At your convenient time appoint a day
  Your friends and kinsmen may confer with me—
  There is a bargain I would strike with you.
  Come, to the supper-room. Do you wait for me,
  To lead Virginia in, or will you do it?

        [ICILIUS *goes eagerly to* VIRGINIA, *and exit with her.*

  Come on, I say, come on. Your hand, Dentatus.

                                        [*Exeunt.*

ACT II

SCENE I. *A Street.*

Enter PUBLIUS *and* SEXTUS.

PUBLIUS. This way! We muster at the Flaminian gate.

SEXTIUS. Shall we not wait for Decius?

PUBLIUS. No, were he ten times Decius. They'll have already begun their march. Come on!

Enter NUMITORIUS.

NUMITORIUS. Do you belong to the fourth legion?

PUBLIUS. We do.

NUMITORIUS. They are upon their march, then.

PUBLIUS. I told you so—Come on, come on!

[*Exeunt* SOLDIERS.

Enter LUCIUS.

LUCIUS. Numitorius, what soldiers were those that just now parted from you?

NUMITORIUS. Soldiers hastening to overtake the army, that's now upon its march.

LUCIUS. 'Tis all confirmed then; the Sabines are in force upon our borders.

NUMITORIUS. I pray you tell me something new! Know you not the Senate has met, and the Decemvirs have come off triumphant in spite of all opposition?

LUCIUS. Should they have been opposed in such a strait as this?

NUMITORIUS. Ay, should they? They dared not have armed a single citizen without the order of the Senate; which, had they not obtained, the country would have been left naked to the foe, and then they had been forced to make room for more popular magistrates.

LUCIUS. Why, were they not opposed then?

NUMITORIUS. Did not I tell you they were opposed? Caius
Claudius, Appius's own uncle, and Honorius, that noble
Senator, opposed them; and it was like to go against them
but for the brawling insolence of Spurius Oppius and the
effrontery of the head Decemvir, backed by the young
Patricians.

LUCIUS. So they are empowered to take up arms?

NUMITORIUS. To be sure they are, and they have done so. One
body has already march'd, and by this time, no doubt, has
come to blows with the enemy. The levy is still proceeding.
All the Decemvirs but Appius take the field. He remains in
Rome to keep good order that is the violater of all order.
Why, where have you been, Lucius, to have felt no movement
of so great and wide a stir? Your brother meets Virginius at
his house to-day. Come with me thither, for you I know are
bid. Lucius, there's no huzzaing for your Decemvirs now.
Come on, we have outstaid the hour.

                                                    [*Exeunt.*

SCENE II. VIRGINIUS'S *House.*

Enter VIRGINIUS, ICILIUS, NUMITORIUS, LUCIUS, *and others.*

VIRGINIUS. Welcome, Icilius! Welcome, friends! Icilius,
    I did design to speak with you of feasting
    And merriment, but war is now the word;
    One that unlovingly keeps time with mirth,
    Unless war's own—whene'er the battle's won,
    And safe carousing comrades drink to victory.

ICILIUS. Virginius! Have you chang'd your mind?

VIRGINIUS. My mind?
    What mind? How now! Are you that boy, Icilius!
    You set your heart so earnestly upon
    A dish of poor confections, that to balk you
    Makes you look blank. I did design to feast you
    Together with your friends. The times are chang'd—
    The march, the tent, the fight becomes us now!

ICILIUS. Virginius!

VIRGINIUS. Well?

ICILIUS. Virginius!

VIRGINIUS. How the boy
Reiterates my name!

ICILIUS. There's not a hope
I have, but is the client of Virginius.

VIRGINIUS. Well, well! I only meant to put it off;
We'll have the revel yet; the board shall smoke;
The cup shall sparkle, and the jest shall soar
And mock us from the roof! Will that content you?
Not till the war be done tho'. Yet ere then
Some tongue, that now needs only wag, to make
The table ring, may have a tale to tell
So petrifying, that it cannot utter it.
I'll make all sure, that you may be my guest
At any rate—altho' you should be forc'd
To play the host for me and feast yourself.
Look here. [*Shows a parchment to* ICILIUS.]
How think you? Will it meet the charge?
Will it not do? We want a witness tho'.
I'll bring one; whom if you approve, I'll sign
The bond. I'll wait upon you instantly.   [*Exit.*

LUCIUS. How feel you now, Icilius?

ICILIUS. Like a man
Whom the next moment makes, or quite unmakes.
With the intensity of exquisite
Suspense my breathing thickens, and my heart
Beats heavily, and with remittant throb
As like to lose its action. See, my hope
Is bless'd! I live, I live!

Enter VIRGINIUS *conducting* VIRGINIA, *with* NUMITORIUS.

VIRGINIUS [*holding his daughters' hand*]. You are my witnesses
That this young creature I present to you
I do pronounce my profitably cherish'd,
And most deservedly beloved child;
My daughter, truly filial—both in word
And act—yet even more in act than word:

And—for the man who seeks to win her love,
A virgin, from whose lips a soul as pure
Exhales, as e'er responded to the blessing
Breath'd in a parent's kiss. [*Kissing her.*] Icilius!

> [ICILIUS *rushes towards* VIRGINIUS *and kneels.*

Since
You are upon your knees, young man, look up;
And lift your hands to heaven. You will be all
Her father has been—added unto all
A lover would be!

ICILIUS. All that man should be
To woman, I will be to her!

VIRGINIUS. The oath
Is register'd! [ICILIUS *rises.*] Didst thou but know, young
   man, [*Takes a hand of each.*]
How fondly I have watch'd her since the day
Her mother died, and left me to a charge
Of double duty bound—how she hath been
My ponder'd thought by day, my dream by night,
My prayer, my vow,
My sweet companion, pupil, tutor, child!
Thou would'st not wonder that my drowning eye
And choking utterance upbraid my tongue
That tells thee, she is thine! Icilius,
I do betroth her to thee; let but the war
Be done—you shall espouse her. Friends, a word.

> [VIRGINIUS *and the rest exeunt.*

ICILIUS [*holding her hand*]. Virginia, my Virginia! I am all
Dissolv'd—o'erpower'd with the munificence
Of this auspicious hour. And thou nor mov'st
Nor look'st—nor speak'st—to bless me with a sign
Of sweet according joy! I love thee but
To make thee happy! If to make thee so
Be bliss denied to me—lo, I release
The gifted hand—that I would faster hold
Than wretches bound for death would cling to life—
If thou would'st take it back—then take it back.

VIRGINIA. I take it back—to give it thee again!

ICILIUS. O help me to a word will speak my bliss,
    Or I am beggar'd. No, there is not one!
    There cannot be; for never man had bliss
    Like mine to name.

VIRGINIA. I'd help thee to
    A hundred words; each one of which would far
    O'er-rate thy gain, and yet no single one
    Rate over high!

ICILIUS. Thou could'st not do it! No,
    Thou could'st not do it! Every term of worth
    Writ down and doubl'd, then the whole sum'd up,
    Would leave with thee a rich remainder still!
    Pick from each rarer pattern of thy sex
    Her rarest charm, till thou hast every charm
    Of soul and body, that can blend in woman,
    I would out-paragon the paragon
    With thee! No, I will not let thee win
    On such a theme as this!

VIRGINIA. Nor will I drop
    The controversy, that the richer makes me
    The more I lose.

ICILIUS. My sweet Virginia,
    We do but lose and lose, and win and win;
    Then let us stop the game—and thus I stop it.

                        [*Kisses her.*

        Re-enter VIRGINIUS, *and the others.*

VIRGINIUS. Witness, my friends, that seal! Observe, it is
    A living one! It is Icilius' seal;
    And stamp'd upon as true and fair a bond—
    Tho' it receive the impress blushingly—
    As ever signet kiss'd. Are all content?
    Speak else! She is thy free affianc'd wife,
    Thou art her free affianc'd husband. Come,
    We have o'erdrawn our time. Farewell, Virginia;
    Thy future husband for a time must be
    Bellona's. To thy tasks again, my child;
    Be thou the bride of study for a time.
    Farewell!

VIRGINIA. My father!

VIRGINIUS. May the gods protect thee.

VIRGINIA. My father!

VIRGINIUS. Does the blood forsake thy cheek?
Come to my arms once more! Remember, girl,
The first and foremost debt a Roman owes,
Is to his country; and it must be paid
If need be with his life. Why, how you hold me!
Icilius, take her from me. Hoa! Within,
Within there! Servia!

Enter SERVIA.

Look to your child.
Come, boy.

ICILIUS. Farewell, Virginia.

VIRGINIUS. Take her in.

VIRGINIA. The gods be with thee my Icilius—Father,
The gods be with thee—and Icilius.

VIRGINIUS. I swear a battle might be fought and won
In half the time. Now, once for all, farewell;
Your sword and buckler, boy! The foe! The foe!
Does he not tread on Roman ground? Come on!
Come on, charge on him, drive him back, or die!

[*Exeunt.*

SCENE III. APPIUS'S *House.*

Enter APPIUS.

It was a triumph, the achieving which
O'erpaid the risk was run—and that was great.
They have made trial of their strength, and learn'd
Its value from defeat. The Senate knows
Its masters now; and the Decemvirate,
To make its reign eternal, only wants
Its own decree, which little pains will win.
Ere this the foe has for his mad invasion
Been paid with chastisement. Now Claudius—

Enter CLAUDIUS.

CLAUDIUS. We have suffer'd a defeat!

APPIUS. What! The Decemvirs fly!

CLAUDIUS. The soldiers fight
  With only half a heart.

APPIUS. Then decimate them. Traitors! Recreants!
  Why, we shall have them at our very doors!
  Have we lost ground, my Claudius?

CLAUDIUS. None, except
  What we've retrac'd in fame. We strove to teach
  The enemy their road lay backwards, but
  They would not turn their faces for us. Each
  Retains his former line.

Enter MARCUS.

APPIUS. What news?

MARCUS. The Œqui
  Still press upon us. Rumours are afloat
  Of new disasters, which the common cry,
  Be sure, still multiplies and swells. Dentatus,
  That over-busy, crabbed veteran,
  Walks up and down among the people, making
  Your plans his theme of laughter. Naught he stints
  That may reflect you in an odious light,
  And lower the Decemvirate.

APPIUS. A dungeon
  Would do good service to him! Once within,
  Strangling were easy. We must stop his mouth.
  Where was he
  When last you heard him?

MARCUS. In the Forum.

APPIUS. So!
  He is past service, is he not? Some way
  To clear the city of him. Come, we'll hear him,
  And answer him, and silence him! 'Tis well
  The dog barks forth his spleen; it puts us on
  Our guard against his bite. Come, to the Forum!

                                        [*Exeunt.*

SCENE IV. *The Forum.*

Enter DENTATUS, TITUS, SERVIUS, *and* CITIZENS.

TITUS. What's to be done?

DENTATUS. We'll be undone—that's to be done.

SERVIUS. We'll do away with the Decemvirate.

DENTATUS. You'll do away with the Decemvirate? The Decemvirate will do away with you! You'll do away with yourselves! Do nothing. The enemy will do away with both of you. In another month, a Roman will be a stranger in Rome. A fine pass we are come to, Masters!

TITUS. But something must be done.

DENTATUS. Why, what would you have? You shout and clap your hands, as if it were a victory you heard of; and yet you cry—something must be done! Truly I know not what that something is, unless it be to make you general. How say you, Masters?

SERVIUS. We'd follow any man that knew how to lead us, and would rid us of our foes and the Decemvirate together.

DENTATUS. You made these Decemvirs! You are strangely discontented with your own work. And you are over-cunning workmen too. You put your materials so firmly together, there's no such thing as taking them asunder. What you build, you build—except it be for your own good. There you are bunglers at your craft. Ha! ha! ha! I cannot but laugh to think how you toiled, and strained, and sweated, to rear the stones of the building one above another, when I see the sorry faces you make at it!

TITUS. But tell us the news again.

DENTATUS. Is it so good? Does it so please you? Then prick your ears again, and listen. We have been beaten again— beaten back on our own soil. Rome has seen its haughty masters fly before chastisement, like slaves—returning cries for blows—and all this of your Decemvirs, gentlemen.

1st CITIZEN. Huzza for it again!   [*The people shout.*

2nd CITIZEN. Hush! Appius comes.

DENTATUS. And do you care for that? You that were just now within a stride of taking him and his colleagues by the throat? You'll do away with the Decemvirs, will you! And let but one of them appear, you dare not, for your life, but keep your spleen within your teeth! Listen to me, now! I'll speak the more for Appius.

Enter APPIUS, CLAUDIUS, *and* MARCUS, *preceded by* LICTORS.

I say, to the eternal infamy of Rome, the foe has chased her sons, like hares, on their own soil, where they should prey like lions—and so they would, had they not keepers to tame them.

APPIUS. What's that you are saying to the people, Siccius Dentatus?

DENTATUS. I am regaling them with the news.

APPIUS. The news?

DENTATUS. Ay, the news—the newest that can be had; and the more novel because unlooked for. Who ever thought to see the eagle in the talons of the kite?

APPIUS. It is not well done in you, Dentatus, to chafe a sore. It makes it rankle. If your surgery has learned no better, it should keep its hands to itself. You have very little to do, to busy yourself after this fashion.

DENTATUS. I busy myself as I like, Appius Claudius.

APPIUS. I know you do, when you labour to spread disaffection among the people, and bring the Decemvirs into contempt.

DENTATUS. The Decemvirs bring themselves into contempt.

APPIUS. Ha! dare you say so?

DENTATUS. Dare! I have dared cry 'Come on!' to a cohort of bearded warriors. Is it thy smooth face should appal me? Dare! it never yet flurried me to use my arm. Shall I not, think you, be at my ease when I but wag my tongue? Dare, indeed! [*Laughing contemptuously.*]

APPIUS. Your grey hairs should keep company with honester speech!

DENTATUS. Shall I show you, Appius, the company they are wont to keep? Look here! and here. [*Uncovering his forehead*

and shewing scars.] These are the vouchers of honest deeds—
such is the speech with which my grey hairs keep company.
I tell you, to your teeth, the Decemvirs bring themselves
into contempt.

APPIUS. What, are they not serving their country at the head
of her armies?

DENTATUS. They'd serve her better in the body of her armies!
I'd name for thee a hundred centurions would make better
generals. A common soldier of a year's active service would
take his measures better. Generals! Our generals were wont
to teach us how to win battles. Tactics are changed. Your
generals instruct us how to lose them.

APPIUS. Do you see my lictors?

DENTATUS. There are twelve of them.

APPIUS. What if I bid them seize thee?

DENTATUS. They'd blush to do it.

APPIUS. Why now, Dentatus, I begin to know you;
I fancied you a man that lov'd to vent
His causeless anger in an under breath,
And speak it in the ear—and only then
When there was safety! Such a one, you'll own,
Is dangerous; and, to be trusted as
A friend or foe, unworthy. But I see
You rail to faces. Have you not so much
Respect for Appius as to take him by
The hand—when he confesses you have some
Pretence to quarrel with his colleagues' plans,
And find fault with himself? Which, yet you'll own,
May quite as well be kindly done, Dentatus,
As harshly. Had you only to myself
Declar'd your discontents, the more you had rail'd,
The more I should have thank'd you.

DENTATUS. Had I thought—

APPIUS. And have you been campaigning then so long,
And prosperously, and mistrust you Siccius,
That a young scarless soldier like myself
Would listen to your tutoring? See, now,
How much you have mistaken me! Dentatus,

In a word—can you assist the generals;
And will you?

DENTATUS. I have all the will—but as
For the ability—

APPIUS. Tut, tut! Dentatus,
You vex me now! This coyness sits not well on you.
You know as well as I you have as much
Ability as will. I would not think you
A man that lov'd to find fault, but to find fault.
Surely the evil you complain of you
Would lend a hand to remedy. See now,
'Tis fairly put to you—what say you?

DENTATUS. Appius,
You may use me as you please.

APPIUS. And that will be,
As you deserve! I'll send you as my legate
To the army! [*Shout from the people.*] Do you hear your
friends, Dentatus?
A lucky omen that! Away, away!
Apprise your house—prepare for setting out.
I'll hurry your credentials. Minutes now
Rate high as hours! Assist my colleagues with
Your counsel; if their plans displease you, why,
Correct them—change them—utterly reject them;
And if you meet obstruction—notice me,
And I will push it by. There now! Your hand!
Again! Away! All the success attend you,
That Appius wishes you!

DENTATUS. Success is from
The gods; whose hand soe'er it pleases them
To send it by—I know not what success
'Tis Appius' wish they send; but this I know—
I am a soldier; and as a soldier I
Am bound to serve. All the success I ask,
Is that which benefits my country, Appius.

[*Exit* DENTATUS.

APPIUS [*aside*]. You have serv'd her overlong! Now for our
    causes. [APPIUS *ascends the Tribunal.*

CLAUDIUS. Do you see the drift of this?

MARCUS. I cannot guess it.

CLAUDIUS. Nor I.

APPIUS [*to a* PLEBEIAN]. Are you the suitor in this cause?
  Speak!

PLEBEIAN. Noble Appius, if there's law in Rome
  To right a man most injur'd, to that law
  Against yon proud Patrician I appeal.

APPIUS. No more of that, I say! Because he's rich
  And great, you call him proud. 'Tis not unlike,
  Because you're poor and mean, you call yourself
  Injur'd. Relate your story; and so please you,
  Spare epithets.

PLEBEIAN. Grant me a minute's pause,
  I shall begin.

> [VIRGINIA *at this moment crosses the stage with* SERVIA,
> *and is met by* NUMITORIUS *who holds her in conversation;*
> APPIUS *rivets his eyes upon her.*

NUMITORIUS. You have heard the news?

VIRGINIA. What news, dear uncle?

NUMITORIUS. Step
  Aside with me, I'll tell you.

> [*Takes her a little farther from the Tribunal.*

APPIUS. Can it be
  A mortal that I look upon?

VIRGINIA. They are safe!
  I thank the gods!

APPIUS. Her eyes look up to heaven
  Like something kindred to it—rather made
  To send their glances down, and fill the earth
  With worship and with gratulation. What
  A thrill runs up and down my veins, and all throughout me!

PLEBEIAN. Now, most noble Appius—

APPIUS. Stop;
  Put off the cause, I cannot hear it now!
  Attend to-morrow! An oppressive closeness

Allows me not to breathe. Lictors, make clear
The ground about the Rostrum!

[*Descends and approaches* CLAUDIUS *with precipitation.*

Claudius, Claudius!
Marcus, go you and summon my physician
To be at home before me. [*Exit* MARCUS.] Claudius,
Claudius, there, there!

VIRGINIA. You send a messenger to-night?

APPIUS. Paint me that smile! I never saw a smile
'Till now. My Claudius, is she not a wonder?
I know not whether in the state of girlhood
Or womanhood to call her. 'Twixt the two
She stands, as that were loth to lose her, this
To win her most impatient. The young year,
Trembling and blushing 'twixt the striving kisses
Of parting spring and meeting summer, seems
Her only parallel!

NUMITORIUS. 'Tis well. I'll send
Your father word of this. But have you not
A message to Icilius?

APPIUS. Mark you, Claudius?
There is a blush! I must possess her.

VIRGINIA. Tell him,
I think upon him. Farewell, Numitorius!

[*Exit with* SERVIA.

NUMITORIUS. Farewell, Virginia.

CLAUDIUS. Master, will you tell me
The name of that young maiden?

NUMITORIUS. She is call'd
Virginia, daughter of Virginius,
A Roman citizen, and a centurion
In the army.

CLAUDIUS. Thank you; she is very like
The daughter of a friend of mine. Farewell.

NUMITORIUS. Farewell.   [*Exit.*

APPIUS. I burn, my Claudius! Brain and heart—there's not
  A fibre in my body but's on fire!
  With what a gait she moves! Such was not Hebe,
  Or Jupiter had sooner lost his heaven
  Than changed his cup-bearer—a step like that
  The rapture glowing clouds might well bear up,
  And never take for human! Find me, Claudius,
  Some way to compass the possession of her.

CLAUDIUS. 'Tis difficult. Her father's of repute;
  The highest of his class.

APPIUS. I guessed it! Friends
  Are ever friends, except when friends are needed.

CLAUDIUS. Nay, Appius—

APPIUS. If thou can'st not give me hope,
  Be dumb!

CLAUDIUS. A female agent may be used
  With some success.

APPIUS. How? How?

CLAUDIUS. To tamper with
  That woman that attends her.

APPIUS. Set about it.

CLAUDIUS. Could she but be induc'd to help you to
  A single meeting with her.

APPIUS. Claudius, Claudius!
  Effect but that!

CLAUDIUS. I'll instantly about it.

APPIUS. Spare not my gold—nor stop at promises.
  I will fulfil them fast as thou can'st make them.
  To purchase such a draught of extacy
  I'd drain a kingdom. Set about it, Claudius!
  Away! I will not eat, nor drink, nor sleep,
  Until I hear from thee!

CLAUDIUS. Depend upon me!

APPIUS. I do, my Claudius, for my life—my life!

                                        [*Exeunt severally.*

ACT III

SCENE I. APPIUS's *House.*

Enter APPIUS.

It is not love, if what I've felt before
And call'd by such a name, be love—a thing
That took its turn—that I could entertain,
Put off, or humour—'tis some other thing;
Or if the same, why in some other state—
Or I am not the same—or it hath found
Some other part of sensibility
More quick, whereon to try its power, and there
Expends it all. Now, Claudius, your success?

Enter CLAUDIUS.

CLAUDIUS. Nothing would do, yet nothing left undone!
She was not to be purchas'd.

APPIUS. Did she guess—

CLAUDIUS. She could not,
So guarded was my agent; who describ'd you
A man of power, of noble family,
And regal fortune—one that ask'd not what
His pleasures cost—no further made disclosure.

APPIUS. And did it nothing move her, Claudius?

CLAUDIUS. Nothing.
The more my agent urg'd, the more the shrunk
And wither'd hag grew callous; further press'd,
And with more urgent importuning, ire
And scorn, in imprecations and invectives
Vented upon the monster (as she call'd him)
That would pollute her child, compell'd my advocate
To drop the suit she saw was hopeless.

APPIUS. Now
Had I a friend indeed!

CLAUDIUS. Has Appius need
  To search for such a friend, and Claudius by him?

APPIUS. Friends ever are provisionally friends—
  Friends for so far—friends just to such a point
  And then 'farewell!' Friends with an understanding—
  As 'should the road be pretty safe'—'the sea
  Not over-rough,' and so on—friends of *ifs*
  And *buts*—no friends! O could I find the man
  Would be a simple, thorough-going friend!

CLAUDIUS. I thought you had one, Appius.

APPIUS. So thought Appius,
  Till Appius thought upon a test of friendship
  He fears he would not give unto himself
  Could he be Appius' friend.

CLAUDIUS. Then Appius has
  A truer friend than Appius is to Appius.
  I'll give that test!

APPIUS. What! you'd remove her father
  And that Icilius whom you told me of?

CLAUDIUS. Count it as done.

APPIUS. My Claudius, is it true?
  Can I believe it? Art thou such a friend,
  That, when I look'd for thee to stop and leave me,
  I find thee keeping with me, step by step,
  And even in thy loving eagerness
  Outstriding me? I do not want thee, Claudius,
  To soil thy hand with their Plebeian blood.

CLAUDIUS. What would'st thou, then?

APPIUS. I was left guardian to thee—

CLAUDIUS. Thou wast.

APPIUS. Among the various property
  Thy father left, were many female slaves.

CLAUDIUS. Well?

APPIUS. It were easy for thee (were it not?)
  To invent a tale that one of them confess'd
  She had sold a female infant (and of course
  Thy slave) unto Virginius' wife, who pass'd it

Upon Virginius as his daughter, which
Supposititious offspring is this same
Virginia?

CLAUDIUS. I conceive you.

APPIUS. To induce
The woman to confirm your tale would ask
But small persuasion. Is it done?

CLAUDIUS. This hour.
I know the school, my Appius, where Virginia
Pursues her studies; thither I'll repair,
And seize her as my slave at once. Do thou
Repair to thy tribunal, whither, should
Her friends molest me in the attempt, I'll bring her,
And plead my cause before thee.

APPIUS. Claudius, Claudius,
How shall I pay thee? O thou noble friend!
Power, fortune, life, whate'er belongs to Appius,
Reckon as thine! Away, away, my Claudius!

[*Exeunt severally.*

SCENE II. *A Street in Rome.*

Enter LUCIUS, *meeting* TITUS, SERVIUS, *and* CNEIUS.

LUCIUS. Well, Masters, any news of Siccius Dentatus from the camp, how he was received by the Decemvirs?

TITUS. He was received well by the Decemvirs.

CNEIUS. It wasn't then for the love they bear him.

TITUS. But they expect he'll help them to return the cuffs they have gotten from the enemy.

SERVIUS. Do you wish for a victory?

LUCIUS. Yes, if Dentatus wins it. 'Tis to our credit, Masters— he's one of us.

SERVIUS. And is not Spurius Oppius one of us?

LUCIUS. He is; but he is in league with the Patricians. He is but half a Plebeian, and that is the worse half. I never lik'd your half-and-half gentry; they generally combine the bad of both kinds, without the good of either.

SERVIUS. Well, we shall have news presently. Your brother Icilius has just arrived with despatches from the camp. I met him passing through the Forum, and asked him what news he brought. He answered, none; but added we might look for news of another kind than what we had been lately accustomed to hear. [*A shriek without.*

CNEIUS. What's that?

TITUS. Look yonder, Masters! See!

SERVIUS. 'Tis Appius's client dragging a young woman along with him.

TITUS. Let us stand by each other, Masters, and prevent him.

Enter CLAUDIUS *dragging along* VIRGINIA, *followed by* SERVIA *and others.*

SERVIA. Help! help! help!

LUCIUS. Let go your hold!

CLAUDIUS. Stand by!
    She is my slave!

SERVIA. His slave? Help! help! His slave?
    He looks more like a slave than she! Good Masters,
    Protect the daughter of Virginius!

LUCIUS. Release the maid.

TITUS. Forbear this violence.

CLAUDIUS. I call for the assistance of the laws;
    She is my slave.

SERVIA. She is my daughter, Masters,
    My foster-daughter; and her mother was
    A free-born woman—and her father is
    A citizen, a Roman—good Virginius,
    As I said before—Virginius, the centurion,
    Whom all of you must know. Help! help! I say,
    You see she cannot speak to help herself;
    Speak for her, Masters—help her, if you're men!

TITUS. Let go your hold.

CLAUDIUS. Obstruct me at your peril.

LUCIUS. We'll make you, if you will not.

CLAUDIUS. Let me pass.

SERVIUS. Let go your hold, once more.

CLAUDIUS. Good Masters, patience—
Hear me, I say. She is my slave—I wish not
To use this violence, my friends; but may not
A master seize upon his slave? Make way,
Or such of you as are dissatisfied,
Repair with me to the Decemvir. Come,
I only want my right!

TITUS. Come on then!

SERVIUS. Ay,
To the Decemvir!

SERVIA. Run, run for Numitorius—alarm our neighbours!
Call out Icilius's friends! I shall go mad! Help! help! help!
[*Exeunt.*

———

SCENE III. *The Forum.*

Enter APPIUS, *preceded by* LICTORS.

APPIUS. Will he succeed? Will he attempt it? Will he
Go through with it? [*Looking out.*] No sign—I almost wish
He had not undertaken it; yet wish
More than I wish for life he may accomplish
What he has undertaken. O the pause
That precedes action! It is vacancy
That o'erweighs action's substance. What I fear
Is that his courage can't withstand her tears,
That will be sure to try and succour her,
Pointing, as 'twere, to every charm, and pleading
With melting eloquence. I hear a sound
As of approaching clamour—and the rush
Of distant feet. He comes! I must prepare
For his reception.   [APPIUS *ascends the Tribunal.*

CLAUDIUS *enters still holding* VIRGINIA, *followed by* SERVIA,
　　WOMEN, *and* CITIZENS *crying "shame!"*

CLAUDIUS. Do not press upon me;
　　Here's the Decemvir—he will satisfy you
　　Whether a master has a right or not
　　To seize his slave when he finds her.

SERVIA. She is no slave
　　Of thine! She never was a slave! Thou slave
　　To call her by that name! Ay, threaten me!
　　She is a free-born maid and not a slave,
　　Or never was a free-born maid in Rome!
　　O you shall dearly answer for it!

APPIUS. Peace!
　　What quarrel's this? Speak, those who are aggriev'd.

　　　　　Enter NUMITORIUS.

NUMITORIUS. Where is Virginia—wherefore do you hold
　　That maiden's hand?

CLAUDIUS. Who asks the question?

NUMITORIUS. I! Her uncle Numitorius!

CLAUDIUS. Numitorius, you think yourself her uncle—
　　Numitorius,
　　No blood of yours flows in her veins, to give you
　　The title you would claim. Most noble Appius!
　　If you sit here for justice—as I think
　　You do, attend not to the clamour of
　　This man, who calls himself this damsel's *uncle*.
　　She is my property—was born beneath
　　My father's roof, whose slave her mother was,
　　Who (as I can establish past dispute)
　　Sold her an infant to Virginius' wife,
　　Who never had a child, and heavily
　　Revolv'd her barrenness. My slave I have found
　　And seiz'd—as who that finds his own (no matter
　　How long soever miss'd) should fear to take it?
　　If they oppose my claim, they may produce
　　Their counter-proofs and bring the cause to trial!
　　But till they prove mine own is not mine own
　　(An undertaking somewhat perilous)

Mine own I shall retain—yet giving them,
Should they demand it, what security
They please for re-producing her.

APPIUS. Why, that
Would be but reasonable.

NUMITORIUS. Reasonable!
Claudius! [*With much vehemence—recollects himself—aside.*]
He's but a mask upon the face
Of some more powerful contriver. Appius,
My niece's father is from Rome, thou know'st,
Serving his country. Is it not unjust,
In the absence of a citizen, to suffer
His right to his own child to be disputed?
Grant us a day to fetch Virginius,
That he himself may answer this most foul
And novel suit. Meanwhile to me belongs
The custody of the maid—her uncle's house
Can better answer for her honour than
The house of Claudius. 'Tis the law of Rome,
Before a final sentence the defendant
In his possession is not to sustain
Disturbance from the plaintiff.

TITUS. A just law.

SERVIUS. And a most reasonable demand.

CITIZENS. Ay! Ay! Ay!

APPIUS. Silence, you citizens; will you restrain
Your tongues, and give your magistrate permission
To speak? The law is just—most reasonable—
I fram'd that law myself and will protect it.
But are you, Numitorius, here defendant?
That title none but the reputed father
Of the young woman has a right to. How
Can I commit to thee what may appear
The plaintiff's property; and if not his,
Still is not thine? I'll give thee till to-morrow
Ere I pass a final judgment. But the girl
Remains with Claudius, who shall bind himself
In such security as you require,

To re-produce her at the claim of him
Who calls her daughter. This is my decree.

NUMITORIUS. A foul decree. Shame, shame!

SERVIUS. Ay, a most foul decree.

CNEIUS. A villainous decree.

SERVIUS. Most villainous.

SERVIA. Good citizens, what do you with our weapons,
When you should use your own? Your hands, your hands!
He shall not take her from us.
Gather round her,
And if he touch her, be it to his cost;
And if ye see him touch her, never more
Expect from us your titles—never more
Be husbands, brothers, lovers, at our mouths,
Or any thing that doth imply the name
Of men—except such men as men should blush for.

APPIUS. Command your wives and daughters, citizens,
They quit the Forum.

SERVIA. They shall not command us,
That care not to protect us.

APPIUS. Take the girl,
If she is yours.

CLAUDIUS. Stand by.

VIRGINIA. O help me, help me!

Enter ICILIUS.

ICILIUS. Virginia's voice—Virginia! [*Rushes to her.*]

VIRGINIA. O Icilius! [*Falls fainting in his arms.*]

ICILIUS. Take her, good Numitorius.

APPIUS. You had better
Withdraw, Icilius; the affair is judged.

CLAUDIUS. I claim my slave.

ICILIUS. Stand back, thou double slave!
Touch her, and I will tear thee limb from limb
Before thy master's face. She is my wife,
My life, my heart, my heart's blood. Touch her
With but a look—

APPIUS. My lictors, there, advance!
  See that Icilius quits the Forum. Claudius,
  Secure your slave.

ICILIUS. Lictors, a moment pause
  For your own sakes. Do not mistake these arms;
  Think not the strength of any common man
  Is that they feel. They serve a charmed frame,
  The which a power pervades that ten times trebles
  The natural energy of each single nerve
  To sweep you down as reeds.

APPIUS. Obey my orders!

ICILIUS. Appius, before I quit the Forum, let me
  Address a word to you.

APPIUS. Be brief, then.

ICILIUS. Is't not enough you have depriv'd us, Appius,
  Of the two strongest bulwarks to our liberties,
  Our tribunes and our privilege of appeal
  To the assembly of the people? Cannot
  The honour of the Roman maids be safe?
  Thou know'st this virgin is betroth'd to me,
  Wife of my hope. Thou shalt not cross my hope
  And I retain my life—attempt it not!
  I stand among my fellow citizens—
  His fellow-soldiers hem Virginius round.
  Both men and gods are on our side; but grant
  I stood alone, with nought but virtuous love
  To hearten me—alone would I defeat
  The execution of thy infamous
  Decree! I'll quit the Forum now, but not
  Alone—my love! my wife! my free-born maid—
  The virgin standard of my pride and manhood,
  I'll bear off safe with me—unstain'd—untouch'd!
                          [*Embracing her.*]

APPIUS. Your duty, lictors—Claudius, look to your right.

ICILIUS. True citizens!

TITUS. Down with the traitor!

SERVIUS. Down with him—slay him!

> [*The* LICTORS *and* CLAUDIUS *are driven back;* CLAUDIUS
> *takes refuge at* APPIUS's *feet, who has descended and throws
> up his arms as a signal to both parties to desist, whereupon the
> people retire a little.*

APPIUS. So, friends! we thank you that you don't deprive us
　　Of every thing; but leave your magistrates,
　　At least their persons, sacred—their decrees,
　　It seems, you value as you value straws,
　　And in like manner break them. Wherefore stop
　　When you have gone so far? You might, methinks,
　　As well have kill'd my client at my feet,
　　As threaten him with death before my face!
　　Rise, Claudius! I perceive Icilius' aim:
　　He labours to restore the tribuneship
　　By means of a sedition. We'll not give him
　　The least pretence of quarrel. We shall wait
　　Virginius's arrival 'till to-morrow.
　　His friends take care to notice him. The camp's
　　But four hours journey from the city. 'Till
　　To-morrow, then, let me prevail with you
　　To yield up something of your right, and let
　　The girl remain at liberty.

CLAUDIUS. If they
　　Produce security for her appearance,
　　I am content.

TITUS. I'll be your security.

SERVIUS. And I.

CITIZENS. We'll all be your security.

> [*They hold up their hands.*

ICILIUS. My friends
　　And fellow citizens, I thank you; but
　　Reserve your kindness for to-morrow, friends,
　　If Claudius still persist. To-day I hope
　　He will remain content with my security,
　　And that of Numitorius, for the maid's
　　Appearance.

APPIUS. See she do appear! And come
  Prepar'd to pay the laws more reverence,
  As I shall surely see that they receive it.

            [*Exeunt* APPIUS, CLAUDIUS, *and* LICTORS.

ICILIUS. Look up, look up! my sweet Virginia,
  Look up, look up! you will see none but friends.
  O that such eyes should e'er meet other prospect!

VIRGINIA. Icilius! Uncle, lead me home! Icilius,
  You did not think to take a slave to wife?

ICILIUS. I thought, and think to wed a free-born maid;
  And thou, and thou alone art she, Virginia!

VIRGINIA. I feel as I were so—I do not think
  I am his slave. Virginius not my father!
  Virginius, my dear father, not my father!
  It cannot be; my life must come from him;
  For, make him not my father, it will go
  From me. I could not live, an he were not
  My father.

ICILIUS. Dear Virginia, calm thy thoughts—
  But who shall warn Virginius?

NUMITORIUS. I've ta'en care
  Of that; no sooner heard I of this claim,
  Than I dispatch'd thy brother Lucius,
  Together with my son, to bring Virginius
  With all the speed they could; and caution'd them
  (As he is something over quick of temper,
  And might snatch justice, rather than sue for it)
  To evade communication of the cause,
  And merely say his presence was required,
  Till we should have him with us. Come, Virginia;
  Thy uncle's house shall guard thee, till thou find'st
  Within thy father's arms a citadel,
  Whence Claudius cannot take thee.

ICILIUS. He shall take
  A thousand lives first.

TITUS. Ay, ten thousand lives.

ICILIUS. Hear you, Virginia! Do you hear your friends?

VIRGINIA. Let him take my life first; I am content
To be his slave then—if I am his slave.

ICILIUS. Thou art a free-born Roman maid, Virginia;
All Rome doth know thee so, Virginia—
All Rome will see thee so.

CITIZENS. We will! We will!

ICILIUS. You'll meet us here to-morrow?

CITIZENS. All, all!

ICILIUS. Cease not to clamour 'gainst this outrage. Tell it
In every corner of the city; and
Let no man call himself a son of Rome,
Who stands aloof when tyranny assails
Her fairest daughter. Come, Virginia,
'Tis not a private, but a common wrong;
'Tis every father's, lover's, freeman's cause;
To-morrow, fellow citizens, to-morrow!

CITIZENS. To-morrow!

[*Exeunt shouting.*

SCENE IV. *The Camp.*

Enter SPURIUS OPPIUS *and* QUINTUS FABIUS VIBULANUS.

OPPIUS. Has he set out?

VIBULANUS. He has, my Oppius,
And never to return! His guard's instructed
To take good care of him. There's not a man
But's ten times sold to us, and of our wishes
Fully possess'd. Dentatus will no more
Obstruct us in our plans. He did not like
The site of our encampment. He will find
At least the air of it was wholesome.

OPPIUS. What
Report are they instructed to bring back?

VIBULANUS. They fell into an ambush. He was slain.

OPPIUS. But should the truth, by any means, come out?

VIBULANUS. Imprison them and secretly despatch them,
　　Or ope' the dungeon doors and let them 'scape.
OPPIUS. I should prefer the latter method.
VIBULANUS. Well,
　　That be our choice. But when it is determined
　　To spill blood otherwise than as it may
　　Be spill'd, to hesitate about some drops
　　Is weakness, may be fatal. Come, my friend,
　　Let us be seen about the camp, and ready
　　With most admiring ear to catch the tidings
　　Will be the wonder of all ears, but ours.
　　Here's one anticipates us!

Enter MARCUS.

　　Well, your news?
MARCUS. Dentatus is no more, but he has dearly sold his life.
　　The matter has been reported as you directed. By few it is
　　received with credence—by many with doubt; while some
　　bold spirits stop not at muttering, but loudly speak suspicion
　　of foul play. A party that we met, a mile beyond the lines, no
　　sooner heard our story than they set off to bring the body to
　　the camp. Others have followed them. Fabius, we have your
　　gage for safety.
VIBULANUS. You have. Come, let us show ourselves. Guilt
　　hides,
　　And we must wear the port of innocence,
　　That more than half way meets accusal. Come.

[*Exeunt.*

SCENE V. *A Mountainous Pass.*

The body of DENTATUS *discovered on a bier,* SOLDIERS *mourning
　　over it.*

Trumpets. Enter VIRGINIUS.

VIRGINIUS. Where is Dentatus? Where is the gallant soldier?
　　Ah, comrade, comrade! warm, yet warm! So lately
　　Gone, when I would have given the world, only
　　To say farewell to thee, or even get

A parting look! O gallant, gallant soldier,
The god of war might sure have spar'd a head
Grown grey in serving him! My brave old comrade!
The father of the field! Thy silver locks
Other anointing should receive, than what
Their master's blood could furnish!

SOLDIER. There has been treachery here.

VIRGINIUS. What!

SOLDIER. The slain are all our own. None of the bodies are stripp'd—these are all Romans. There is not the slightest trace of an enemy's retreat. And now I remember they made a sudden halt when we came in sight of them at the foot of the mountain. Mark'd you not, too, with what confused haste they told their story, directed us, and hurried on to the camp?

VIRGINIUS. Revenge! The Decemvirs! Ay, the Decemvirs!
For every drop of blood thou shalt have ten,
Dentatus!

LUCIUS [*without*]. What hoa! Virginius, Virginius!

VIRGINIUS. Here, here!

Enter LUCIUS.

LUCIUS. 'Tis well you're found, Virginius.

VIRGINIUS. What makes you from the city? Look!
My Lucius, what a sight you've come to witness.
My brave old comrade! Honest Siccius!
Look, comrades,
Here are the foes have slain him! Not a trace
Of any other—not a body stripp'd—
Our father has been murdered. We'll revenge him
Like sons! Take up the body. Bear it to
The camp; and as you move your solemn march,
Be dumb—or if you speak, be it but a word;
And be that word—revenge!

[*The* SOLDIERS *bear off the body*—VIRGINIUS *following is stopp'd by* LUCIUS.

LUCIUS. Virginius.

VIRGINIUS. I did not mind thee, Lucius.
  Uncommon things make common things forgot.
  Hast thou a message for me, Lucius? Well,
  I'll stay and hear it—but be brief; my heart
  Follows my poor Dentatus.

LUCIUS. You are wanted
  In Rome.

VIRGINIUS. On what account?

LUCIUS. On your arrival
  You'll learn.

VIRGINIUS. How! is it something can't be told
  At once? Speak out, boy! Ha! Your looks are loaded
  With matter. Is't so heavy that your tongue
  Cannot unburden them? Your brother left
  The camp on duty yesterday—hath ought
  Happen'd to him? Did he arrive in safety?
  Is he safe? Is he well?

LUCIUS. He is both safe and well.

VIRGINIUS. What then? What then? Tell me the matter,
  Lucius.

LUCIUS. I have said
  It shall be told you.

VIRGINIUS. Shall! I stay not for
  That shall, unless it be so close at hand
  It stop me not a moment. 'Tis too long
  A coming. Fare you well, my Lucius.

LUCIUS. Stay
  Virginius. Hear me then with patience.

VIRGINIUS. Well,
  I am patient.

LUCIUS. Your Virginia—

VIRGINIUS. Stop, my Lucius!
  I am cold in every member of my frame!
  If 'tis prophetic, Lucius, of thy news,
  Give me such token as her tomb would, Lucius—
  I'll bear it better. Silence.

LUCIUS. You are still—

VIRGINIUS. I thank thee, Jupiter! I am still a father!

LUCIUS. You are, Virginius, yet.

VIRGINIUS. What, is she sick?

LUCIUS. No.

VIRGINIUS. Neither dead nor sick! All well! No harm,
Nothing amiss! Each guarded quarter safe,
That fear may lay him down and sleep, and yet
This sounding the alarm! I swear thou tell'st
A story strangely. Out with't! I have patience
For any thing, since my Virginia lives,
And lives in health.

LUCIUS. You are requir'd in Rome
To answer a most novel suit.

VIRGINIUS. Whose suit?

LUCIUS. The suit of Claudius.

VIRGINIUS. Claudius!

LUCIUS. Him that's client
To Appius Claudius, the Decemvir.

VIRGINIUS. What!
That pander! Ha! Virginia! You appear
To couple them. What makes my fair Virginia
In company with Claudius? Innocence
Beside lasciviousness! His suit! What suit?
Answer me quickly! Quickly, lest suspense,
Beyond what patience can endure, coercing,
Drive reason from his seat!

LUCIUS. He has claim'd Virginia.

VIRGINIUS. Claim'd her! Claim'd her!
On what pretence?

LUCIUS. He says she is the child
Of a slave of his, who sold her to thy wife.

VIRGINIUS. Go on, you see I'm calm.

LUCIUS. He seiz'd her in
The school, and dragg'd her to the Forum, where
Appius was giving judgment.

VIRGINIUS. Dragg'd her to
  The Forum! Well? I told you, Lucius,
  I would be patient.

LUCIUS. Numitorius there confronted him.

VIRGINIUS. Did he not strike him dead?
  True, true, I know it was in presence of
  The Decemvir. O had I confronted him!
  Well, well! The issue—well; o'erleap all else,
  And light upon the issue! Where is she?

LUCIUS. I was despatch'd to fetch thee, ere I could learn.

VIRGINIUS. The claim of Claudius—Appius's client. Ha!
  I see the master cloud—this ragged one,
  That lowers before, moves only in subservience
  To the ascendant of the other. Jove,
  With its own mischief break it and disperse it,
  And that be all the ruin! Patience! Prudence!
  Nay, prudence, but no patience. Come! a slave
  Dragg'd through the streets in open day! my child,
  My daughter! my fair daughter, in the eyes
  Of Rome! O I'll be patient. Come! The essence
  Of my best blood in the free common ear
  Condemn'd as vile! O I'll be patient. Come;
  O they shall wonder—I will be so patient.

                                    [*Exeunt.*

ACT IV

VIRGINIA *discovered, supported by* SERVIA.

VIRGINIA. Is he not yet arriv'd? Will he not come?

SERVIA. He surely will.

VIRGINIA. He surely will! More surely
He had arriv'd already, had he known
How he is wanted. Where's
My uncle?

SERVIA. Finding you had fallen asleep
After such watching, he went forth to hear
If there were any tidings of Virginius.
He's here.

Enter NUMITORIUS. VIRGINIA *looks at him inquisitively for some time.*

VIRGINIA. Not come, not come! I am sure of it!
He will not come! Do you not think he'll come?
Will not my father come? What think you, uncle?
Speak to me, speak; o give me any words,
Rather than what looks utter!

NUMITORIUS. Be compos'd!
I hope he'll come.

VIRGINIA. A little while ago
You were sure of it—from certainty to hope
Is a poor step; you hope he'll come. One hope,
One little hope to face a thousand fears!
'Tis near the time.

NUMITORIUS. It is indeed.

VIRGINIA. Must I go forth with you? Must I again
Be dragg'd along by Claudius as his slave,
And none again to succour me? Icilius,

Icilius! Does your true betrothed wife
Call on you, and you hear not? My Icilius!
Am I to be your wife or Claudius' slave?
Where—where are you Icilius?

Enter ICILIUS.

ICILIUS. My Virginia!
[*To* NUMITORIUS.] What's to be done, my friend? 'tis almost
time.

VIRGINIA. I hear what you are saying—it is time—
And will you give me up?
Can you devise no means to keep me from him?
Could we not fly?

    [ICILIUS *looks earnestly at* NUMITORIUS, *who fixes his eyes
    stedfastly on the ground:* ICILIUS *droops his head.*

I see! Your pledge
Must be redeem'd, although it cost you your
Virginia.

VIRGINIUS [*without*]. Is she here?

VIRGINIA. Ah!

Enter VIRGINIUS.

    [VIRGINIA *rushes into her father's arms.*

VIRGINIUS. My child! My child!

VIRGINIA. I am! I feel I am! I know I am!
My father! my dear father.

VIRGINIUS. Brother! Icilius! thank you, thank you. All
Has been communicated to me. Ay!
And would they take thee from me? Let them try it!
You've ta'en your measures well—I scarce could pass
Along, so was I check'd by loving hands
Ready to serve me. Hands with hearts in them!
So thou art Claudius' slave? And if thou art,
I'm surely not thy father! Blister'd villain!
You have warn'd our neighbours, have you not, to attend
As witnesses? To be sure you have. A fool
To ask the question. Dragg'd along the streets too!
'Twas very kind in him to go himself

And fetch thee—such an honour should not pass
Without acknowledgment. I shall return it
In full! In full!

NUMITORIUS. Pray you be prudent, brother.

VIRGINIA. Dear father, be advis'd. Will you not, father?

VIRGINIUS. I never saw you look so like your mother
In all my life!

VIRGINIA. You'll be advis'd, dear father?

VIRGINIUS. It was her soul—her soul that play'd just then
About the features of her child, and lit them
Into the likeness of her own. When first
She plac'd thee in my arms—I recollect it
As a thing of yesterday—she wish'd, she said,
That it had been a man. I answer'd her,
It was the mother of a race of men,
And paid her for thee with a kiss. Her lips
Are cold now—could they but be warm'd again
How they would clamour for thee!

VIRGINIA. My dear father,
You do not answer me! Will you not be advis'd?

VIRGINIUS. I will not take him by the throat and strangle him!
But I could do it! I could do it! Fear not:
I will not strike while any head I love
Is in the way. It is not now a time
To tell thee—but would'st thou believe it—honest
Siccius Dentatus has been murder'd by them.

ICILIUS. Murder'd!

NUMITORIUS. Dentatus murder'd!

VIRGINIA. O how much
Have we to fear.

VIRGINIUS. We have the less to fear.
I spread the news at every step. A fire
Is kindled that will blaze at but a breath
Into the fiercest flame!

NUMITORIUS. 'Tis time. Let's haste
To the Forum. [*Going.*]

VIRGINIUS. Let the Forum wait for us!
  Put on no show of fear, when villany
  Would wrestle with you. It can keep its feet
  Only with cowards. I shall walk along
  Slowly and calmly, with my daughter thus
  In my hand: though with another kind of gripe
  Than that which Claudius gave her. Well, I say,
  I'll walk along thus, in the eyes of Rome.
  Go you before, and what appeal soe'er
  You please make you to rouse up friends. For me,
  I shall be mute—my eloquence is here—
  Her tears—her youth—her innocence—her beauty!
  If orators like these can't move the heart,
  Tongues surely may be dumb.
ICILIUS. A thousand hearts
  Have spoke already in her cause!
VIRGINIUS. Come on!
  Fear not! it is your father's grasp you feel.
  O he'll be strong as never man was, that
  Will take thee from it. Come, Virginia;
  We trust our cause to Rome and to the gods!

               [VIRGINIUS *leads her off.* ICILIUS *etc. follow.*

SCENE II. *The Forum.*

Enter APPIUS *and* LICTORS.

APPIUS. See you keep back the people! Use your fasces
  With firmer hands, or hearts. Your hands are firm
  Enough, would but your hearts perform their office.
  Look to it!

Enter MARCUS.

MARCUS. News has arriv'd that speaks as if Dentatus
  Was murder'd by the order of your colleagues!
  There's not a face I meet but lowers with it:
  The streets are fill'd with thronging groups, that as
  You pass grow silent, and look sullen round on you,
  Then fall again to converse.

APPIUS. 'Tis ill tim'd.

MARCUS. What say you, Appius?

APPIUS. Murder's ill tim'd, I say,
Happen when 'twill; but now is most ill tim'd,
When Rome is in a ferment on account
Of Claudius and this girl he calls his slave;
Look out and see
If Claudius be approaching yet.

MARCUS. Claudius is here!

Enter CLAUDIUS.

APPIUS. Well, Claudius, are the forces
At hand?

CLAUDIUS. They are, and timely too; the people
Are in unwonted ferment.

APPIUS. I have heard
Word has arriv'd of old Dentatus' death;
Which, as I hear, and wonder not to hear it,
The mutinous citizens lay to our account.

CLAUDIUS. That's bad enough; yet—

APPIUS. Ha! what's worse?

CLAUDIUS. 'Tis best
At once to speak what you must learn at last,
Yet last of all would learn.

APPIUS. Virginius!

CLAUDIUS. Yes!
He has arriv'd in Rome.

MARCUS. They are coming, Appius.

CLAUDIUS. Fly, Marcus, hurry down the forces! [*Exit* MARCUS.
Appius,
Be not o'erwhelm'd!

APPIUS. There's something awes me at
The thought of looking on her father!

CLAUDIUS. Look
Upon her, my Appius! Fix your gaze upon
The treasures of her beauty, nor avert it
Till they are thine. Haste! Your tribunal! Haste!

APPIUS *ascends his Tribunal. Enter* NUMITORIUS, ICILIUS,
LUCIUS, VIRGINIUS *leading* VIRGINIA, SERVIA, *and*
CITIZENS. *A dead silence prevails.*

VIRGINIUS. Does no one speak? I am defendant here.
    Is silence my opponent? Fit opponent
    To plead a cause too foul for speech! What brow
    Shameless gives front to this most valiant cause,
    That tries its prowess 'gainst the honour of
    A girl, yet lacks the wit to know that they
    Who cast off shame should likewise cast off fear.

APPIUS. You had better,
    Virginius, wear another kind of carriage:
    This is not of the fashion that will serve you.

VIRGINIUS [*having left* VIRGINIA *with* ICILIUS]. The fashion,
    Appius! Appius Claudius, tell me
    The fashion it becomes a man to speak in,
    Whose property in his own child—the offspring
    Of his own body, near to him as is
    His hand, his arm—yea, nearer—closer far,
    Knit to his heart—I say, who has his property
    In such a thing, the very self of himself,
    Disputed—and I'll speak so, Appius Claudius;
    I'll speak so. Pray you tutor me!

APPIUS. Stand forth,
    Claudius. If you lay claim to any interest
    In the question now before us, speak; if not,
    Bring on some other cause.

CLAUDIUS. Most noble Appius—

VIRGINIUS. And are you the man
    That claims my daughter for his slave? Look at me,
    And I will give her to thee.

CLAUDIUS. She is mine, then:
    Do I not look at you?

VIRGINIUS. Your eye does, truly,
    But not your soul. I see it through your eye
    Shifting and shrinking—turning every way
    To shun me. Your soul
    Dares as soon show its face to me. Go on,

I had forgot; the fashion of my speech
May not please Appius Claudius.

CLAUDIUS. I demand
Protection of the Decemvir!

APPIUS. You shall have it.

VIRGINIUS. Doubtless!

APPIUS. Keep back the people, lictors! What's
Your plea? You say the girl's your slave—produce
Your proofs.

CLAUDIUS. My proof is here, which if they can
Let them confront. The mother of the girl—

[VIRGINIUS, *about to speak, is withheld by* NUMITORIUS.

NUMITORIUS. Hold, brother! Hear them out, or suffer me
To speak.

VIRGINIUS. Man, I must speak, or else go mad!
And if I do go mad, what then will hold me
From speaking? She was thy sister, too!
Well, well, speak thou. I'll try, and if I can
Be silent. [*Retires.*]

NUMITORIUS. Will she swear she is her child?

VIRGINIUS [*starting forward*]. To be sure she will—a most
wise question that!
Is she not his slave! Will his tongue lie for him—
Or his hand steal—or the finger of his hand
Beckon, or point, or shut, or open for him?
To ask him if she'll swear! Will she walk or run,
Sing, dance, or wag her head; do any thing
That is most easy done? She'll as soon swear!
What mockery it is to have one's life
In jeopardy by such a bare-fac'd trick!
Is it to be endur'd? I do protest
Against her oath!

APPIUS. No law in Rome, Virginius,
Seconds you. If she swear the girl's her child,
The evidence is good, unless confronted
By better evidence. Look you to that,
Virginius. I shall take the woman's oath.

VIRGINIA. Icilius!

ICILIUS. Fear not, love; a thousand oaths
  Will answer her.

APPIUS. You swear the girl's your child,
  And that you sold her to Virginius' wife,
  Who pass'd her for her own. Is that your oath?

SLAVE. It is my oath.

APPIUS. Your answer now, Virginius.

VIRGINIUS. Here it is! [*Brings* VIRGINIA *forward.*]
  Is this the daughter of a slave? I know
  'Tis not with men, as shrubs and trees, that by
  The shoot you know the rank and order of
  The stem. Yet who from such a stem would look
  For such a shoot? My witnesses are these—
  The relatives and friends of Numitoria,
  Who saw her, ere Virginia's birth, sustain
  The burden which a mother bears, nor feels
  The weight with longing for the sight of it.
  Here are the ears that listen'd to her sighs
  In nature's hour of labour, which subsides
  In the embrace of joy—the hands, that when
  The day first look'd upon the infant's face,
  And never look'd so pleas'd, help'd them up to it,
  And bless'd her for a blessing. Here, the eyes
  That saw her lying at the generous
  And sympathetic fount, that at her cry
  Sent forth a stream of liquid living pearl
  To cherish her enamell'd veins. The lie
  Is most unfruitful then that takes the flower—
  The very flower our bed connubial grew—
  To prove its barrenness! Speak for me, friends;
  Have I not spoke the truth?

WOMEN *and* CITIZENS. You have, Virginius.

APPIUS. Silence! keep silence there. Mo more of that!
  You're very ready for a tumult, citizens.

                   [SOLDIERS *appear behind.*

Lictors, make way to let these troops advance.
We have had a taste of your forbearance, Masters,
And wish not for another.

VIRGINIUS. Troops in the Forum!

APPIUS. Virginius, have you spoken?

VIRGINIUS. If you have heard me,
I have; if not, I'll speak again.

APPIUS. You need not,
Virginius; I have evidence to give,
Which should you speak a hundred times again
Would make your pleading vain.

VIRGINIUS [aside]. Your hand, Virginia!
Stand close to me.

APPIUS. My conscience will not let me
Be silent. 'Tis notorious to you all,
That Claudius' father, at his death, declar'd me
The guardian of his son. This cheat has long
Been known to me. I know the girl is not
Virginius' daughter.

VIRGINIUS [aside]. Join your friends, Icilius,
And leave Virginia to my care.
Don't tremble, girl, don't tremble.

APPIUS. Virginius,
I feel for you; but, though you were my father,
The majesty of justice should be sacred—
Claudius must take Virginia home with him.

VIRGINIUS. And if he must, I should advise him, Appius,
To take her home in time, before his guardian
Complete the violation, which his eyes
Already have begun. Friends! Fellow citizens!
Look not on Claudius—look on your Decemvir!
He is the master claims Virginia!
The tongues that told him she was not my child
Are these—the costly charms he cannot purchase,
Except by making her the slave of Claudius,
His client, his purveyor, that caters for
His pleasures—markets for him—picks and scents
And tastes, that he may banquet—serves him up

PLATE 5

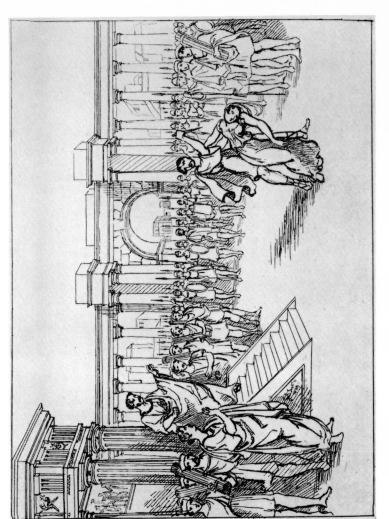

Virginius. Scharf's drawing of Macready's 1837 production: The death of Virginia. Act Four, scene one.

His sensual feast, and is not now asham'd,
In the open, common street, before your eyes—
Frighting your daughters and your matrons' cheeks
With blushes they ne'er thought to meet—to help him
To the honour of a Roman maid, my child,
Who now clings to me, as you see, as if
This second Tarquin had already coil'd
His arms around her. Look upon her, Romans!
Befriend her! succour her! see her not polluted
Before her father's eyes! He is but one.
Tear her from Appius and his lictors, while
She is unstain'd. Your hands, your hands, your hands!

CITIZENS. They are yours, Virginius.

APPIUS. Keep the people back—
Support my lictors, soldiers! Seize the girl,
And drive the people back.

ICILIUS. Down with the slaves!

> [*The people make a show of resistance, but upon the advancing of the* SOLDIERS, *retreat, and leave* ICILIUS, VIRGINIUS, *and* VIRGINIA *in the hands of* APPIUS *and his party.*

Deserted! Cowards! Traitors!

VIRGINIUS. Icilius, peace!
You see how 'tis, we are deserted, left
Alone by our friends, surrounded by our enemies,
Nerveless and helpless.

APPIUS. Away with him!

ICILIUS. Virginia! Tyrant! My Virginia!

APPIUS. Away with him!   [ICILIUS *is borne off.*
Separate them, lictors!

VIRGINIUS. Let them forbear awhile, I pray you, Appius:
It is not very easy. Though her arms
Are tender, yet the hold is strong by which
She grasps me, Appius. Forcing them will hurt them,
They'll soon unclasp themselves. Wait but a little—
You know you're sure of her.

APPIUS. I have not time
To idle with thee; give her to my lictors.

VIRGINIUS. Appius, I pray you wait! If she is not
  My child, she hath been like a child to me
  For fifteen years. If I am not her father
  I have been like a father to her, Appius,
  For even such a time. Let me take
  The maid aside, I pray you, and confer
  A moment with her nurse; perhaps she'll give me
  Some token will unloose a tie, so twin'd
  And knotted round my heart, that if you break it
  My heart breaks with it.

APPIUS. Have your wish. Be brief!
  Lictors! look to them.

VIRGINIA. Do you go from me!
  Do you leave! Father! Father!

VIRGINIUS. No, my child;
  No, my Virginia—come along with me.

VIRGINIA. Will you not leave me? Will you take me with
      you?
  Will you take me home again? O bless you, bless you!
  My father, my dear father! Art thou not
  My father?

      [VIRGINIUS, *perfectly at a loss what to do, looks anxiously
      around the Forum: at length his eye falls on a butcher's stall,
      with a knife upon it.*

VIRGINIUS. This way, my child. No, no! I am not going
  To leave thee, my Virginia! I'll not leave thee.

          [VIRGINIUS *secures the knife in the folds of his toga.*

APPIUS. Well, have you done?

VIRGINIUS. Short time for converse, Appius;
  But I have.

APPIUS. I hope you are satisfied.

VIRGINIUS. I am—
  I am—that she is my daughter!

APPIUS. Take her, lictors!

[VIRGINIA *shrieks, and falls half dead upon her father's shoulder.*

VIRGINIUS. Another moment, pray you. Bear with me.
  A little. 'Tis my last embrace. 'Twont try

Your patience beyond bearing, if you're a man.
Lengthen it as I may I cannot make it
Long. My dear child! My dear Virginia! [*Kissing her.*]
There is one only way to save thine honour—
'Tis this!

      [*Stabs her, and draws out the knife. She falls and dies.*

Lo, Appius! with this innocent blood,
I do devote thee to th' infernal gods!
Make way there!

APPIUS. Stop him! Seize him!

VIRGINIUS. If they dare
To tempt the desperate weapon that is madden'd
With drinking my daughter's blood, why let them: Thus
It rushes in amongst them. Way there! Way!

           [*Exit through the* SOLDIERS.

ACT V

SCENE I. *A Street.*

Enter APPIUS.

APPIUS. I do abjure all further league with them:
    They have most basely yielded up their pow'r,
    Power gone, life follows! Well, 'tis well we know
    The worst! The worst? The worst is yet to come,
    And if I err not, hither speeds a messenger
    Whose heel it treads upon.

Enter VIBULANUS, *hastily, and other* DECEMVIRS, *with*
MARCUS.

VIBULANUS. Honorius and Valerius are elected
    To the Consulate. Virginius is made Tribune.
    Employ the present time
    In looking to your safety.

APPIUS. I am in your hands,
    Lead me which way you please.

ICILIUS [*without*]. Hold! Stand!

ICILIUS *enters, with* HONORIUS *and* VALERIUS *as Consuls,*
NUMITORIUS *and* LICTORS.

    Did I not tell you 'twas the tyrant? Look,
    Was I not right? I felt that he was present
    Ere mine eye told it me. You are our prisoner.

APPIUS. On what pretence, Icilius?

ICILIUS. Ask of poor
    Virginius, tottering between despair
    And madness, as he seeks the home where once
    He found a daughter!

APPIUS. I demand due time
    To make up my defence.

ICILIUS. Demand due time!
    Appius! Assign the cause, why you denied

A Roman maid, of free condition,
Her liberty provisionally, while
Her plea remain'd unjudg'd. No answer, Appius?
Lictors, lay hold upon him—to prison with him!
Look to him well. To prison with the tyrant!

> [*Exeunt* APPIUS *and* LICTORS *on one side,* ICILIUS *and*
> NUMITORIUS *on the other.*

VIBULANUS. Let all his friends, that their own safety prize,
Solicit straight for his enlargement; doff
Their marks of station, and to the vulgar eye
Disguise it with the garb of mourning: 'twill
Conciliate the crowd. We know them well:
But humour them; they are water soon as fire!

> [*Exeunt severally.*

SCENE II. VIRGINIUS's *House.*

Enter LUCIUS *and* SERVIA.

LUCIUS. Is he not yet come home?

SERVIA. Not since her death.
I dread his coming home, good Lucius.

LUCIUS. A step! 'Tis Numitorius and Virginius.

SERVIA. Gods, how he looks! See, Lucius, how he looks!

Enter VIRGINIUS, *attended by* NUMITORIUS *and others.*

VIRGINIUS. 'Tis ease, 'tis ease! I am content! 'Tis peace,
'Tis any thing that is most soft and quiet.
And after such a dream! I want my daughter;
Send me my daughter!

NUMITORIUS. Yes, his reason's gone.
Scarce had he come in sight of his once sweet
And happy home, ere with a cry he fell
As one struck dead. When to himself he came,
We found him as you see. How is it, brother?

VIRGINIUS. How should it be but well? Our cause is good.
Think you Rome will stand by and see a man

Robb'd of his child? We are bad enough, but yet
They should not so mistake us.
Call my daughter to me.
What keeps her thus? I never stept within
The threshold yet, without her meeting me
With a kiss. She's very long coming. Call her!

NUMITORIUS. Icilius comes! See, my Icilius, see!

Enter ICILIUS.

VIRGINIUS. Come, come, make ready. Brother, you and he
Go on before: I'll bring her after you.

ICILIUS. Ha!

NUMITORIUS. My Icilius, what a sight is there!
Virginius' reason is a wreck, so stripp'd
And broken up by wave and wind, you scarce
Would know it was the gallant bark you saw
Riding so late in safety.

ICILIUS [*taking* VIRGINIUS's *hand*]. Father! Father!
That art no more a father!

VIRGINIUS. Ha! what wet
Is this upon my hand? A tear, boy! Fie,
For shame! Is that the weapon you would guard
Your bride with? First assay what steel can do!

NUMITORIUS. Not a tear has bless'd his eye since her death!
If we could make him weep—

ICILIUS. I have that will make him,
If aught will do it. 'Tis her urn. 'Twas that
Which first drew tears from me. I'll fetch it. But
I cannot think you wise, to wake a man
Who's at the mercy of a tempest. Better
You suffer him to sleep it through. [*Exit* ICILIUS.

VIRGINIUS. Gather your friends together: tell them of
Dentatus' murder. Screw the chord of rage
To the topmost pitch. Mine own is not mine own! [*Laughs.*]
That's strange enough. Why does he not dispute
My right to my own flesh, and tell my heart
Its blood is not its own? He might as well. [*Laughs.*]
But I want my child.

Enter LUCIUS.

LUCIUS. Justice will be defeated!

VIRGINIUS. Who says that?
He lies in the face of the gods! She is immutable,
Immaculate, and immortal! And though all
The guilty globe should blaze, she will spring up
Through the fire, and soar above the crackling pile,
With not a downy feather ruffled by
Its fierceness!

NUMITORIUS. He is not himself. What new
Oppression comes to tell us to our teeth
We only mock'd ourselves to think the days
Of thraldom past?

LUCIUS. The friends of Appius
Beset the people with solicitations.
The fickle crowd, that change with every change,
Begin to doubt and soften. Every moment
That's lost a friend is lost. Appear among
Your friends, or lose them!

NUMITORIUS. Lucius, you
Remain, and watch Virginius.

[*Exit, followed by all but* LUCIUS *and* SERVIA.

VIRGINIUS. You remember,
Don't you, nurse?

SERVIA. What, Virginius?

VIRGINIUS. That she nurs'd
The child herself. Will she come or not?
I'll call myself! She will not dare! O when
Did my Virginia dare—Virginia!
Is it a voice, or nothing answers me?
I hear a sound so fine—there's nothing lives
'Twixt it and silence. Aha! She is not here!
They told me she was here: they have deceiv'd me;
And Appius was not made to give her up,
But keeps her, and effects his wicked purpose
While I stand talking here, and ask you if
My daughter is my daughter! Though a legion

Sentried that brothel, which he calls his palace,
I'd tear her from him!

LUCIUS. Hold, Virginius! Stay!
Appius is now in prison.

VIRGINIUS. With my daughter!
He has secur'd her there! Ha! has he so?
Gay office for a dungeon! Hold me not,
Or I will dash you down, and spoil you for
My keeper. My Virginia, struggle with him!
Appal him with thy shrieks; ne'er faint, ne'er faint!
I am coming to thee! I am coming to thee!

[VIRGINIUS *rushes out, followed by* LUCIUS, SERVIA, *and others.*]

SCENE III. *A Dungeon.*

APPIUS *discovered.*

APPIUS. From the palace to the dungeon is a road
Trod oft, not oft retrod. What hope have I
To pace it back again? I know of none.
I am as one that's dead! I am as much the carcass
Of myself, as if the string were taken from
My neck. Their hands long for the office. O
'Tis worth the half of a Plebeian's life
To get his greasy fingers on the throat
Of a Patrician! But I'll baulk them. Come!
Appius shall have an executioner
No less illustrious than himself.

He is on the point of swallowing poison, when VIBULANUS *enters.*

Who's there?

VIBULANUS. Your friend!

APPIUS. My Vibulanus!

VIBULANUS. Appius, what
Was that you hid in such confusion as
I enter'd?

APPIUS. 'Tis a draught for life, which, swallow'd,
  She relishes so richly, that she cares not
  If she ne'er drink again. Here's health to you!

VIBULANUS. Not out of such a cup as that, my Appius.
  Your friends are busy for you with your foes—
  Your foes become your friends. Where'er a frown
  Appears against you, nothing's spar'd to make
  The wearer doff it, and put up a smile
  In its stead.

APPIUS. Thou giv'st me life
  Indeed!

VIBULANUS. That I may give thee life indeed,
  I'll waste no longer time with thee.
  Farewell, my Appius! If my absence takes
  A friend from thee, it leaves one with thee—hope!   [*Exit.*

APPIUS. And I will clasp it to me! Never friend
  Made sweeter promises. But snatch me from
  Beneath the feet of the vile herd that's now
  Broke loose and roams at large, I'll show them who
  They'd trample on. At liberty!
  Again at liberty! O give me power
  As well, for every minute of my thraldom
  I'll pick a victim from the common herd
  Shall groan his life in bondage.
  Are ye not open yet, ye servile gates?
  Let fall your chains, and push your bolts aside!
  It is your past and future lord commands you!

                VIRGINIUS *rushes in.*

VIRGINIUS. Give me my daughter!

APPIUS. Ha!

VIRGINIUS. My child, my daughter!
  My daughter, my Virginia! Give her me!

APPIUS. Thy daughter!

VIRGINIUS. Ay! Deny that she is mine
  And I will strangle thee, unless the lie
  Should choke thee first.

APPIUS. Thy daughter!

VIRGINIUS. Play not with me!
Provoke me not! Equivocate, and lo!
Thou sport'st with fire. I am wild, distracted, mad!
I am all a flame—a flame! I tell thee once
For all, I want my child, and I will have her;
So give her to me.

APPIUS. Cag'd with a madman! Hoa!
Without there!

VIRGINIUS. Not a step thou stirr'st from hence,
Till I have found my child.
Please you, give me back
My daughter.

APPIUS. In truth she is not here, Virginius;
Or I would give her to thee.

VIRGINIUS. Would? Ay, should!
Tho' would were would not. Do you say, indeed
She is not here? You nothing know of her?

APPIUS. Nothing, Virginius! good Virginius, nothing.

VIRGINIUS. How if I thrust my hand into your breast,
And tore your heart out, and confronted it
With your tongue? I'd like it. Shall we try it? Fool!
Are not the ruffians leagued? The one would swear
To the tale o' the other.

APPIUS. By the gods, Virginius,
Your daughter is not in my keeping.

VIRGINIUS. Well,
Then I must seek her elsewhere. I did dream
That I had murder'd her. 'Tis false! 'twas but
A dream. She isn't here, you say. Well, well!
Then I must go and seek her elsewhere. Yet
She's not at home—and where else should I seek her
But there or here? Here, here, here! Yes, I say,
But there or here—I tell you I must find her—
She must be here, or what do you here? What
But such a wonder of rich beauty could
Deck out a dungeon so as to despoil
A palace of its tenant? Art thou not
The tyrant Appius? Did'st thou not decree

My daughter to be Claudius' slave, who gave her
To his master? Have you not secur'd her here
To compass her dishonour, ere her father
Arrives to claim her?

APPIUS. No.

VIRGINIUS. Do you tell me so?
Vile tyrant! Think you, shall I not believe
My own eyes before your tongue? Why, there she is!
There at your back—her locks dishevell'd and
Her vestment torn! Her cheeks all faded with
Her pouring tears, as flowers with too much rain!
Her form no longer kept and treasur'd up.
Villain! is this a sight to show a father?
And have I not a weapon to requite thee?

> [*Searches about his clothes.*

Ha, here are ten!

APPIUS. Keep down your hands! Help! Help!

VIRGINIUS. No other look but that! Look on, look on!
It turns my very flesh to steel. Brave girl!
Keep thine eye fix'd—let it not wink. Look on!

> [*Exeunt, struggling.*

Enter NUMITORIUS, ICILIUS, LUCIUS, GUARD, *and* SOLDIER.

NUMITORIUS. Not here!

LUCIUS. Is this the dungeon? Appius is not here,
Nor yet Virginius. You have sure mistaken.

GUARD. This is the dungeon. Here Virginius entered.

NUMITORIUS. Yet is not here! Hush! The abode of death
Is just as silent. Gods! should the tyrant take
The father's life, in satisfaction for
The deed that robb'd him of the daughter's charms—
Hush! hark! A groan! There's something stirs.

LUCIUS. 'Tis this way!

NUMITORIUS. Come on! Protect him, gods, or pardon me
If with my own hand I revenge his death.

> [*Exeunt.*

SCENE IV. *Another Dungeon.*

VIRGINIUS *discovered on one knee, with* APPIUS *lying dead before him. Enter* NUMITORIUS, ICILIUS *with the urn of* VIRGINIA, *and* LUCIUS.

NUMITORIUS. What's here? Virginius! with the tyrant prostrate and dead!

LUCIUS. His senses are benumb'd; there is no audit to his mind by which our words can reach it. Help to raise him: the motion may recal perception.

NUMITORIUS. His eye is not so deathlike fix'd: it moves a little.

LUCIUS. Speak to him, Numitorius; he knows your voice the best.

NUMITORIUS. Virginius!

LUCIUS. I think he hears you; speak again.

NUMITORIUS. Virginius!

VIRGINIUS. Ah! [VIRGINIUS *rises and comes forward, supported by* NUMITORIUS *and* LUCIUS.]

LUCIUS. That sigh has burst the spell which held him.

NUMITORIUS. Virginius, my dear brother!

VIRGINIUS. Lighter, lighter! My heart is ten times lighter! What a load it has heav'd off! Where is he? I thought I had done it.

NUMITORIUS. Virginius!

VIRGINIUS. Well, who are you? What do you want? I'll answer what I've done.

NUMITORIUS. Do you not know me, brother? Speak, Icilius, try if he knows you.

ICILIUS. Virginius!

NUMITORIUS. Try again.

ICILIUS. Virginius!

VIRGINIUS [*sinking*]. That voice—that voice—I know that voice!
It minds me of a voice was coupled with it,

And made such music, once to hear it was
Enough to make it ever after be
Remembered! [ICILIUS *places the urn in his hand.*] What's
    this?

ICILIUS. Virginia!

> [VIRGINIUS *looks alternately at* ICILIUS *and the urn—looks
> at* NUMITORIUS *and* LUCIUS—*seems particularly struck by
> his mourning—looks at the urn again—bursts into a passion of
> tears, and exclaims,* 'Virginia!' *Falls on* ICILIUS's *neck.
> Curtain drops.*

EPILOGUE

by BARRY CORNWALL, Esq.

Spoken by MISS BRUNTON

―――――

Leaving the common path, which many tread,
We will not wake with jokes our poets dead:
Nor shame the young creations of his pen,
By bidding all who've perish'd be again.
The pale Virginia, in her bloody shroud,
Lies like a shrined saint. Oh! then, aloud
Shall we break scurril jests, and bid depart
Those thoughts of her, which fill and teach the heart?
No moral now we offer, squar'd in form,
But Pity, like the sun-light, bright and warm,
Comes mix'd with showers; and, fading, leaves behind
A beauty and a blossom on the mind.
We do not strain to show that 'thus it grows',
And 'hence we learn' what every body knows:
But casting idle dogmas (words) aside,
We paint a villain in his purple pride;
And tearing down a pow'r, that grew too bold,
Show merely what was done in days of old.
Leaving this image on the soul, we go
Unto our gentler story, touch'd with woe;
(With woe that wantons not, nor wears away
The heart) and love too perfect for decay.
But whatsoe'er we do, we will not shame
Your better feeling with an idle game
Of grin and mimicry (a loathsome task);
Or strip the great Muse of her mighty mask,
And hoot her from her throne of tears and sighs,
Until from folly and base jest she dies.
No; let her life be long, her reign supreme—
If but a dream, it is a glorious dream.

Dwell then upon our tale; and bear along
With you deep thoughts—of love—of bitter wrong—
Of freedom—of sad pity—and lust of pow'r.
The tale is fitted for an after hour.

BLACK-EYED SUSAN

OR ALL IN THE DOWNS

A NAUTICAL DRAMA IN THREE ACTS

BY

DOUGLAS JERROLD (1803–1857)

———

First performed at the Surrey Theatre, 8 June 1829

———

CAST

WILLIAM	Mr. T. P. Cooke
CAPTAIN CROSSTREE	Mr. Forester
RAKER	Mr. Warwick
HATCHET	Mr. Yardley
DOGGRASS	Mr. Dibdin Pitt
ADMIRAL	Mr. Gough
LIEUTENANT	Mr. Almar
JACOB TWIG	Mr. Rogers
GNATBRAIN	Mr. Buckstone
BLUE PETER	Mr. Williamson
SEAWEED	Mr. Asbury
QUID	Mr. Lee
LIEUTENANT PIKE	Mr. Hicks
SMUGGLER	Mr. Dowsing
PLOUGHSHARE, a rustic	Mr. Webb
BLACK-EYED SUSAN	Miss Scott
DOLLY MAYFLOWER	Mrs. Vale

Sailors, Midshipmen, Officers, &c.

———

*The Music throughout this piece is chiefly
Selections from Dibdin's Naval Airs*

PREFACE TO *BLACK-EYED SUSAN*

WHILE Gothic drama satisfied the Romantic taste for the extravagant and the spectacular on a level the new popular audiences could appreciate, it did not present material directly related to the contemporary world. However, melodramatists were not slow in filling the gap left by the legitimists' concern with history and what was remote from modern experience. Almost as soon as melodrama became a recognizable form it drew on the existing events of the war between England and France. Militant patriotism first found stage expression in military and nautical spectacle drama, in plays like *The Siege, Storming, and Taking of Badajoz* and *The Siege of Salamanca*, both performed in 1812, or *The Siege of Gibraltar* (1804), *The Battle of Trafalgar* (1806), and *The Battle of the Nile* (1815), whose engagements were all fought in the specially constructed water tank on the stage of Sadler's Wells, in which model navies manœuvred and battered each other with cannon-fire. Astley's circus ring was the right size for equestrian military dramas such as J. H. Amherst's *The Battle of Waterloo* (1824); for the whole century Astley's recreated British military triumphs on an elaborate scale. The roar of guns, the blowing up of enemy fortresses, the clash of arms, the heroism and patriotic declamation of British officers, seamen, and common soldiers, pleased and thrilled spectators living in the great age of Wellington, Nelson, the Peninsular Army, and the glorious fleet.

Out of the welter of flame, smoke, and rhetoric grew a new melodrama and a new hero. Military melodrama that displayed the heroism of the British soldier remained popular for the rest of the century, but more interesting and much more popular on the stage were nautical melodrama and the honest British tar, ideally embodied in William of *Black-Eyed Susan*. By the early 1820s nautical melodrama was a fully fledged form of its own, its popularity concurrent with that of the still lively Gothic. The origins of the noble sailor lay in the songs and music-dramas of the Dibdins and earlier natuical spectacle-drama as well as in contemporary events,[1] and he appealed immensely to audiences of theatres like the Surrey, a centre of nautical melodrama for many years. Such audiences were almost entirely working and lower middle class: watermen, shipbuilders, seamen, chandlers, dockworkers, and their womenfolk, all acutely aware of the Thames and the sea, their livelihoods dependent on Britain's maritime supremacy and trade. Thus their stage idols were watermen and sailors like themselves, with names positively smelling of salt water and courage: Jack Gallant, Jack Stedfast, Bill Bluff, Union Jack, Ben Billows—all characters played by the inimitable Thomas Potter Cooke, the creator of William and dozens of other nautical parts, himself a sailor who had faced death in shipwreck and in battle against the French. These heroes bravely fought wreckers, pirates, slavers, smugglers, and the French. They spoke glowingly, in a curious sea-metaphor, of their true loves, their ships, their officers, and their country, and they remained faithful to their sweethearts and wives on shore. Creatures of fact and fantasy simultaneously, the sailor heroes dominated the melodramatic stage in the 1820s and 1830s, sharing it by the 1840s with their domestic counterparts. After 1850 they appeared less often, more in working-class theatres than in the West End, although even here, somewhat more sophisticated and perhaps elevated in rank, they survived until the end of the century.

Unlike Fitzball's *The Red Rover* (1829), John Haines's *My Poll and My Partner Joe* (1835), Wilks's *Ben the Boatswain* (1839), and others with violent action against pirates, slavers, or the enemy, as well as explosions, shipwrecks, and similar sensations, *Black-Eyed Susan* is more quietly domestic and thus indicative of a growing trend which begins in Gothic melodrama and culminates in domestic melodrama itself. In fact, all nautical melodrama contains much domestic matter. Susan's simple cottage, her distress and poverty, and the landlord's attempt to evict her are thoroughly typical of hundreds of domestic melodramas to follow. Conversely, the brave sailor

---

[1] Black-Eyed Susan and William are taken from John Gay's song, verses from which are sung in Jerrold's play. Similarly, the heroes and titles of nautical melodramas such as *My Poll and My Partner Joe*, *Tom Bowling*, *Ben the Boatswain*, and *Ben Block* come from nautical songs by the Dibdins.

was so popular that he kept appearing in non-nautical melo-drama.

Jerrold is credited with about seventy plays in a career of writing for the stage extending from 1821 to 1854. Several of these plays are nautical melodramas; indeed, the verisimilitude of the shipboard settings comes from Jerrold's two years' service as a young midshipman in the Napoleonic wars. Among his other melodramas are the first English temperance play, *Fifteen Years of a Drunkard's Life* (1828), and *The Rent Day* (1832), long popular, about an honest farmer and an evicting steward. Later Jerrold turned more to legitimate plays for the patent theatres, like the comedies *Bubbles of the Day* (1842) and *The Prisoner of War* (1842). Although he was for a period resident dramatist of the Coburg and the Surrey, neither these positions nor his plays brought him sufficient income, and he went into journalism, becoming a regular contributor to *Punch* and editor of several other periodicals.

Elliston, the manager of the Surrey, made £5,000 out of *Black-Eyed Susan* and T. P. Cooke received £60 a week for acting William, but Jerrold got only £50 from Elliston and £10 for the copyright. After a run of 150 consecutive nights at the Surrey, *Black-Eyed Susan* opened at Covent Garden at the end of November 1829; in all it was performed 400 times in 1829 at different London theatres, and before the year was over it had also been done at Cambridge, Norwich, Exeter, Durham, Liverpool, and Dublin. The play remained the most popular nautical melodrama of the century. By 1854 Cooke (who retired from the stage in 1860) had played William over 800 times. *Black-Eyed Susan* received revivals at several London theatres after 1850; among them the Princess's in 1853, the Holborn in 1871, and the Adelphi in 1896. F. C. Burnand and Montagu Williams burlesqued it with great success in 1866,[1] and W. G. Wills adapted it as the heavily pathetic *William and Susan* in 1880. Of the 1896 Adelphi revival, which ran for five months, one reviewer wrote that aside from its interest as a picture of life long ago, the story 'is so true, so pathetic, and so

---

[1] Like most successful melodramas, *Black-Eyed Susan* was promptly burlesqued. *Black-Eyed Sukey, or All in the Dumps*, by Frederick Cooper, appeared in 1829. Creswick of the Surrey told Burnand that his burlesque would not be acceptable to Surrey patrons, who revered old favourites.

human, as to render its appeal to the emotions perennially irresistible. That even the most hardened playgoer could witness the parting of William and Susan with dry eyes we do not believe.'[1] Shaw praised the same revival and Terriss as William, who played 'with perfect judgment, producing just the right effect of humble but manly sincerity and naturalness in great distress by the most straightforward methods'.[2] *Black-Eyed Susan* was revived in London at the Bedford in 1950, and the Toynbee Theatre in 1967, the latter production transferring to Richmond, Yorkshire.

The authoritative text for *Black-Eyed Susan* is the copy licensed by the Lord Chamberlain's office for the Covent Garden production in November 1829, and already performed at the Surrey. (The Surrey Theatre was legally outside the Lord Chamberlain's jurisdiction and did not need to submit plays to his Examiner.) This copy is printed by *Duncombe*, but differs materially from the *Black-Eyed Susan* in *Duncombe's* acting edition, v. 4. The edition in *Lacy*, v. 23, departs from *Duncombe* in shortening the play and altering the order of several passages of dialogue; nevertheless it is still useful and obviously based on a different production entirely from the 1829 Surrey and Covent Garden ones, probably the Princess's production of 1853. *Dicks's* no. 230 is a much later acting edition.

[1] *The Theatre* (February 1897), p. 98.
[2] *The Saturday Review*, lxxxiii, 2 January 1897.

ACT I

SCENE I. *A View of the Country in the Vicinity of Deal.*

Enter DOGGRASS *and* GNATBRAIN.

DOGGRASS. Tut! if you are inclined to preach, here is a mile-stone—I'll leave you in its company.

GNATBRAIN. Aye, it's all very well—very well; but you have broken poor Susan's heart, and as for William—

DOGGRASS. What of him?

GNATBRAIN. The sharks of him, for what you care. Didn't you make him turn a sailor and leave his young wife, the little delicate black-ey'd Susan, that pretty piece of soft-speaking womanhood, your niece? Now say, haven't you qualms? On a winter's night, now, when the snow is drifting at your door, what do you do?

DOGGRASS. Shut it.

GNATBRAIN. And what, when you hear the wind blowing at your chimney corner?

DOGGRASS. Get closer to the fire.

GNATBRAIN. What, when in your bed, you turn up one side at the thunder?

DOGGRASS. Turn round on the other. Will you go on with your catechism?

GNATBRAIN. No, I'd rather go and talk to the echoes. A fair day to you, Master Doggrass. If your conscience—

DOGGRASS. Conscience! Phoo! my conscience sleeps well enough.

GNATBRAIN. Sleeps! Don't wake it then—it might alarm you.

DOGGRASS. One word with you—no more of your advice: I go about like a surly bull, and you a gadfly buzzing around me. From this moment throw off the part of counsellor.

GNATBRAIN. But don't you see—

DOGGRASS. Don't you see these trees growing about us?

GNATBRAIN. Very well.

DOGGRASS. If a cudgel was cut from them for every knave who busies himself in the business of others—don't you think it would mightily open the prospect?

GNATBRAIN. Perhaps it might: and don't you think that if every hard-hearted, selfish rascal that destroys the happiness of others were strung up to the boughs before they were cut for cudgels, don't you think, instead of opening the prospect, it would mightily darken it?

DOGGRASS. I have given you warning—take heed, take heed! And with this counsel, I give you a goodday.   [*Exit.*

GNATBRAIN. Aye, it's the only thing good you can give: and that only good because it's not your own. The rascal has no more heart than a bagpipe! One could sooner make Dover cliffs dance a reel to a penny whistle, than move him with words of pity or distress. No matter, let the old dog bark, his teeth will not last for ever; and I yet hope to see the day when poor black-ey'd Susan, and the jovial sailor, William, may defy the surly cur that now divides them.   [*Exit.*

SCENE II. *The Town of Deal.*

Enter RAKER *and* HATCHET.

RAKER. A plague on him! if I thought he meant us foul play—

HATCHET. Not he—'twas a mistake.

RAKER. Aye, a mistake that nearly threw us into the hands of the Philistines. But I know why you have ever a good word for this same Doggrass.

HATCHET. Know! you know as much as the weathercock that answers every wind, yet cannot tell the point from which it blows. And what do you know?

RAKER. I know that Mrs. Susan, Doggrass's niece, has two black eyes.

HATCHET. Umph! your knowledge proves that, though a fool, you are not yet blind.

RAKER. Civil words, Master Hatchet.

HATCHET. What! be you as dumb as the figure-head of the Starling; as soft and as yielding as teazed oakum—let my little finger be your helm and see you answer it. Who am I?

RAKER. Tom Hatchet, the smuggler of Deal, captain of the Redbreast, and trading partner with old Doggrass.

HATCHET. Thank'ee: now I'll tell you what you are—Bill Raker, first mate of the Redbreast, as great a rogue as ever died at the fore-yard, and consequently—

RAKER. The best person to go on your errands.

HATCHET. Just so; see you do them well. Now, bear up, whilst I pour a broadside of intelligence into you. I'm going to be married.

RAKER. You generally are at every port you put into.

HATCHET. Belay your jokes. To whom do you think—you can't guess?

RAKER. No. It isn't to the last port-admiral's widow? Perhaps to big Betsy, the bumboat woman.

HATCHET. No, you albatross—to Susan—black-ey'd Susan.

RAKER. Steady there—steady! I'm no younker. The lass is married already.

HATCHET. Aye, she *had* a husband. [*Significantly.*]

RAKER. What! why no!

HATCHET. How blows the wind now—what do you stare at? He's dead.

RAKER. William dead! Then there's not so fine, so noble, so taut-rigged a fellow in His Majesty's navy. Poor lad—poor lad!

HATCHET. Turning whimperer?

RAKER. Why not? Such news would make a mermaid cry in the middle of her singing.

HATCHET. Avast with your salt water! William is not dead: what think you now?

RAKER. That there is one more brave fellow in the world and one more liar.

HATCHET. Ha!

RAKER. Slack your fore-sheet, Captain Hatchet; if you must spin such galley yarns, let it be to the marines, or the landlady of the Ship; but see that you don't again bring tears into an old sailor's eyes, and laugh at him for hoisting an answering pendant to signals of distress. You marry Susan! Now belay, belay the joke.

HATCHET. Listen to my story: it shall be short—short as a marlin-spike. I must marry Susan; she knows not you—you must swear that you were her husband's shipmate—that you saw him drowned. Susan now lives with old Dame Hatley— she has no other home; and if she refuse, Doggrass will seize her for long arrears of rent on the old woman's goods, and turn Susan adrift; then the girl has no chance left but to marry. Is it not a good scheme?

RAKER. Has the devil been purser, he could not have made a better.

HATCHET. I'm going now to Doggrass, to see further about it; meantime, do you think of the part you are to play, and I'll think how I can best reward you. [*Exit.*

RAKER. I must certainly look a scoundrel. There must be an invitation in my figure-head to all sorts of wickedness, else Captain Hatchet could never have offered such dirty work to an old sailor. I must look a villain, and that's the truth. Well, there is no help for an ugly countenance; but if my face be ill-favoured, I'll take care to keep my heart of the right colour. Like the Dolphin tap, if I hang out a badly painted sign post I'll see and keep good cheer within. [*Exit.*

SCENE III. DAME HATLEY'S *Cottage.*

SUSAN *is heard without, singing a verse of* 'Black-Ey'd Susan'.

Enter SUSAN.

SUSAN. Twelve long tedious months have passed, and no, no tidings of William. Shame upon the unkind hearts that parted us—that sent my dear husband to dare the perils of the ocean, and made me a pining, miserable creature. Oh! the pangs, the dreadful pangs that tear the sailor's wife, as, wakeful on her tear-wet pillow, she lists and trembles at the roaring sea.

Enter GNATBRAIN *at the cottage door in flat.*

GNATBRAIN. There she is, like a caged nightingale, singing her heart out against her prison bars—for this cottage is little better than a gaol to her. Susan!

SUSAN. Gnatbrain!

GNATBRAIN. In faith, Susan, if sorrow makes such sweet music, may I never turn skylark, but always remain a goose.

SUSAN. Have you seen my uncle?

GNATBRAIN. Oh, yes!

SUSAN. Will he show any kindness?

GNATBRAIN. I cannot tell. You may have flowers from an aloe tree if you wait a hundred years.

SUSAN. He has threatened to distress the good dame.

GNATBRAIN. Aye, for the rent. Oh, Susan, I would I were your landlord. I should think myself well paid if you would allow me every quarter-day to put my ear to the key-hole, and listen to one of your prettiest ditties. Why, for such payment, were I your landlord, I'd find you in board, washing, and lodging, and the use of a gig on Sundays. I wish I—But, la! what's the use of my wishing? I'm nobody but half-gardener, half-waterman—a kind of alligator, that gets his breakfast from the shore, and his dinner from the sea—a—

[DOGGRASS *passes window.*

SUSAN. Oh, begone! I see Mr. Doggrass; if he finds you here—

GNATBRAIN. He must not; here's a cupboard—I'm afraid there's plenty of room in it.

SUSAN. No, no, I would not for the world—there is no occasion —meet him.

GNATBRAIN. Not I, for quiet's sake. We never meet but, like gunpowder and fire, there is an explosion. This will do

[*Goes into closet.*

Enter DOGGRASS.

DOGGRASS. Now, Susan, you know my business—I say, you know my business. I come for money.

SUSAN. I have none, sir.

DOGGRASS. A pretty answer, truly. Are people to let their houses to beggars?

SUSAN. Beggars! Sir, I am your brother's orphan child.

DOGGRASS. I am sorry for it. I wish he were alive to pay for you. And where is your husband?

SUSAN. Do *you* ask where he is? I am poor, sir—poor and unprotected; do not, as you have children of your own, do not insult me.   [*Weeps.*

DOGGRASS. Aye, this is to let houses to women; if the tax-gatherer were to be paid with crying, why, nobody would roar more lustily than myself; let a man ask for his rent, and you pull out your pocket-handkerchief. Where's Dame Hatley?

SUSAN. In the next room—ill, very ill.

DOGGRASS. An excuse to avoid me; she shall not.   [*Going.*

SUSAN. You will not enter.

DOGGRASS. Who shall stop me?

SUSAN. If heaven give me power, I! Uncle, the old woman is sick—I fear dangerously. Her spirit, weakened by late misfortune, flickers like a dying light—your sudden appearance might make all dark. Uncle—*landlord!* Would you have murder on your soul?

DOGGRASS. Murder?

SUSAN. Yes; though such may not be the common word, hearts are daily crushed, spirits broken—whilst he who slays destroys in safety.

DOGGRASS. Can Dame Hatley pay me the money?

SUSAN. No.

DOGGRASS. Then she shall go to prison.

SUSAN. She will die there.

DOGGRASS. Well?

SUSAN. Would you make the old woman close her eyes in a gaol?

DOGGRASS. I have no time to hear sentiment. Mrs. Hatley has no money—you have none. Well, though she doesn't merit lenity of me, I'll not be harsh with her.

SUSAN. I thought you could not.

DOGGRASS. I'll just take whatever may be in the house, and put up with the rest of the loss.

Enter DOLLY MAYFLOWER.

DOLLY. So, Mr. Doggrass, this is how you behave to unfortunate folks—coming and selling them up, and turning them out. Is this your feeling for the poor?

DOGGRASS. Feeling! I pay the rates. What business have you here? Go to your spinning.

DOLLY. Spinning! if it were to spin a certain wicked old man a halter, I'd never work faster. Ugh! I always thought you very ugly, but now you look hideous.

SUSAN. Peace, good Dolly.

DOLLY. Peace! oh, you are too quiet—too gentle. Take example by me: I only wish he'd come to sell me up, that's all. [DOGGRASS *goes to door.*] Oh, I know who you are looking after—your man, Jacob Twig; he hops after you on your dirty work, like a tom-tit after a jackdaw—I saw him leering in at the door. I wish my dear Gnatbrain was here. Oh, Susan, I wish he was here; he's one of the best, most constant of lovers—he'd befriend you for my sake.

DOGGRASS. Jacob!

Enter JACOB TWIG. *He has a memorandum book in his hand, a pen in his ear, and an ink bottle in the button-hole of his coat.*

You know your business.

JACOB. What, here, master? What, at old Dame Hatley's?

DOLLY. To be sure, good Jacob, if your master had a tree, and but one squirrel lived in it, he'd take its nuts, sooner than allow it lodging gratis.

SUSAN. Uncle, have compassion—wait but another week—a day.

DOGGRASS. Not an hour—a minute. Jacob, so do your duty. Now begin; put down everything you see in the cottage.

JACOB. Master, hadn't you better wait a little? Perhaps the Dame can find friends. [DOGGRASS *is imperative*.] Well, here goes: I'll first begin with the cupboard.

SUSAN [*anxiously*]. No, let me entreat you do not. Come this way, if you are still determined.

DOGGRASS. Eh! why that way? why not with the cupboard? I suspect—

JACOB. And now, so do I.

DOLLY. You suspect! I dare say, suspicion is all your brain can manage; what should you suspect—a thing that never had a thought deeper than a mug of ale? You suspect Susan! Why, we shall have the crows suspecting the lilies.

JACOB. You say so, do you? Now I'll show you my consequence. I'll put everything down, master, and begin with the cupboard. Ah! it's fast: I'll have it open—and I'll put the first thing down.

> [*Pulls open the door of the cupboard, when* GNATBRAIN *knocks* JACOB *prostrate, and stands* C. *in attitude;* SUSAN *in* R. *corner;* DOLLY *in surprise;* DOGGRASS *standing* L. *corner exulting.*

GNATBRAIN. No, I'll put the first thing down.

DOLLY. Gnatbrain! Oh, Susan, Susan!

DOGGRASS. Oh, oh! we shall have the crows suspecting the lilies! Pretty flower! how it hangs its head! Go on with your duty, Jacob; put down everything in the house.

GNATBRAIN. Do, Jacob; and begin with one broken head— then, one stony-hearted landlord—one innocent young woman—ditto, jealous—one man tolerably honest—and one somewhat damaged.

JACOB. I'll have you up before the justices—you have broken my crown.

GNATBRAIN. Broken your crown! Jacob, Jacob, it was cracked before!

JACOB. How do you know that?

GNATBRAIN. By the ring of it, Jacob—by the ring: I never heard such a bit of Brummagem in my life.

DOGGRASS. Well, Susan, it is sometimes convenient, is it not, for a husband to be at sea?

SUSAN. Sir, scorn has no word—contempt no voice to speak my loathing of your insinuations. Take, sir, all that is here; satisfy your avarice—but dare not indulge your malice at the cost of one who has now nothing left her in her misery but the sweet consciousness of virtue.   [*Exit.*

DOGGRASS. The way with all women when they are found out, is it not, Mrs. Dolly?

DOLLY. I can't tell, sir; I never was found out.

DOGGRASS. Aye, you are lucky.

DOLLY. Yes—we don't meet often. But as for you, Mr. Gnatbrain—

GNATBRAIN. Now, no insinuations. I wish I could remember what Susan said about virtue: it would apply to my case admirably; nothing like a sentiment to stop accusation—one may apply it to a bleeding reputation, as barbers do cobwebs to a wound.

DOGGRASS. Jacob, do you stay here—see that nothing of the least value leaves the house.

GNATBRAIN. In that case, Jacob, you may let your master go out.

DOGGRASS. Some day, my friend, I shall be a match for you.

[*Exit.*

GNATBRAIN. Perhaps so, but one of us must change greatly to make us pairs. Jacob, I never look upon your little carcase but it puts me in mind of a pocket edition of the Newgate Calendar—a neat Old Bailey duodecimo; you are a most villanous-looking rascal—an epitome of noted highwaymen.

JACOB. What!

GNATBRAIN. True as the light. You have a most Tyburnlike physiognomy: there's Turpin in the curl of your upper lip—Jack Sheppard in the under one—your nose is Jerry Abershaw himself—Duval and Barrington are your eyes—and as for your chin, why, Sixteen-String Jack lives again in it. [G N A T B R A I N *goes to window, affecting to see what is passing outside.*] Eh! well done—excellent! There's all the neighbours getting the furniture out of the garden window.

J A C O B. Is there? It's against the law; I'm His Majesty's officer, and I'll be among them in a whistle.

[*Runs out at door.* G N A T B R A I N *instantly bolts it.*

G N A T B R A I N. A bailiff, like a snow-storm, is always best on the outside. Now Dolly, sweet Dolly Mayflower—

D O L L Y. Don't talk to me—the cupboard, sir—the cupboard.

G N A T B R A I N. Hear my defence. On my word, I had not the least idea that you would have found me, or the cupboard is the last place I should have gone into.

D O L L Y. It's no matter, there's Mr. James Rattlin, boatswain's mate of the Bellerophon—

G N A T B R A I N. What! you wouldn't marry a sailor?

D O L L Y. And why not?

G N A T B R A I N. Your natural timidity wouldn't allow you.

D O L L Y. My timidity?

G N A T B R A I N. Yes; you wouldn't like to be left alone o' nights. Your husband would be at sea for six months out of the twelve; there would be a wintry prospect for you.

D O L L Y. But he would be at home the other six—and there's summer, sir.

G N A T B R A I N. True, but when you can have summer all the year round, don't you think it more to your advantage?

D O L L Y. No—for if it always shone we should never really enjoy fine weather.

G N A T B R A I N. Oh, my dear, when we are married, we'll get up a thunder-storm or two, depend upon it. But come, Dolly, your heart is too good—your head too clear, to nourish idle suspicion—let us go and see poor Susan. There is real calamity enough in our every-day paths; we need not add to it by our idle follies. [*Exeunt.*

SCENE IV. *A View of the Country about Deal.*

Enter HATCHET.

HATCHET. Doggrass has made the seizure by this time. Now I'll step in, pay the money, and thus buy the gratitude of Susan, before I tell her the story of her husband's death.

Enter JACOB, *running.*

Bring up, there, my young skiff. Whither bound?

JACOB. I'm in a hurry.

HATCHET. Bring up, I say, or I'll spoil your figure-head.

[*Lifting his cudgel.*

JACOB. Do you know who I am?

HATCHET. No; what are you, my young flying-fish?

JACOB. I'm a bailiff—aren't you frightened? I serve Mr. Doggrass.

HATCHET. The very craft I was sailing after. You have been to Susan's—black-ey'd Susan as she's called?

JACOB. How do you know that?

HATCHET. You have made a seizure there?

JACOB. Right again.

HATCHET. Have secured everything?

JACOB. Wrong. I had made as pretty a piece of business of it as any of my craft—a very pretty stroke of handiwork; but somehow or the other—

HATCHET. You frighten me. Nobody paid the money, I hope?

JACOB. Oh, don't be alarmed at that; no, but somehow or other, quite by mistake, when I thought I was in possession, I found myself on the wrong side of the house. Ah, here comes Susan.

Enter SUSAN.

Aren't you ashamed of yourself, Mrs. Susan, to make one to cozen so innocent a little bailiff as myself—aren't you ashamed of yourself?

HATCHET [*to* JACOB]. Stand o' one side! What, in trouble, my pretty Susan? What, have the land sharks got aboard of the cottage? Come, cheer up.

susan. What, do you indeed pity me? This is kind, and from a stranger, unexpected.

hatchet. Not such a stranger as you may think.

susan. No?

hatchet. No, I knew your husband—sailed with him.

susan. You did! Oh, tell me everything.

hatchet. All in good time. [*To* jacob.] What do you want here—sticking like a barnacle to a ship's copper.

jacob. Want! Oh, here comes my master, he'll tell you what I want; I'll leave you with him, he'll answer all questions.

[*Exit.*

Enter doggrass.

doggrass. So, madam, you must show contempt to a king's officer—put a servant of the law out of doors!

hatchet. Steady there—none of your overhauling! What do you want with the young woman?

doggrass. What's that to you?

susan. Oh, pray don't quarrel on my account—do not, I entreat you.

hatchet [*aside*]. I'll swagger a little. Quarrel, my dear! I'd fight yard-arm to yard-arm for you—go on a boarding party, cut out, row under a battery, or fight in a rocket boat; anything for the pretty black-ey'd Susan.

doggrass. Well, as you'll do all this, perhaps you'll pay the money she owes.

hatchet. That will I, though it were the last shot in my locker.

susan. No, no, there is no occasion; I would not have it for the world.

doggrass. You wouldn't? I would—but don't be afraid, he'll talk, but he'll be long ere he pays twelve pounds seventeen and sixpence for you, black-ey'd and pretty as you are.

hatchet. See how little you know of a sailor; there's thirteen pounds—I'm not much of an accountant, but it strikes me that that will pay your little bill, and just leave a dirty two-and-sixpence for young Jib-boom, the bailiff.

SUSAN. Oh, my good, kind friend! this generosity—my thanks, my prayers!

HATCHET. Not a word, not a word—good day.

SUSAN. Yet do not leave me; you said you knew my husband—had a tale to tell of him.

HATCHET. Yes, but not now; tomorrow. If I had done any-thing to oblige you, let me ask the delay. Besides, then I will bring one with me who can tell you more of William than I can myself; meantime, farewell. [*Aside.*] She's softened; a woman is like sealing wax, only melt her, and she will take what form you please. I've bought her heart with the chink, and tomorrow will secure it.   [*Exit.*

SUSAN. Wait till tomorrow! Alas! there is no remedy but patience; yet spite of myself, I feel forebodings which I know 'tis weakness to indulge.

DOGGRASS. I suppose, Mrs. Susan, as the case at present stands, neither you or the old dame will now think of leaving the cottage?

SUSAN. Indeed, landlord, we shall.

DOGGRASS. Landlord! why not uncle? It is a much better word.

SUSAN. It might have been, but your unkindness has taught me to forget it.

DOGGRASS. Now, hear reason. [*She turns from him.*] Well, to be sure, a plain spoken man can't expect it from one of your sex, so I'll leave you. You'll think again about the cottage? It has a pretty situation, and as for the rent, why, as one may say, it's a nothing. [*Aside.*] Now to my jolly boys, the smugglers; they carouse tonight at their haunt, and will be expecting me.   [*Exit.*

SUSAN. Cruel man. Oh, William! when, when will you return to your almost heart-broken Susan? Winds, blow pros-perously, be tranquil, seas, and bring my husband to my longing eyes.   [*Exit.*

SCENE V. *The Cave of the Smugglers. It is supposed to lead to a subterraneous passage, opening on the seashore. Casks on each side of the stage—tables, cans, etc.*

Enter LIEUTENANT PIKE, *disguised as a French Officer.*

PIKE. The smugglers are caught—we'll roast them in their own trap. The fools! I have gulled them with a story as long as the maintop-bowline. They think me a French officer, escaped from a prison-ship, and have stowed me away here until an opportunity shall serve to take me over to France. Eh! who have we here?   [*Retires.*

Enter RAKER.

RAKER. Captain Hatchet promises well; it is but a lie—aye, but such a one! No, I'm determined not to join such a plot, yet I'll seem to do so, too. Mounseer!

PIKE. Who dat?

RAKER. A friend.

PIKE. Ma foi! dis place is de veritable enfer—'tis de diable.

RAKER. Yes, you are not used to it; it isn't so pleasant as Paris, I dare say. Well, you have paid us decently for the job, else I don't think it altogether right that having been taken fighting against us, we ought to aid in your escape—the captain says so, however.

Enter HATCHET. SMUGGLERS *come in from different parts, seat themselves at table, and prepare for feasting.*

HATCHET. What's that about the captain?

RAKER. Only talking a bit with the Mounseer.

HATCHET. Well, Frenchman, about midnight the craft gets under weigh, and tomorrow you may sup in France.

PIKE. *Avec beaucoup de plaisir. Ce sera bien agréable.* [*Aside.*] Are all the gang here, I wonder.

RAKER. Hullo! What's that? why, the Mounseer is speaking English!

HATCHET. English! poor fellow, not he—he hasn't sense enough, like you or me.

Enter SMUGGLER *from back of Cave.*

SMUGGLER. A prize! a prize!

ALL. Where?

SMUGGLER. At the mouth of the creek. It is the excise-cutter's boat—her crew are somewhere about. Let us first scuttle the craft, and then—

PIKE. Villains!

HATCHET. Ha! treachery! You are no Frenchman!

ALL. Down with him! Down with him!

PIKE. Fifty on one! nay, then, let's make a bout of it—Skylark's crew, ahoy!

> [*A huzza is given,* SAILORS *rise up from behind various parts of the Scene from the butts, and present their pistols at the* SMUGGLERS, *who, after a brief struggle, yield—a Picture is formed and the Act closes.*

ACT II

SCENE I. *A View of the Downs. The Fleet at Anchor.*

Enter DOGGRASS *and* JACOB TWIG.

JACOB. Well, master, I think they have made a lucky escape.

DOGGRASS. They have for this time; but they had to fight for it. Had it not been for a sudden reinforcement, Hatchet, Raker, and all the jolly boys would have been taken; it would have spoilt the roaring trade of Deal.

JACOB. Yes, and your trade as innkeeper and chief encourager of the smugglers.

DOGGRASS. No such ill luck in the stars, I trust; and see what a fleet has dropped anchor during the night! I must run to Hatchet and see how he fares with Susan—if she stands out, she's less of the woman than I take her for.   [*Exit.*

JACOB. After all, I don't much like this trade of bailiff. I've a great mind to give it up, go back to my native Dover again, and turn ploughman. [*Three cheers.*] Holloa! the boats are putting off from the ships. Deal will be crowded again; there will be no getting a sweetheart for these six months.

Music. Enter SEAWEED, BLUE PETER, SAILORS, *and* WILLIAM.

WILLIAM. Huzza, huzza! My noble fellows, my heart jumps like a dolphin—my head turns round like a capstern; I feel as if I were driving before the gale of pleasure for the haven of joy.

SEAWEED. But I say, William, there's nobody here to meet us.

WILLIAM. Why, no! that is, you see, because we dropped anchor afore the poor things had turned out of their hammocks. Ah! if my Susan knew who was here, she'd soon lash and carry, roused up by the whistle of that young boatswain's

mate, Cupid, piping in her heart. Holloa! what craft is this?
Cutter ahoy! what ship?

JACOB [*taking off his hat*]. My name is Jacob Twig.

WILLIAM. You needn't bring to under bare poles—cover
your truck, and up with your answering pendant. Come,
clear your signal halyards, and hoist away. What service?

JACOB. I'm in the law.

WILLIAM. Umph! belongs to the rocket boats. May my
pockets be scuttled if I didn't think so. His Beelzebub's ship,
the Law! She's neither privateer, bomb-ship, nor letter-of-
mark; she's built of green timber, manned with lob-lolly
boys and marines; provisioned with mouldy biscuit and bilge
water, and fires nothing but red hot shot: there's no grappling
with or boarding her. She always sails best in a storm, and
founders in fair weather. I'd sooner be sent adrift in the North
Sea, in a butter cask, with a 'bacco-box for my store room,
than sail in that devil's craft, the Law. My young grampus, I
should like to have the mast-heading of you in a stiff north-
wester.

SEAWEED. Avast there, messmate! don't rake the cock-boat
fore and aft.

WILLIAM. Why, yes; I know it's throwing away powder and
shot, to sink cockle-shells with forty-two pounders. But
warn't it the lawyers that turned me and Susan out of our
stowage? Why, I'd as soon have met one of Mother Carey's
chickens, as—eh! [*Looking out.*] There's a fleet bearing down.

PETER. A fleet? Aye, and as smart as a seventy-four on the
king's birthday.

WILLIAM. A little more to port, messmate. There's my Susan!
now pipe all hands for a royal salute; there she is, schooner-
rigged—I'd swear to her canvas from a whole fleet. Now she
makes more sail—outs with her studding booms—mounts
her royals, moon-rakers and sky-scrapers; now she lies to—
now—now—eh? May I be put on six-water grog for a lubber.

PETER. What's the matter?

WILLIAM. 'Tisn't she—'tisn't my craft.

Enter RUSTICS, MEN *and* WOMEN, *and* PLOUGHSHARE, *who welcome all the* SAILORS. *Every one except* WILLIAM *is met by a* FEMALE. *He looks anxiously at every one. Music. All go off except* PLOUGHSHARE *and* WILLIAM.

WILLIAM. What! and am I left alone in the doctor's list, whilst all the crew are engaging? I know I look as lubberly as a Chinese junk under a jewry-mast. I'm afraid to throw out a signal—my heart knocks against my timbers, like a jolly-boat in a breeze, alongside a seventy-four. Damn it, I feel as if half of me was wintering in the Baltic, and the other half stationed in Jamaica. It's no use, I must ask for despatches. Damn it, there can be no black seal to them. Messmate!

PLOUGHSHARE. Now, friend.

WILLIAM. Give us your grappling-iron! Mayhap you don't know me.

PLOUGHSHARE. No.

WILLIAM. Well, that's hard to a sailor come to his native place. We have ploughed many an acre together in Farmer Sparrow's ground.

PLOUGHSHARE. What—William! William that married Susan!

WILLIAM. Avast there! hang it— that name, spoke by another, has brought the salt water up; I can feel one tear standing in either eye like a marine at each gangway: but come, let's send them below. [*Wipes his eyes.*] Now, don't pay away your line till I pipe. I have been three years at sea; all that time I have heard but once from Susan—she has been to me a main-stay in all weathers. I have been piped up—roused from my hammock, dreaming of her—for the cold black middle watch. I have walked the deck, the surf beating in my face, but Susan was at my side, and I did not feel it. I have been reefing on the yards, in cold and darkness, when I could hardly see the hand of my next messmate—but Susan's eyes were on me, and there was light. I have heard the boatswain pipe to quarters—a voice in my heart whispered 'Susan', and I strode like a lion. The first broadside was given—shipmates whose words were hardly off their lips, lay torn and mangled about me—their groans were in my ears, and their blood hot on my face—I whispered 'Susan!' It was a word that seemed to turn the balls aside, and keep me safe. When land was cried from the mast head, I seized the glass—my shipmates saw the cliffs of England—I, I could see but Susan! I leap upon the beach; my shipmates find hands to grasp and lips to press— I find not Susan's.

PLOUGHSHARE. Believe me—

WILLIAM. Avast there! if you must hoist the black flag— gently. Is she yet in commission? Does she live?

PLOUGHSHARE. She does.

WILLIAM. Thank heaven! I'll go to church next Sunday, and you shall have a can of grog—eh, but your figure-head changes like a dying dolphin! she lives, but perhaps hove down in the port of sickness. No! what then, eh—avast! avast! not dead— not sick—yet—why there's a galley-fire lighted up in my heart—there's not an R put in her name?

PLOUGHSHARE. What do you mean?

WILLIAM. Mean! grape and cannister! She's not run—not shown false colours?

PLOUGHSHARE. No, no.

WILLIAM. I deserve a round dozen for the question. Damn it, none of your small arms; but open all your ports and give fire.

PLOUGHSHARE. Susan is well—is constant; but has been made to feel that poverty is too often punished for crime.

WILLIAM. What, short of ammunition to keep off the land-sharks? But her uncle?

PLOUGHSHARE. He has treated her very unkindly.

WILLIAM. I see it! Damn it, I'll overhaul him—I'll bring him on his beam ends. Heave a-head, shipmate! Now for my dear Susan, and no quarter for her uncle.

[*Music. Exeunt* PLOUGHSHARE *and* WILLIAM.

Enter CAPTAIN CROSSTREE.

CROSSTREE. In faith that's the prettiest little vessel I ever saw in a long cruise. I threw out signals to her, but she wouldn't answer. Here comes the fellow that passed me whilst I was talking to her.

Enter GNATBRAIN.

CROSSTREE. Shipmate, there is a dollar for you.

GNATBRAIN. Truly, sir, I would we had been messmates, you might then have made it ten shillings.

CROSSTREE. You passed me a few minutes since, when I was in company with a petticoat.

GNATBRAIN. Aye; it's no use, Captain; she's a tight little craft, and as faithful to all that is good, as your ship to her helm.

CROSSTREE. What is her name? who is she?

GNATBRAIN. We simply call her Susan—black-ey'd Susan; she is the wife of a sailor.

CROSSTREE. Ah! What? Fond of the blue jackets?

GNATBRAIN. Yes, so fond of the jacket that she'll never look at your long coat—good-day, Captain.   [*Exit.*

CROSSTREE. The wife of a sailor! wife of a common seaman! why, she's fit for an admiral. I know it is wrong, but I will see her—and come what may I must and will possess her.

[*Exit.*

SCENE II. *Interior of* SUSAN's *Cottage.*

Enter WILLIAM.

WILLIAM. Well, here I am at last! I've come fifteen knots an hour, yet I felt as if I was driving astern all the time. So, this is poor Susan's berth—not aboard—out on liberty, and not come to the beach? Eh! that's she; ha! and with two strange-rigged craft in convoy. I'll tack a bit, and—damn it, if there's foul play! chain-shot and bar-shot! I'll rake 'em fore and aft.

[*Retires.*

Slow music. Enter SUSAN, HATCHET, *and* RAKER.

WILLIAM [*aside*]. What, hanging out signals of distress?

SUSAN. Oh, these are heavy tidings indeed.

HATCHET. Don't take on so, pretty Susan! If William is dead, there are husbands enough for so pretty a face as yours.

WILLIAM [*aside*]. Dead! May I never splice the mainbrace if that swab don't want to get into my hammock. [HATCHET *approaches nearer to* SUSAN.] Now he's rowing alongside her with muffled oars, to cut her cable! I'll tomahawk his rigging for him.

SUSAN. But is there no hope?

HATCHET. Hope! none. I tell you, Susan, this honest fellow was William's messmate; he saw him go down—you didn't rightly hear him when he first told the story—tell it again, Tom. [RAKER *sullenly indicates his unwillingness*.] Poor fellow! he was William's friend, and the story hurts him. I'll tell it you. You see, the ship had got upon the rocks, and it came on to blow great guns; her timbers opened, then she broke her back—all her masts were overboard, and orders were given to take to the boats. William was in the jolly-boat —well, she hadn't got the length of a boarding-pike from the wreck, when she shipped a sea and down she went. William and twelve other brave fellows were in the water—his shipmate here threw out a rope: it was too late. William sunk, and was never seen more. His shipmate turned round and saw —[*During this speech,* RAKER *has moved into the corner of the stage, his back to* HATCHET, *as if unwilling to hear the story.* WILLIAM *by the conclusion of this speech has placed himself between* HATCHET *and* SUSAN.] Damnation!

SUSAN [*shrieking and throwing herself into* WILLIAM's *arms*]. William!

WILLIAM. Damn it, I'm running over at the scuppers, or, you lubbers, I'd been aboard of you before this. What, hang out false signals to the petticoat—may you both have the yellow flag over you, and go up in the smoke of the fore-castle-chaser. Bring to a minute, and I'll be yard-arm and yard-arm with you. What, Susan, Susan! See, you swabs, how you've brought the white flag into her pretty figure-head. [*Puts* SUSAN *aside—draws his cutlass*.] Now then I'll make junk of one of you.

SUSAN. William! William! for heaven's sake—

WILLIAM. Just one little bout, Susan, to see how I'll make small biscuit of 'em. You won't fight? Then take *that* to the paymaster and ask him for the change.

> [*Strikes* HATCHET *with the flat part of his cutlass.*

HATCHET. Struck! then here's one of us for old Davey!

> [*Music. Runs at* WILLIAM *with a drawn cutlass, who catches his arm—they struggle round.* WILLIAM *throws him off and stands over him,* HATCHET *on his knee; at the same time* LIEUTENANT PIKE *appears—two* MARINES *appear at window. Tableau.*

PIKE. Smugglers, surrender, or you have not a moment's life!

> [HATCHET *and* RAKER, *startled by the appearance of* PIKE'S *party, recoil. The* MARINES *march on and take them into custody.*

WILLIAM. Smugglers! I thought they were not men-of-war's-men; true blue never piloted a woman on a quick-sand.

PIKE. We dogged you here, though you gave us the slip last night. Come, my lads; as you have cheated the king long enough, you shall now serve him—the fleet wants hands, and you shall aboard.

WILLIAM. If they are drafted aboard of us, all I wish is that I was boatswain's mate for their sake.

> [*Music. Exeunt all but* WILLIAM *and* SUSAN.

Now, Susan, [*Embraces her.*] may I be lashed here until death gives the last whistle.

SUSAN. Oh, William, I never thought we should meet again.

WILLIAM. Not meet! why, we shall never part again. The Captain has promised to write to the Admiralty for my discharge; I saved his life in the Basque Roads. But I say Sue, why wasn't you on the beach?

SUSAN. I knew not of your arrival.

WILLIAM. Why, a sailor's wife, Susan, ought to know her husband's craft, if he sailed in a washing-tub, from a whole fleet. But how is this, Sue—how is it? Poverty aboard—and then your uncle—

Enter DOGGRASS.

The very griffin I was talking of. Now, what are you staring at? what are you opening your mouth for like the main hold of a seventy-four? I should like to send you to sea in a leaky gun-boat, and keep you at the pumps for a six months' cruise.

DOGGRASS. What! William!

[*In a fawning tone, offering his hand.*

WILLIAM. Avast, there! don't think to come under my lee in that fashion. Aren't you a neat gorgon of an uncle now, to cut the painter of a pretty pinnace like this, and send her drifting down the tide of poverty, without ballast, provisions, or compass? May you live a life of ban-yan days, and be put six upon four for't.

DOGGRASS. But you mistake, William—

WILLIAM. No palaver; tell it to the marines. What, tacking and double tacking! Come to what you want to say at once— if you want to get into the top, go up the futtock shrouds like a man—don't creep through lubber's hole. What have you got to say?

DOGGRASS. Don't—you have put my heart into my mouth.

WILLIAM. Have I? I couldn't put a blacker morsel there. Just come alongside here. [*Pulls him by neckcloth.*] I am not much of a scholar, and don't understand fine words. Your heart is as hard as a ring-bolt—to coil it up at once, you are a d——d rascal. If you come here after your friends, you'll find 'em in the cock-pit of one of the fleet: you have missed the rattlins this time, but brought yourself up by the shrouds. Now take my advice, strike your false colours, or I wouldn't give a dead marine for the chance of your neck.

DOGGRASS. Well, we shall meet again. Goodbye to you. [*Aside.*] As Hatchet's taken I must look to myself.

[*Exit.*

WILLIAM. That fellow would sit still at his grog, at the cry of 'a man overboard!' Oh, Susan, when I look at your eyes, you put me in mind of a frigate with marines firing from the tops. Come along, Sue; first to fire a salute to old Dame Hatley, then to my shipmates. Today we'll pitch care overboard,

without putting a buoy over him—call for the fiddles—start
the rum cask—tipple the grog—and pipe all hands to mischief.   [*Exeunt.*

SCENE III. *A View near Deal. Public House,* R.

BLUE PETER, SEAWEED, GNATBRAIN, DOLLY, SAILORS,
RUSTICS, MEN *and* WOMEN, *discovered drinking.*

SEAWEED. Belay that galley yarn, Peter, belay! Though you
have got among the landsmen, don't pay out so much cable.

GNATBRAIN. Oh, let him go on—he lies like a purser at
reckoning day.

SEAWEED. No, no, we'll have no more of it. Where's William,
I wonder? he promised to meet us. I suppose he's with his
Susan now.

PETER. And where can he be better, do you think? But suppose,
just to pass the time away, I give you the song that was made
by Tom Splinter upon Susan's parting with William in the
Downs?

ALL. Aye, the song—the song!

SEAWEED. Come, pipe up, my boy. Poor Tom Splinter! he
was cut in half by a bar-shot from the Frenchman; well,
every ball's commissioned. The song, the song!

PETER. Here goes, but I know I can't sing it now.

SEAWEED. Can't sing! bless you, [*To* RUSTICS.] whenever
we want to catch a mermaid, we only make him chant a
stave, and we've twenty round the ship in the letting go of
an anchor.

Song—BLUE PETER.

All in the Downs the fleet was moor'd,
  The streamers waving in the wind.
When black-ey'd Susan came on board,
  Oh! where shall I my true love find?
Tell me, ye jovial sailors, tell me true,
If my sweet William sails among your crew?

William, who high upon the yard,
  Rock'd with the billows to and fro;
Soon as her well-known voice he heard,
  He sigh'd and cast his eyes below.
The cord slides swiftly through his glowing hands,
And quick as lightning on the deck he stands.

The boatswain gave the dreadful word,
  The sails their swelling bosom spread;
No longer must she stay on board.
  They kiss'd; she sighed; he hung his head.
Her less'ning boat unwilling rows to land;
Adieu! she cries, and wav'd her lily hand.

Hallo, who have we here? Man the yards, my boys—here comes the Captain.

Enter CAPTAIN CROSSTREE; SAILORS *take off their hats;* LASSES *curtsey.*

CROSSTREE. I am sorry, my fine fellows, to interrupt your festivities, but you must aboard tonight.

ALL. Tonight, your honour?

CROSSTREE. Yes; it is yet uncertain that we may not be ordered to set sail tomorrow.

PETER. Set sail tomorrow! Why, the Lords of the Admiralty will break the women's hearts, your honour.

CROSSTREE. Where is William?

PETER. He's with Susan, your honour; pretty black-ey'd Susan, as she is called.

CROSSTREE. With black-ey'd Susan! how is that?

PETER. How, your honour? why, they are spliced together for life.

CROSSTREE. Married! I never heard of this?

PETER No! why, your honour, I thought it was as well known as the union-jack. They were spliced before we went upon the last station. Not know it, your honour? Why, many a time has the middle-watch sung the parting of William and Susan.

CROSSTREE [*aside*]. Married! I had rather forfeited all chance
of being an admiral. Well, my lads, you hear my advice,
so make the best of your time, for tomorrow you may be
sailing for blue water again.

[SAILORS *bow*—CROSSTREE *exits into Inn.*

PETER. Them Lords of the Admiralty know no more about the
pleasures of liberty, plenty of grog, and dancing with the
lasses, than I knows about 'stronomy.

Music. Enter WILLIAM *and* SUSAN. *They cheer them.*

WILLIAM. Here are my shipmates, Susan! Look at her, my
hearties—I wouldn't give up the command of this craft, no—
not to be made Lord High Admiral. What, honest Gnatbrain,
Susan has told me about you—give us a grapple! [*Takes out
box.*] Here, take a bit from St. Domingo Billy.

GNATBRAIN. From what? [SAILORS *gather round* WILLIAM.

WILLIAM. From St. Domingo Billy. I see you are taken back—
steering in a fog; well, I'll just put on my toplights to
direct your course.

GNATBRAIN. Now I am a bit of a sailor—but none of your
hard words.

WILLIAM. Hard words! no, I always speak good English. You
don't think I'm like Lieutenant Lavender, of the Lily-white
schooner?

GNATBRAIN. But about St. Domingo Billy?

WILLIAM. It's lucky for you that you've been good to Susan, or
I shouldn't spin you these yarns. You see it was when the
fleet was lying off St. Domingo, in the West Indies. The
crew liked new rum and dancing with the niggers; well, the
Admiral (a good old fellow, and one as didn't like flogging)
wouldn't give the men liberty; some of 'em, howsomever,
would swim ashore at night, and come off in the morning.
Now, you see, to hinder this, the Admiral and the Captains
put St. Domingo Billy on the ships' books, and served him
out his mess every morning.

GNATBRAIN. Who was St. Domingo Billy?

WILLIAM. Why, a shark, as long as the Captain's gig. This
shark, or Billy, for that's what the sailors called him, used to

swim round the fleet, and go from ship to ship, for his biscuit and raw junk, just like a Christian.

GNATBRAIN. Well, but your 'bacco-box, what about that?

WILLIAM. Steady! I'm coming to it. Well, one morning, about eight bells, there was a black bumboat woman aboard, with a little piccaninny, not much longer than my hand. Well, she sat just in the gangway, and there was Billy along side, with his three decks of grinders, ready for what might come. Well, afore you could say about-ship, the little black baby jumped out of its mother's grappling, and fell into Billy's jaws—the black woman gave a shriek that would have split the boatswain's whistle! Tom Gunnel saw how the wind was: he was as fine a seaman as ever stept—stood six feet two, and could sit upon his pig-tail. Well, he snatches up a knife, overboard he jumps, dives under Billy, and in a minute the sea was as red as a marine. All the crew hung like a swarm of bees upon the shrouds, and when Tom came up, all over blood with the corpse of the baby and the shark turned upon its side—my eyes! such a cheer—it might have been heard at Greenwich. We had 'em aboard, cut up Billy, and what do you think we found in him? All the watches and 'bacco-boxes as had been lost for the last ten years—an Admiral's cocked hat, and three pilots' telescopes. This is one on 'em!

[*Showing box.*

GNATBRAIN. What, one of the telescopes?

WILLIAM. No, of the boxes, you lubber.

GNATBRAIN. Well, friend William, that's a tolerable yarn.

WILLIAM. True, true as the Nore Light. But come, my hearties, we are not by the galley fire—let's have a dance!

PETER. A dance! what should you say now if you were to see Blue Peter flying at the fore?

WILLIAM. Blue Peter! Belay, there—we shan't touch cable these six weeks.

PETER. The captain blows from another point: eh, and here's Quid the boatswain, with the crew of an admiral's barge after him.

Enter QUID, LIEUTENANT PIKE, *with* RAKER *and* HATCHET *guarded by* MARINES.

QUID. We'll see 'em in the bilboes, your honour.

PIKE. That's right, for there's a whole nest of them up along the coast, and I know a rescue is meditated.

QUID. Rescue! They'd as soon get a twelvemonth's pay out of our purser. Now lads, all hands on board.

WILLIAM. On board, Master Quid! Why, you are not in earnest?

QUID. Indeed, but I am: there's the first lieutenant waiting on the beach for all the liberty men.

[SAILORS *and* LASSES *retire and converse together, bidding each other farewell.*

WILLIAM. The first lieutenant!

SUSAN. Oh, William, must you leave me so early?

WILLIAM. Why, duty, you know, Susan, must be obeyed. [*Aside.*] Cruise about here a little while—I'll down to the lieutenant and ask him for leave 'till tomorrow. Well, come along, shipmates, if so be that Blue Peter must fly at the fore, why, it's no use putting a black face on the matter.

[SAILORS *go off with* LASSES. QUID, RAKER, *and* HATCHET *follow*, WILLIAM *turning round and looking contemptuously at the two latter.*

GNATBRAIN. This it is, you see, pretty Susan, to be married to a sailor; now don't you think it would be much better if William had a little cot, with six feet square for the cultivation of potatoes, than the forecastle for the rearing of laurels? To be obliged to leave you now!

SUSAN. Yes, but I trust he will be enabled to return; nay, there are hopes that he will gain his discharge; and then, with his prize money—

GNATBRAIN. Aye, I see, go into the mercantile line—take a shop for marine stores. But come along, Susan, the evening is closing in—I'll see you to your cottage.

SUSAN. I thank you, good Gnatbrain, but I would for a time be alone.

GNATBRAIN. Ah, I see, melancholy and fond of moonlight; well, poor thing; it's not to be wondered at. I was melancholy when I was first in love, but now I contrive to keep a light heart, though it is stuck by an arrow.   [*Exit.*

PLATE 6

Black-Eyed Susan. West's print of T. P. Cooke as William.

SUSAN. I hope he will return—surely his officer will not be so unkind as to refuse him.

Enter CAPTAIN CROSSTREE *from Inn, rather intoxicated.*

CROSSTREE [*singing*]. 'Cease, rude Boreas.' Confound that fellow's wine! or mischief on that little rogue's black eyes, for one or the other of them has made sad havoc here.

SUSAN [*aside*]. The stranger officer that accosted me.

CROSSTREE. Well, now for the boat. [*Sees* SUSAN.] May I never see salt water again, if this is not the very wench. My dear! my love! come here.

SUSAN. Intoxicated, too! I will hence.   [*Going.*

CROSSTREE [*staying her*]. Stop! why, what are you fluttering about? Don't you know I've found out a secret—ha, ha! I'm your husband's captain.

SUSAN. I am glad of it, sir.

CROSSTREE. Are you so? well, that sounds well.

SUSAN. For I think you will give my husband leave of absence, or, if that is impossible, allow me to go on board his ship.

CROSSTREE. Go on board, that you shall! you shall go in the captain's gig—you shall live in the captain's cabin.

SUSAN. Sir!

CROSSTREE. Would it not be a shame for such a beautiful black-ey'd, tender little angel as yourself to visit between decks? Come, think of it—as for William, he's a fine fellow, certainly, but you can forget him.

SUSAN. Sir, let me go!

CROSSTREE. Forget him and live for me—by heavens, I love you, and must have you!

SUSAN. If you are a gentleman, if you are a sailor, you will not insult a defenceless woman.

CROSSTREE. My dear, I have visited too many seaports not to understand all this. I know I may be wrong, but passion hurries me—the wine fires me—your eyes dart lightning into me, and you shall be mine!   [*Seizes* SUSAN.

SUSAN. Let me go! in mercy—William, William!

CROSSTREE. Your cries are vain, resistance useless!

SUSAN. Monster! William, William!

> WILLIAM *rushes in, with his drawn cutlass.*

WILLIAM. Susan! and attacked by the buccaneers! Die!

> [WILLIAM *strikes at the* CAPTAIN, *whose back is turned towards him—he falls.*

CROSSTREE. I deserve my fate.

WILLIAM *and the rest of the* SAILORS, GNATBRAIN, *etc., who have re-entered—*The Captain!

> [WILLIAM *turns away horror-struck.* SUSAN *falls on her knees, the* SAILORS *bend over the* CAPTAIN. *Slow music. Tableau.*

ACT III

SCENE I. *A Street in Deal.*

Enter GNATBRAIN.

GNATBRAIN. The Court-Martial is ordered: the Captains, with the Admiral at their head, are assembling on board the ship, [*Gun heard without.*] and there goes the signal gun for the commencement of the proceedings. Poor William!

Enter DOGGRASS.

DOGGRASS. Poor William! aye, if pity would save him, his neck would be insured. Didn't he attempt to kill his Captain?

GNATBRAIN. True; he deserves hanging for that. You would have doubtless gone a different way to work. William cut down his officer in defence of his wife—now you, like a good, prudent man, would have thrust your hands into your pockets and looked on.

DOGGRASS. None of your sneering, sirrah. William—hanging is too good for him!

GNATBRAIN. You know best what hanging is good for—but I know this, if all the rascals who, under the semblance of a smug respectability, sow the world with dissensions and deceit, were fitted with a halter, rope would double its price, and the executioner set up his carriage.

DOGGRASS. Have you any meaning in this?

GNATBRAIN. No—none: you can couple my meaning with your honesty.

DOGGRASS. When will your tongue change its pertness?

GNATBRAIN. When your heart changes its colour.

DOGGRASS. My heart! I have nothing to reproach myself with; I feel strong in—

GNATBRAIN. Yes, you must be strong, there's no doubting that—else you'd never be able to carry that lump of marble in your bosom—that's a load would break the back of any porter.

DOGGRASS. I tell you what, my friend, I had some thoughts—

GNATBRAIN. Stop! I'll tell you what I had only just now—a dream.

DOGGRASS. A dream?

GNATBRAIN. Aye; I dreamt that a young lamb was set upon by a wolf, when, strange to say, a lion leapt upon it, and tore it piecemeal. At this moment a band of hunters came up, and secured the noble brute. They were about to kill the lion, their guns were pointed, their swords drawn, when a thing, at first no bigger than my hand, appeared in the sky— it came closer, and I saw it was a huge vulture. It went wheeling round and round the victim lion, and appeared to anticipate the feast of blood—and with a red and glaring eye, and grasping talons, seemed to demand the carcase, ere the lion yet was dead.

DOGGRASS. And this was a dream?

GNATBRAIN. Yes, a day-dream.

DOGGRASS. And what, since you will talk, said you to the vulture?

GNATBRAIN. Nothing; but I looked at it—and with a loathing left it.   [*Exit, looking significantly at* DOGGRASS.

DOGGRASS. I shall never sleep quietly until I lay that rascal by the heels. Confusion take him! I'm ashamed to say I am almost afraid of him.

Enter JACOB TWIG.

Now Jacob, how fares Captain Crosstree?

JACOB. Better; it is thought he will recover.

DOGGRASS. Another disappointment; yet by the rules of the service William must die. Here, Jacob, I've something for you to—

JACOB. I've something for you, sir.   [*Gives him money.*

DOGGRASS. Why, what's this?

JACOB. Three guineas, two shillings, and sixpence half-penny! That's just, sir, what I've received of you since I've been in your employ.

DOGGRASS. Well, and what of that?

JACOB. I don't feel comfortable with it, sir; I'd thank you to take it.

DOGGRASS. Take it! Are you mad?

JACOB. No, sir—I have been; I have been wicked, and I now think—and I wish you would think so too—that all wickedness is madness.

DOGGRASS. How is all this brought about?

JACOB. A short tale, sir; it's all with the Captain.

DOGGRASS. The Captain!

JACOB. Yes; I was in the public-house when the Captain was brought in with that gash in his shoulder. I stood beside his bed, it was steeped in blood—the doctor shook his head— the parson came and prayed; and when I looked on the Captain's blue lips and pale face, I thought what poor creatures we are; and then something whispered in my heart, 'Jacob, thou hast been a mischief-making, wicked lad —and suppose, Jacob, thou wert at a moment's notice to take the Captain's place!' I heard this—heard it as plain as my own voice—and my hair moved, and I felt as if I'd been dipped in a river, and I fell like a stone on my knees—when I got up again I was quite another lad.

DOGGRASS. Ha, ha!

JACOB. That's not a laugh; don't deceive yourself. It sounds to my ears like the croak of a frog, or the hoot of an owl.

DOGGRASS. Fool!

JACOB. I ran as hard as I could run to Farmer Arable—told him what a rascal I was, and begged he'd hire me—he did, and gave me half-a-year's wages in advance, that I might return the money you had paid me—there it is.

DOGGRASS. Idiot! take the money.

JACOB. Every coin of it is a cockatrice's egg—it can bring forth nought but mischief.

DOGGRASS. Take it, or I'll throw it into the sea.

JACOB. Don't, for coming from your hand it would poison all the fishes.

DOGGRASS. You will be a fool, then?

JACOB. Yes; one of your fools, Master Doggrass—I will be honest.   [*Exit.*

DOGGRASS. All falling from me; no matter. I'll wait to see William disposed of; then, since the people here seem leagued against me, sell off my stock, and travel. The postman brought this packet [*Producing one.*] to my house directed to Captain Crosstree. What can it contain? No matter —it is a virtue on the right side to be over cautious; so go you into my pocket until William is settled for. [*Distant gun heard without.*] The Court has opened—now to watch its progress.   [*Exit.*

SCENE II. *The State Cabin of* WILLIAM'*s ship. The Court-Martial—three guns on each side of the cabin. The* ADMIRAL *sits at the head of the table—a union jack flying over his chair; six* CAPTAINS *sit on each side of the table.* WILLIAM *is brought in by the* MASTER-AT-ARMS *and* MARINE OFFICER; *a* MARINE *at each side, and one behind. A* MIDSHIPMAN *is in attendance. Music.*

ADMIRAL. Prisoner, as your ship is ordered for instant service, and it has been thought expedient that your shipmates should be witnesses of whatever punishment the Court may award you, if found guilty of the crime wherewith you are charged, it will be sufficient to receive the depositions of the witnesses without calling for the attendance of Captain Crosstree, whom it is yet impossible to remove from shore. One of the witnesses, I am sorry to say, is your wife; however, out of mercy to your peculiar situation, we have not summoned her to attend.

WILLIAM. Bless you, your honours, bless you. My wife, Susan, standing here before me, speaking words that would send me to the fore-yard—it had been too much for an old sailor. I thank your honours! If I must work for the dead reckoning, I wouldn't have it in sight of my wife.

ADMIRAL. Prisoner, you are charged with an attempt to slay Robert Crosstree, Captain of His Majesty's navy, and your superior officer. Answer, are you guilty or not guilty?

WILLIAM. I want, your honour, to steer well between the questions. If it be asked, whether I wished to kill the Captain, I could, if I'd a mind to brag, show that I loved him—loved him next to my own Susan; all's one for that. I am not guilty of an attempt to kill the Captain, but if it be guilt to strike in defence of a sailor's own sheet-anchor, his wife, why, I say guilty, your honour; I say it, and think I've no cause to hang out the red at my fore.

ADMIRAL. You plead guilty—let me as one of your judges advise you to reconsider the plea. At least take the chances which the hearing of your case may allow.

WILLIAM. I leave that chance to your own hearts, your honours; if they have not a good word for poor Will, why, it is below the honesty of a sailor to go upon the half-tack of a lawyer.

ADMIRAL. You will not retract the plea?

WILLIAM. I'm fixed; anchored to it, fore-an-aft, with chain cable.

ADMIRAL. Remove the prisoner! [WILLIAM *is removed as brought in.*] Gentlemen, nothing more remains for us than to consider the justice of our verdict. Although the case of the unfortunate man admits of many palliatives, still, for the upholding of a necessary discipline, any commiseration would afford a dangerous precedent, and I fear cannot be indulged. Gentlemen, are you all determined in your verdict? Guilty or not guilty? Guilty? [*After a pause, the* CAPTAINS *bow assent.*] It remains then for me to pass the sentence of the law? [CAPTAINS *bow.*] Bring back the prisoner.

Enter WILLIAM, *guarded as before.*

Does no one of your shipmates attend to speak to your character? Have you no one?

WILLIAM. No one, your honour? I didn't think to ask them—but let the word be passed, and may I never go aloft, if from the boatswain to the black cook there's one that could spin a yarn to condemn me.

ADMIRAL. Pass the word forward for witnesses.

[*Music.* MIDSHIPMAN *goes to cabin door and returns with* QUID.

ADMIRAL. What are you?

QUID. Boatswain, your honour.

ADMIRAL. What know you of the prisoner?

QUID. Know, your honour! The trimmest sailor as ever handled
rope; the first on his watch, the last to leave the deck; one as
never belonged to the after-guard—he has the cleanest top
and the whitest hammock; from reefing a main top-sail to
stowing a netting, give me taut Bill afore any able seaman
in His Majesty's fleet.

ADMIRAL. But what know you of his moral character?

QUID. His moral character, your honour? Why, he plays upon
the fiddle like an angel.

ADMIRAL. Are there any other witnesses?   [*Exit* QUID.

Enter SEAWEED.

What do you know of the prisoner?

SEAWEED. Nothing but good, your honour.

ADMIRAL. He was never known to disobey command?

SEAWEED. Never but once, your honour, and that was when he
gave me half his grog when I was upon the black list.

ADMIRAL. And what else do you know?

SEAWEED. Why, this I know, your honour, if William goes
aloft there's sartin promotion for him.

ADMIRAL. Have you nothing else to show? Did he never do any
great, benevolent action?

SEAWEED. Yes, he twice saved the Captain's life, and once
ducked a Jew slopseller.

[ADMIRAL *motions him to retire.*

ADMIRAL. Are there any more witnesses?

WILLIAM. Your honours, I feel as if I were in irons, or seized
to the grating, to stand here and listen—like the landlord's
daughter of the Nelson—to nothing but yarns about sarvice
and character. My actions, your honours, are kept in the log
book aloft—if, when that's over-hauled, I'm not found a trim
seaman, why, it's only throwing salt to the fishes to patter
here.

ADMIRAL. Gentlemen, are your opinions still unchanged? [CAPTAINS *bow assent.*] Prisoner, what have you to say in arrest of judgment? Now is your time to speak.

WILLIAM. In a moment, your honours. Damn it, my top-lights are rather misty. I have been three years at sea, and had never looked upon or heard from my wife—as sweet a little craft as was ever launched. I had come ashore, and I was as lively as a petterel in a storm; I found Susan—that's my wife, your honours—all her gilt taken by the land-sharks; but yet all taut, with a face as red and rosy as the king's head on the side of a fire bucket. Well, your honours, when we were as merry as a ship's crew on a pay-day, there comes an order to go on board. I left Susan, and went with the rest of the liberty men to ax leave of the first lieutenant. I hadn't been gone the turning of an hour-glass, when I heard Susan giving signals of distress. I out with my cutlass, made all sail, and came up to my craft. I found her battling with a pirate— I never looked at his figure-head, never stopped—would any of your honours? long live you and your wives say I! Would any of your honours have rowed alongside as if you'd been going aboard a royal yacht? No, you wouldn't; for the gilt swabs on the shoulders can't alter the heart that swells beneath. You would have done as I did—and what did I? Why, I cut him down like a piece of old junk; had he been the first lord of the Admiralty, I had done it!

[*Overcome with emotion.*]

ADMIRAL. Prisoner, we keenly feel for your situation; yet you, as a good sailor, must know that the course of justice cannot be evaded.

WILLIAM. Your honours, let me be no bar to it; I do not talk for my life. Death! why, if I 'scaped it here—the next capful of wind might blow me from the yard-arm. All I would strive for is to show I had no malice; all I wish, whilst you pass sentence, is your pity. That your honours, whilst it is your duty to condemn the sailor, may, as having wives you honour and children you love, respect the husband.

ADMIRAL. Have you anything further to advance?

WILLIAM. All my cable is run out—I'm brought to.

ADMIRAL [*all the* CAPTAINS *rise*]. Prisoner, it is now my most painful duty to pass the sentence of the Court upon you. The Court commiserates your situation and in consideration of your services will see that every care is taken of your wife when deprived of your protection.

WILLIAM. Poor Susan!

ADMIRAL. Prisoner, your case falls under the twenty-second Article of War. [*Reads.*] 'If any man in, or belonging to the Fleet, shall draw, or offer to draw, or lift up his hand against his superior officer, he shall suffer death.' [*Putting on his hat.*] The sentence of the Court is that you be hanged at the fore-yard-arm of this His Majesty's ship, at the hour of ten o'clock. Heaven pardon your sins, and have mercy on your soul! This Court is now dissolved.

> [*Music.* ADMIRAL *and* CAPTAINS *come forward.* ADMIRAL *shakes hands with* WILLIAM *who, overcome, kneels—after a momentary struggle, he rises, collects himself, and is escorted from the cabin in the same way that he entered. The scene closes —gun fires.*]

SCENE III. *A Street in Deal.*

Enter GNATBRAIN *and* JACOB TWIG.

JACOB. But is it true, Gnatbrain—is Master Doggrass really drowned?

GNATBRAIN. True! I tell you I saw the old piece of wickedness go down.

JACOB. Tell me all—tell me.

GNATBRAIN. Why, the old villain was hovering, whilst the Court Martial was going on, like a raven about the vessel. The whole sea was covered with boats—there was scarcely room enough to put out an oar. Well, the word was given that the sentence was about to be passed, when old Doggrass, as he would have snuffed up the words of death, as a kite snuffs carrion, sprang hastily up in the boat—she gave a lurch, threw him backward, he went down—not a hand was out to catch him; he went down with the horror of the good and the laughter of the wicked weighing on his drowning head.

JACOB. Then he is really lost?

GNATBRAIN. Aye, no matter for that: poor William is lost, too.

JACOB. Is there no hope of mercy—won't his judges have compassion?

GNATBRAIN. Yes; but not that compassion which will save him. Why, I'm told that every captain there, the good old Admiral himself—men who had looked upon shipwrecks, wounds and death with dry eyes, cried when the business was over, like soft-hearted girls. He is to be—he's to die to-morrow.

JACOB. Tomorrow!

GNATBRAIN. Yes, and the day is now closing in: I must away to poor Susan. That Captain Crosstree, I wouldn't wear his epaulets for all his prize-money.

JACOB. The Captain! Why, they tell me he's gone raving mad, ever since he heard of the Court Martial: that he curses himself, calls William his brother, and prays for him. I wish our squire could but look upon the Captain as he lies, shrieking and foaming; it would cure him of pride for the rest of his life.

GNATBRAIN. Farewell, Jacob; I must on my melancholy errand.

JACOB. Honest Gnatbrain, I was near being a little bit of a rogue—thank heaven that's over; still, I am afraid I angered Susan's husband when he first came on shore. I don't know how it is, yet if he would let me press his five fingers before tomorrow, I—I don't know, but I feel that it would make me more comfortable. He won't refuse it, think ye?

GNATBRAIN. Refuse it! No—all William's life has been goodness, and think you he would forget it at the end? Come, boy, brace up your heart, for you are about to see a sight enough to banish smiles for ever from your face, and turn the young hair grey.   [*Exeunt.*

SCENE IV. *The Gun-room of the Ship*—SENTRY *at the door* —*tiller working over head*—*screen canvas berths at the side*— *tomahawks crossed, and fire-buckets in a row.* WILLIAM *is seated, double-ironed, on a spare tiller.* LIEUTENANT, OFFICER OF MARINES, *and* MASTER-AT-ARMS *in attendance.* WILLIAM'*s chest is opened before him. The* LIEUTENANT *motions to* MASTER- AT-ARMS *to release the prisoner.* QUID, SEAWEED, *and others discovered.*

LIEUTENANT. Now, William.

WILLIAM [*with emotion*]. Bless you, your honour.

LIEUTENANT. Come, summon all your firmness.

WILLIAM. I will, your honour; but just then I couldn't help thinking that when I used to keep the middle watch with you, I never thought it would come to this.

LIEUTENANT. But you are a brave fellow, William, and fear not death.

WILLIAM. Death! No—since I first trod the king's oak, he has been about me—I have slept near him, watched near him—he has looked upon my face, and saw I shrunk not—in the storm I have heeded him not—in the fury of the battle I've thought not of him. Had I been mowed down by ball or cutlass, my shipmates, as they had thrown me to the sharks, would have given me a parting look of friendship, and over their grog have said I did my duty—this, your honour, would not have been death, but lying-up in ordinary. But to be swayed up like a wet jib to dry—the whole fleet—nay, the folks of Deal, people that knew me, used to pat me on the head when a boy—all these looking at me. Oh! thank heaven, my mother's dead.

LIEUTENANT. Come, William; [*Shakes his hand.*] there, think no more after that fashion. Here is your chest—perhaps there are some of your shipmates on whom you would wish to bestow something.

WILLIAM. Thankee, your honour. Lieutenant, I know you won't despise the gift because it comes from one who walked the forecastle—here's my box, keep it for poor Will's sake. You and I, your honour, have laid yard-arm and yard-arm with many a foe—let us hope we shall come gunwale to gunwale in another climate. [*Gives him box—to* MARINE OFFICER.] Your honour's hand—Blue Peter's flying—the vessel of life has her anchor a-trip, and must soon get under way for the ocean of eternity. Your honour will have to march me to the launching-place—you won't give a ship a bad name because she went awkwardly off the stocks? Take this, your honour, [*Opens watch.*] this paper was cut by Susan's fingers before we left the Downs; take it, your honour, I can't look at it. Master Quid, take this for my sake. [*Gives chain and seals, among which is a bullet.*] You see that bullet; preserve that more than the gold—that ball was received by Harry Trunnion in my defence. I was disarmed, and the Frenchman was about to fire, when Harry threw himself before me, and received that bullet in his breast. I took it flattened from his dead body—have worn it about me—it has served to remind me that Harry suffered for my sake, and that it was my duty, when chance might serve, to do the like for another.

[*Music.* WILLIAM *is overcome by his feelings and hurriedly distributes the contents of his chest among the rest of his shipmates.*]

LIEUTENANT. And now, William, have you any request to make?

WILLIAM. Lieutenant, you see this locket. [*Points to locket at his neck.*] It is Susan's hair—when I'm in dock, don't let it be touched. I know you won't: you have been most kind to me, Lieutenant, and if those who go aloft may know what passes on the high sea, I shall yet look down upon you in the middle watch, and bless you. Now, one word more. How fares the Captain?

LIEUTENANT. Very ill, so ill that he has been removed from the command, and the first lieutenant acts until the new Captain arrives.

WILLIAM. His case then is desperate; well, if he go out of commission, I can't tremble to meet him—I bear no malice, your honour, I loved the Captain.

LIEUTENANT. You have nothing to ask?

WILLIAM. Nothing, your honour. Susan and some friends will shortly be on board—all I want is that I may ask for strength to see my wife—my poor young, heart-broken wife, for the last time, and then die like a seaman and a man.

[*Music. Exeunt all but* WILLIAM.

I am soon to see poor Susan! I should like first to beat all my feelings to quarters, that they may stand well to their guns in this their last engagement. I'll try and sing that song which I have many a time sung in the mid-watch, that song which has often placed my heart, though a thousand miles at sea, at my once happy home. [WILLIAM *sings a verse of* 'Black-Ey'd Susan'.] My heart is splitting.   [*Overcome.*

SUSAN *shrieks without—rushes in, and throws herself in*
WILLIAM'S *arms.*

WILLIAM. Oh, Susan! Well, my poor wench, how fares it?

SUSAN. Oh, William! and I have watched, prayed for your return—smiled in the face of poverty, stopped my ears to the reproaches of the selfish, the worse pity of the thoughtless—and all, all for this!

WILLIAM. Ay, Sue, it's hard; but that's all over—to grieve is useless. Susan, I might have died disgraced—have left you the widow of a bad, black-hearted man. I know 'twill not be so—and in this, whilst you remain behind me, there is at least some comfort. I died in a good cause; I died in defence of the virtue of a wife—her tears will fall like spring rain on the grass that covers me.

SUSAN. Talk not so—your grave! I feel it is a place where my heart must throw down its heavy load of life.

WILLIAM. Come, Susan, shake off your tears. There, now, smile a bit—we'll not talk again of graves. Think, Susan, that I am a going on a long foreign station—think so. Now, what would you ask—have you nothing, nothing to say?

SUSAN. Nothing! Oh, when at home, hoping, yet trembling for this meeting, thoughts crowded on me, I felt as if I could have talked to you for days, stopping for want of power, not words. Now the terrible time is come—now I am almost tongue-tied—my heart swells to my throat, I can but look and weep. [*Gun fires.*] That gun! oh, William, husband, is it so near! You speak not—tremble.

WILLIAM. Susan, be calm. If you love your husband, do not send him on the deck a white-faced coward. Be still, my poor girl, I have something to say—until you are calm, I will not utter it; now Susan—

SUSAN. I am cold and motionless as ice.

WILLIAM. Susan, you know the old aspen that grows near to the church porch; you and I, when children, almost before we could speak plainly, have sat and watched, and wondered at its shaking leaves. I grew up, and that tree seemed to me a friend that loved me, yet had not the tongue to tell me so. Beneath its boughs our little arms have been locked together —beneath its boughs I took the last kiss of your white lips when hard fortune made me turn sailor. I cut from the tree this little branch. [*Produces it.*] Many a summer's day aboard, I've lain in the top and looked at these few leaves, until I saw green meadows in the salt sea, and heard the bleating of the sheep. When I am dead, Susan, let me be laid under that tree —let me—

> [*Gun fires*—SUSAN *falls—at this moment a voice without cries* 'A body overboard!' BLUE PETER *and* SAILORS *come in, with* MASTER-AT-ARMS *and* MARINE OFFICER. *Music.* WILLIAM *gives* SUSAN *into charge of* SAILORS, *and she is borne off.*

WILLIAM. What cry was that—a shipmate overboard?

PETER. No, William—but as the gun was fired, a body rose up just at the port-hole; they have taken it aboard. It is the body of Susan's uncle—a packet, directed to the Captain, was taken from it.

WILLIAM. What, Susan's uncle! Villain, may the greatest— [*Bell tolls.*]—no, no,—I shall soon be like him; why should the dying triumph over the dead? [*After a moment.*] I forgive him.   [*Music. Exeunt.*

SCENE V. *The Forecastle of the ship. Procession along the starboard gangway; minute bell tolls.* MASTER-AT-ARMS *with a drawn sword under his arm, point next to the prisoner;* WILLIAM *follows without his neckcloth and jacket, a* MARINE *on each side;* OFFICER OF MARINES *next;* ADMIRAL, CAPTAIN, LIEUTENANTS, *and* MIDSHIPMEN, *following.* WILLIAM *kneels, and all aboard appear to join in prayer with him. The procession then marches on and halts at the gangway;* MARINE OFFICER *delivers up prisoner to the* MASTER-AT-ARMS *and* BOATSWAIN, *a* SAILOR *standing at one of the forecastle guns, with the lock-string in his hand. A platform extends from the cathead to the fore-rigging. Yellow flag flying at the fore. Colours halfmast down. Music.* WILLIAM *embraces the union jack—shakes the* ADMIRAL's *hand.*

MASTER-AT-ARMS. Prisoner, are you prepared?

WILLIAM. Bless you! bless you all—   [*Mounts the platform.*

CAPTAIN CROSSTREE *rushes on from gangway.*

CROSSTREE. Hold! Hold!

ADMIRAL. Captain Crosstree—retire, sir, retire.

CROSSTREE. Never! If the prisoner be executed, he is a murdered man. I alone am the culprit—'twas I who would have dishonoured him.

ADMIRAL. This cannot plead here—he struck a superior officer.

CROSSTREE. No!

ALL. No?

CROSSTREE. He saved my life; I had written for his discharge. Villainy has kept back the document—'tis here dated back. When William struck me he was not the king's sailor—I was not his officer.

ADMIRAL [*taking the paper—music*]. He is free!

[*The* SAILORS *give three cheers;* WILLIAM *leaps from the platform.* SUSAN *is brought on by* CROSSTREE, *followed by* GNATBRAIN, TWIG, *etc. Picture.*

CURTAIN

THE FACTORY LAD

A DOMESTIC DRAMA IN TWO ACTS

BY

JOHN WALKER

———

First performed at the Surrey Theatre,
15 October 1832

———

CAST

GEORGE ALLEN		Mr. Waldron
WILSON		Mr. Lee
SIMS	Lately discharged from the factory of ******	Mr. Brunton
SMITH		Mr. Gardner
HATFIELD		Mr. C. Hill
WILL RUSHTON, an outcast		Mr. Stuart
SQUIRE WESTWOOD, master of the factory		Mr. Dibdin Pitt
TAPWELL, landlord of the 'Harriers'		Mr. Young
GRIMLEY		Mr. Bannister
JUSTICE BIAS		Mr. Clarkson
CRINGE, his clerk		Mr. Smith
JANE ALLEN		Mrs. W. West
MARY, her eldest girl, about eleven		Miss. H. Pitt
MILLY, her second, about six		Miss Clarke
A CHILD IN CRADLE		

Constables, Soldiers

PREFACE TO *THE FACTORY LAD*

By 1820 the third main kind of melodrama had emerged with distinctive characteristics of its own. Though domestic melodrama in a foreign setting had existed for some years, it was only after 1820 that it developed native settings, situations, and character types. From about 1840 it displaced the nautical in popular esteem, and well before the middle of the century its range of subject matter, far wider and more varied than that of other sorts of melodrama, included shops and city streets, village, farm, and mill, factories, family life, drink, gambling, and crime. Its favourite characters were the villainous peer or squire (seducer as well as rent collector), the old farmer and his wife, the virtuous peasant or workman, the gullible village girl driven in disgrace for her sin from her heartbroken father's cottage, her city equivalent forlorn and despairing in the London slums, eccentric comic men and women drawn from the ranks of servants, shop assistants, and streetsellers. While domestic melodrama offered audiences a dream world of ideal justice and eventual happiness, it simultaneously presented increasingly realistic settings of streets and buildings they knew by sight and people they encountered on their daily business. Dramatizations of crimes in their own neighbourhoods or from the newspapers lent further reality, and authors were careful not to omit thrills and sensations rarely a part of drab real life but most welcome on the stage.

Since there is such a mass and variety of domestic melodrama before 1850, one can do no more in a short preface than name a few examples. Village melodrama, in part a nostalgic re-creation of the rural past of the majority of the new urban population, is a large section of its own, extended further by plays contrasting country and city, pretty cottage and dreary streets, village virtue and urban vice. The village type is represented by Payne's *Clari* (1823), J. B. Buckstone's *Luke the Labourer* (1826), Jerrold's *The Rent Day* (1832), and Bernard's *The Farmer's Story* (1836). Realistic metropolitan settings and themes of urban squalor and degradation mark Moncrieff's *The Scamps of London* (1843) and Charles Selby's *London by*

Night (1845), both adaptations of the influential *Les Bohémiens de Paris*, itself a stage version of Eugène Sue's novel *Les Mystères de Paris* (1842–3). Many versions exist of the famous crime melodramas *Maria Marten* and *Sweeny Todd*; better crime plays are Fitzball's *Jonathan Bradford* (1833), with its advanced staging of four rooms and action going forward in all simultaneously, and Dibdin Pitt's *Simon Lee* (1839) and *Susan Hopley* (1841), the latter with a vision of murder and a vengeance-seeking ghost.[1] Gambling is the subject of Raymond Clayton's *The Gambler's Life in London* (1829) and *The London Banker* (1845). The horrible consequences of drink are grimly portrayed in Jerrold's *Fifteen Years of a Drunkard's Life* (1828) and T. P. Taylor's *The Bottle* (1847), which was based on Cruikshank's temperance engravings.

There are comparatively few factory melodramas; of these the most interesting by far is *The Factory Lad*. Set in Lancashire, it is the first treatment in English drama of industrial violence and antagonism between master and man;[2] it also contains a savage attack upon the dispensation of justice and parish welfare. The play antedates Frances Trollope's *Michael Armstrong, the Factory Boy* (1840), a novel about the appalling working conditions for children in cotton mills, by eight years, and Disraeli's *Sybil* (1845) and Mrs. Gaskell's *Mary Barton* (1847) by considerably more. Its themes were not socially new—the Luddites began smashing machines in 1811 and again after the war, and the replacement of handlooms by steam machinery in the Lancashire cotton mills had developed rapidly since 1800—but its artistic treatment was. *The Factory Lad* is exceptional for a melodrama in having no comic relief and an unhappy ending. Its radical social consciousness is advanced even for socially aware domestic melodrama, and its unrelenting severity and power of serious dramatic expression also place it well ahead of its time.

Other melodramas deal with similar material. In G. F.

---

[1] Crime and criminals are universal in melodrama and a separate crime category can hardly be distinguished, but the crimes of daily life were especially well suited to treatment in domestic melodrama.

[2] Nine days before the first night of *The Factory Lad* in 1832, Jerrold's *The Factory Girl* appeared at Drury Lane. The latter is not closely related to factory life, but it does touch on the utter weariness and early death of children in a cotton mill. The master is a good man; the villain is his foreman.

Taylor's *The Factory Strike, or Want, Crime, and Retribution* (1838), a generous mill-owner is compelled by competition from mechanized factories to reduce his workmen's pay. The villain persuades the men to strike; the factory is fired and the employer murdered. This play condemns strikes and is on the side of the owner, but Haines's *The Factory Boy* (1840), with a Merseyside setting, is very much anti-employer. The villains are the rich mill-owner Magnus Mule and his foreman. The Factory Boy's mother died in a snowstorm at the gates of the mill because Mule refused her food; his innocent father was hanged for theft because of Mule's scheming. Finally justice triumphs: Mule is stabbed to death and the foreman shot. After 1850 authors continued to write factory melodramas. Boucicault adapted *Mary Barton* in *The Long Strike* (1866), in which Manchester mill-owners declare a lockout after rejecting the just demands of their employees, whose delegates they jail. Two scenes not in the novel show strike funds doled out to hungry families, and the mill-owning villain pursued by an angry mob. Tom Taylor's *Arkwright's Wife* (1873), set in the eighteenth century, is unsympathetic to mob violence and machine-smashing, but George Fenn's *The Foreman of the Works* (1886) pits an honest bell-foundry foreman against his evil employer. A strike occurs, and the play concludes with the strike-leader, a fanatic demagogue who had plotted to blow up the foundry, hurling the villain over a cliff and being arrested. In Arthur Moss's *The Workman's Foe* (*ca* 1900) a factory manager boasts of his power to crush workmen and seduce factory girls. Such factory melodramas are the ancestors of Galsworthy's *Strife* (1909) and later plays with themes of industrial discontent and struggle.

I know nothing of John Walker, the author of *The Factory Lad*. Between 1825 and 1843 he wrote for minor theatres at least six other melodramas and one comedy, *Nell Gwynne*. Most of the melodramas, such as *The Mysterious Stranger*, *The Wizard Priest*, *The Wild Boy of Bohemia*, and *The Outlaw's Oath*, are Gothic. *The Factory Lad* was performed only six times when it first came out, but that it had at least some acting life is indicated by its presence in *Duncombe's* and *Dicks'* acting editions.[1] As *The Factory Lad* was a Surrey play, there is no

---

[1] Jerrold's *The Factory Girl* was given only three times at Drury Lane, and there

Lord Chamberlain's copy; the text here published comes from *Duncombe's British Theatre*, v. 11, and *Dicks'* no. 230, which although much later is virtually a reprint of *Duncombe.*

is evidence that melodramas with factory themes were slow to win popularity on the London stage, being concerned as they were with northern cotton mills.

ACT I

SCENE I. *Exterior of a Factory, lighted.*

As the curtain rises the clock strikes eight, and the men, including ALLEN, WILSON, SMITH, SIMS, *and* HATFIELD, *enter from Factory.*

ALLEN. Now my lads, the glad sound—eight o'clock, Saturday night. Now for our pay, and for the first time from our new master, the son of our late worthy employer.

WILSON. The poor man's friend!

HATFIELD. And the poor man's father, too!

ALLEN. Aye; who, as he became rich by the industry of his men, would not desert them in a time of need, nor prefer steam machinery and other inventions to honest labour.

WILSON. May his son be like him!

ALLEN. Aye; he was a kind man, truly. Good as good could be, an enemy to no man but the slothful! Ah, a tear almost starts when I think of him! May he be happy, may—. He must be as happy above as he made those on this earth. But come, come, we won't be melancholy. Saturday night! We won't put a dark side upon things, but let us hope his son, our present master, may be like his father, eh?

HATFIELD. Ah, half like, and I shall be content!

WILSON. And I—and all of us.

ALLEN. Hush! He comes.

Enter WESTWOOD, *from Factory.*

WESTWOOD. Gentlemen!

HATFIELD [*aside to* ALLEN *and rest*]. Gentlemen! There's a pleasing way.

ALLEN. Gentlemen, sir! We're no gentlemen, but only poor, hard-working men, at your honour's service.

HATFIELD. Hard-working and honest, we hope.

WESTWOOD. Well, well, gentlemen or hard-working men, it's not what I've come about.

ALLEN. No complaint, I hope? Work all clean and right?

WESTWOOD. It may be.

HATFIELD. It may be! It is, or I'll forfeit my wages. Your father, sir, never spoke in doubt, but always looked, spoke his mind, and—

WESTWOOD. And that's what *I've* come to do. I've come to speak my mind. Times are now altered!

ALLEN. They are indeed, sir. A poor man has now less wages for more work.

WESTWOOD. The master having less money, resulting from there being less demand for the commodity manufactured.

ALLEN. Less demand!

WESTWOOD. Hear me! If not less demand, a greater quantity is thrown into the markets at a cheaper rate. Therefore, to the business I've come about. As things go with the times, so must men. To compete with my neighbours—that is, if I wish to prosper as they do—in plain words, in future I have come to the resolution of having my looms propelled by steam.

ALLEN.
HATFIELD. } By steam!
WILSON.

WESTWOOD. Which will dispense with the necessity of manual labour, and save me some three thousand a year.

ALLEN. And not want us, who have been all our lives working here?

WESTWOOD. I can't help it. I am sorry for it; but I must do as others do.

ALLEN. What, and turn us out, to beg, starve, steal, or—

HATFIELD. Aye; or rot for what he cares.

WESTWOOD. Turn you out are words I don't understand. I don't want you, that's all. Surely I can say that? What is here is mine, left me by my father to do the best with, and that is now my intention. Steam supersedes manual labour. A ton of coals will do as much work as fifty men, and for less wages than ten will come to, is it not so?

ALLEN. It may be as you say, sir; but your poor father made the old plan do, and died, they say, rich. He was always well satisfied with the profits our industry brought him, he lived cheerful himself and made others so; and often I have heard him say his greatest pleasure was the knowledge that so many hard-working men could sit down to a Sunday's dinner in peace, and rear up their children decently through his means.

WILSON. Ah, heaven bless him!

HATFIELD. Heaven has blessed him, I trust, for he was a man— an Englishman who had feeling for his fellow creatures, and who would not, for the sake of extra gain, that he might keep his hounds and his hunters, turn the poor man from his door who had served him faithfully for years.

WESTWOOD. I hear you, and understand you, sir. Sentiments in theory sound well, but not in practice; and as you seem spokes- man in this affair, I will—though I consider myself in no way compelled—reply to you in your own way. Don't you buy where you please, at the cheapest place? Would you have bought that jerkin of one man more than another, if he had charged you twice the sum for it, or even a sixpence more? Don't you, too, sow your garden as you please, and dig it as you please?

HATFIELD. Why, it's my own!

WESTWOOD. There it is! Then have *I* not the same right to do as I please with *my own*?

ALLEN. Then you discharge us?

HATFIELD. Oh, come along! What's the use of asking or talking either? You cannot expect iron to have feelings!

WESTWOOD. I stand not here to be insulted; so request you'll to the counting-house, receive your wages, and depart.

ALLEN. And for ever?

WESTWOOD. For ever! I want you not.

ALLEN. Will you not think of it again once more?

WESTWOOD. I'm resolved.

ALLEN [*aside*]. My poor wife and children! [*To* WESTWOOD.] No, no; not quite—not quite resolved! Things, mayhap ha' run cross, so you be hasty! Think, think again! [*Kneels.*] On my knees hear a poor man's prayer.

WESTWOOD. It is useless! I *have* thought and decided!

ALLEN [*rises*]. My wife! My children!   [*Rushes off.*

WILSON. Poor fellow!

HATFIELD. Then, if ye will not hear a poor man's prayer, hear his curses! May thy endeavours be as sterile land, which the lightning has scath'd, bearing nor fruit, nor flower, nor blade, but never-dying thorns to pierce thee on thy pillow! Hard-hearted, vain, pampered thing as thou art, remember, the day will come thou'lt be sorry for this night's work! Come, comrades—come!

[HATFIELD, WILSON, SIMS, *and* SMITH *exeunt.* WESTWOOD *into Factory, sneeringly.*

SCENE II. *A Country Lane. Dark.*

Enter RUSHTON, *cautiously, with snare, bag, and gun. Sets a snare.*

RUSHTON. That be sure for a good 'un! Ha, ha! The Game Laws, eh? As if a poor man hadn't as much right to the bird that flies and the hare that runs as the rich tyrants who want all, and gripe and grapple all too? I care not for their laws. While I have my liberty, or power, or strength, I will live as well as the best of 'em. [*Noise without.*] But who comes here? Ah, what do I see? Some of the factory lads, and this way too! What can this mean? I'll listen!   [*Stands aside.*

Enter HATFIELD, WILSON, SIMS, *and* SMITH.

WILSON. Well, here's a pretty ending to all our labours, after nine years, as I've been—

SIMS. And I ten.

SMITH. And I, since I was a lad.

HATFIELD. And I, all my life. But so it is. What are working men like us but the tools that make others rich, who, when we become old—

OMNES. Ah!

HATFIELD. We're kicked from our places, like dogs, to starve, die, and rot, for what they care!

SIMS. Or beg!

HATFIELD. Ah, that I'll never do!

WILSON. Nor I!

SMITH. Nor I, either!

SIMS. Then rob, mayhap?

WILSON. That may be!

HATFIELD. Aye; be like poor Will Rushton—an outcast, a poacher, or anything!

RUSHTON [*starting forward. The others stand amazed*]. Aye, or a pauper, to go with your hat in your hand, and after begging and telling them what they know to be the truth—that you have a wife and five, six, or eight children, one perhaps just born, another mayhap just dying—they'll give you eighteen pence to support them all for the week; and if you dare to complain, not a farthing; but place you in the stocks, or scourge you through the town as a vagabond! This is parish charity! I have known what it is. My back is still scored with the marks of their power. The slave abroad, the poor black whom they affect to pity, is not so trampled on, hunted, and ill-used as the peasant or hard-working fellows like your-selves, if once you have no home nor bread to give your children!

WILSON. But this I'll never submit to!

SIMS. Nor I!

SMITH. Nor I!

HATFIELD. Nor I! I'll hang first!

WILSON. Thank heaven, I have no children!

SMITH. Nor more have I, nor Sims; but some have both, wives and children.

WILSON. 'Tis true. I have a wife, but she's as yet young, healthy, and can work and does work; but think of poor

Allen, with a wife and three small children and an aged mother to support.

RUSHTON. What! And is he discharged too? What, Allen—George Allen?

HATFIELD. Aye, along with the rest. Not wanted now!

RUSHTON. My brother George, as I do call him still—for though my poor wife be dead and gone, she were his wife's sister. Ah, but let me not think of that. Where—where be poor George? He be not here!

WILSON. He rushed off home, I do believe, like to one broken-hearted.

RUSHTON. Ah, to his poor wife and children! There will I go to him, and say though all the world do forsake him, Will Rushton never will! No; while there be a hare or bird he shall have one; and woe to the man who dare prevent or hold my hand!

HATFIELD. You're a brave and staunch fellow.

RUSHTON. Aye, and desperate and daring, too.

WILSON. Give me your hand.

HATFIELD And here's mine. What say you? Suppose we go to the 'Harriers', and, in the back room by ourselves, just ha' a drop of something and talk o' things a bit.

WILSON. We will go.

SMITH. Aye, we will.

HATFIELD [to RUSHTON]. And you to George, and say where we are.

RUSHTON. I will—and bring him with me! But he'll not want asking. These times cannot last long. When man be so worried that he be denied that food that heaven sends for all, then heaven itself calls for vengeance! No, the time has come when the sky shall be like blood, proclaiming this shall be the reward of the avaricious, the greedy, the flinty-hearted, who, deaf to the poor man's wants, make him what he now is, a ruffian—an incendiary!

WILSON. Remember Allen. Yet stay! Now I think again, will it not alarm his wife to see *you*?

RUSHTON. Ah!

HATFIELD. And bring things to mind that had not best be thought of just now.

RUSHTON. Ah, my wife—

HATFIELD. Was her sister. So, suppose Smith here goes instead. She do not know him, does she, Smith?

SMITH. But bare—perhaps not. I ha' passed her once or twice.

HATFIELD. 'Twill do then. You go then and whisper in his ear where we are.

SMITH. Aye, the 'Harriers'.

HATFIELD [to RUSHTON]. What say you, isn't it better so?

RUSHTON. Aye, aye!

WILSON. 'Tis much better.

HATFIELD. Remember then! To the 'Harriers'.

RUSHTON. And shall I be there?

SMITH. To be sure.

WILSON. But won't our all meeting in a room by ourselves, and Will with us too, excite suspicion?

HATFIELD. That's well thought again. Then we'll drop in one by one, or two together so—and Will, you can look in too, as 'twere by accident, for a drink o' summat—that way.

RUSHTON. I care not how, lads. In Will Rushton you see one who has been so buffetted he thinks not of forms. But be it as you will. To the last drop I have, I'll be your friend—aye, the friend of poor George Allen!

HATFIELD. George! Away—away!

[*Music. They shake hands earnestly and exeunt.*

━━━

SCENE III. *Interior of* ALLEN's *House. Fireplace, saucepan on. A Clock—time twenty minutes past eight. A Cradle with Child.*
JANE ALLEN, *and* MARY *and* MILLY *assisting her in pearling lace, and drawing ditto.*

MARY. I've done another length, mother, and that makes five, and sister hasn't done four yet.

JANE. Never mind! She does very well. You're both very good children! Only now you may lay the cloth, and get out the supper. It's past eight, and your father will be coming home, and he'll be very tired, I dare say, and hungry too, and at the end of the week a bit of supper and a draught of ale is a thing he looks for! And, his family around him, who so happy as George Allen?

MARY. And you too, mother, and me too, and sister too, and little brother in the cradle.

JANE. All—all, bless you, and thank heaven!

MARY. Then I'll not begin another, mother?

JANE. No; but make haste and lay the cloth.

MILLY. And shan't I finish mine neither, mother?

JANE. No, never mind, that's a good girl. Get out the bread, and be quick. [*Clock chimes half-past.*] Hear? It's half-past! A fork—the potatoes must be done.

MARY. Yes, mother.

[*Hands fork.* JANE *goes to fire, and* MILLY *gets bread out.*

JANE. Oh, I think I hear him!

MARY. And so do I, mother—I can hear him! But oh dear, how he's banging to the gate!

Enter GEORGE ALLEN, *who throws himself in a chair fretfully.*

JANE. Why, George, what's the matter? Dear me, how pale you are! Are you not well, George? You seem feverish.

ALLEN. I am—I am!

JANE. You'll be better after supper. Children, quick!

MARY. Oh, father, we've been so busy, and done such a deal! See, father!

[*Shows him lace.* ALLEN *takes it, throws it down, rises, and stamps on it.*

ALLEN. Curses on it!

MARY. Oh, mother—mother, father's thrown down all my work and has stamped on it, and I'm sure it's done very well! [*Cries.*]

MILLY. Oh, mother, see what father's done!

JANE. George, oh, tell me what means this!

ALLEN. It means that—

MARY. What, father? What makes you angry?

JANE. Say, George!

ALLEN [*looks at his children, and then clasps them*]. God—God bless you! [*Picks up the lace and gives it them.*] There, there! You're good children!   [*Sits down.*

MARY. I'm sure, father, I never do anything to make you angry.

MILLY. No more do I, father—do I?

MARY. Nor does mother, either?

ALLEN. No—no, I know she does not!

JANE. Then what is it, George? I never saw you thus before! You're so pale, and you tremble so. Why did you throw down the lace, that which is a living to us?

ALLEN. Because it will never be so again!

JANE. Not a living to us?

ALLEN. No! George Allen must beg now! Ah, beg or as bad—work and starve. And that I'll never do!

JANE. Oh, speak! Work and starve? Impossible!

ALLEN. Naught be impossible these days! What has ruined others will now ruin us. It's been others' turn first, now it be ours.

JANE. What, George?

ALLEN. That steam—that curse on mankind, that for the gain of a few, one or two, to ruin hundreds, is going to be at the factory! Instead of five-and-thirty good hands, there won't be ten wanted now, and them half boys and strangers. Yes, steam be now going to do all the work, and poor, hard-working, honest men, who ha' been for years toiling to do all for the good of a master, be now turned out o' doors to do what they can or what they like. And you know what that means, and what it must come to.

JANE. Oh, dreadful—dreadful! But don't fret, husband—don't fret! We will all strive to do something!

ALLEN [*again rising*]. But what be that something? Think I can hear my children cry for food and run barefoot? Think I don't know what 'twill come to?

JANE. But some other place will perhaps give us employ.

ALLEN. Aye, some foreign outlandish place; to be shipped off like convicts to die and starve. Look at Will Rushton, who was enticed, or rather say ensnared there with his wife and four children. Were not the children slaughtered by the natives, who hate white men and live on human flesh? And was not his wife seized too, your own sister, and borne away and never returned; shared perhaps the same fate as her children, or perhaps worse? And has not poor Will, since he returned, been crazed, heart-broken, a pauper, a poacher, or anything?

JANE. Oh, no, no! We shall meet with friends here, George.

ALLEN. Aye, Jane, such friends that if thou wert dying, starving, our children stretched lifeless, and I but took a crust of bread to save thee, would thrust me in a prison, there to rot. I have read, Jane—I have seen, Jane, the fate of a poor man. And you know we have nothing now, no savings after the long sickness of father and burying, and the little one we lost, too.

JANE. They are in heaven now, I hope!

Door opens and SMITH *appears.*

ALLEN. Who's there?

SMITH. It's only me, George.

ALLEN. Ah! [SMITH *approaches and whispers in* ALLEN's *ear.*] I will!

JANE [*apart*]. What can this mean?

SMITH. Be secret.

ALLEN. As the grave!

SMITH [*whispers again*]. There, too!

ALLEN. He will?

SMITH. As by chance, you know.

JANE [*apart*]. Heaven, what can it mean?

ALLEN. I'll be there.

> [*Shakes* SMITH *by the hand, who leaves at door.*

JANE. Oh, George—George, what is this, that your eyes roll so? Now think!

ALLEN. I do think, Jane.

JANE. Sit—come, come, sit—sit down and have some supper, then you'll be better! Remember it is Saturday night. I know it is enough to make you vexed; but think, George—think, and remember there is One who never forsakes the good man, if he will but pray to him.

ALLEN. I will—I will; but I must now to see the lads that be like myself, poor fellows—just to talk, you know—to think, as like—to plan—e'es to plan—merely to plan.

JANE. But not yet. Sit awhile. Take some ale.

ALLEN. Why, I can get ale there, and I can't eat, my tongue and throat be so dry. God bless you!   [*Going.*

MARY. Not going, father?

MILLY. Not going, father?

JANE. See, George! Don't go yet!

ALLEN [*kisses children*]. I must—I must! Only for a short time, and it be growing late.

> [*Approaches door.*

JANE. Don't! Stay, George—stay!

> [*Kneels and catches hold of him.*

ALLEN. I must—I must!

> [*Rushes out. Music.* JANE *falls.*

MARY [*cries*]. Mother—mother! Oh, father!

> [*They fall on their mother, and scene closes.*

SCENE IV. *An Apartment in* WESTWOOD's *House.*

Enter WESTWOOD.

WESTWOOD. I must be on the alert, and keep my doors well fastened, and have, too, an armed force to welcome these desperadoes if they should dare to violate the laws, well framed to subject them to obedience. I did not half like the menace of that fellow. However, I'll be secure, and if they dare, let them take the consequences. [*Muses, and repeats* HATFIELD's *words.*] 'The day will come, I shall be sorry for what I have done!' Ha, ha! Sorry! Fool, and fools! What have I to fear or dread? Is England's proud aristocracy to tremble when brawling fools mouth and question? No; the hangman shall be their answer.

Enter SERVANT.

SERVANT. The dinner's ready, sir.

WESTWOOD. Is it eight, then?

SERVANT. Yes, sir.

WESTWOOD. Is that old grumbler, my father's late housekeeper, gone, who dared to talk and advise, as she called it?

SERVANT. She went at six, sir. We trundled her out, sir.

WESTWOOD. And the French cook, is he arrived yet?

SERVANT. He has sent his valet to say he'll be here in three days, after his excursion to Brighton.   [*Exit.*

WESTWOOD. What, because our fathers acted foolishly, shall we also plod on in the same dreary route? No; science has opened to us her stores, and we shall be fools indeed not to take advantage of the good it brings. The time must come, and shortly, when even the labourer himself will freely acknowledge that our improvements in machinery and the aid afforded us by the use of steam will place England on a still nobler eminence than the proud height she has already attained.   [*Exit.*

———

SCENE V. *A Room in the 'Harriers'.*

WILSON, SIMS, SMITH, *and* HATFIELD *discovered at a table, drinking.* TAPWELL, *the Landlord, just entering.*

TAPWELL. *Another* mug, did you say?

HATFIELD. Aye, and another to that. What stare you at?

TAPWELL. Eh? Oh, very well!   [*Exit.*

SIMS. Master Tapwell seems surprised at our having an extra pot.

HATFIELD. Let him be. We care not, no more will he, if we have twenty, so he gets the money.

WILSON [*to* SMITH]. He said he'd come, did he—Allen?

SMITH. For certain.

HATFIELD. His wife, no doubt, was there? Did you manage all well? Whisper secretly?

SMITH. Not a word out.

HATFIELD. That's well, for women are bad to trust in these things. I've read in books where the best plots have failed through women being told what their husbands or their fathers were going to do, though it was to free a nation from the yoke of tyranny.

WILSON. Aye, right; and so have I.

Re-enter TAPWELL, *with beer.*

TAPWELL. The beer.
                    [*Holds out his hand without delivering it.*

WILSON. What's that for?

TAPWELL. Another mug, and you didn't pay for the last, which makes one-and-fourpence.

HATFIELD. What, you know, do you, already, that we're discharged?

TAPWELL. Why, yes, if truth must be told, young Squire—

HATFIELD. Young who?

TAPWELL. Young Squire—Master Westwood.

HATFIELD. Young damnation! Squire such a rascal as that again while we're here, and this pot with its contents shall make you call for a plaster quicker than you may like. Squire Westwood! Squire Hard-heart! No man, no feeling! Call a man like that a squire! An English gentleman—a true English gentleman is he who feels for another, who relieves the distressed, and not turns out the honest hard-working man to beg or starve because he, forsooth, may keep his hunters and drink his foreign wines.

sims. Aye; and go to foreign parts. Englishmen were happy when they knew naught but Englishmen; when they were plain, blunt, honest, upright, and downright—the master an example to his servant, and both happy with the profits of their daily toil.

ALLEN enters at door.

smith. Allen!

hatfield [to tapwell]. Off, thou lickshoe! There, take that. That will do, I suppose, for another pot, or a gallon?
[Throws him down a crown piece on the floor.

tapwell. Oh, certainly, Master Hatfield—certainly gentlemen! Another pot now, did you say?

smith. Off!   [Thrusts him out and shuts the door.

hatfield [to allen]. Come, come, don't look so down—come, drink!

wilson. Aye, drink!

allen. Nay, I—

hatfield. Not drink? Not 'Destruction to steam machinery'?

allen. Destruction to steam machinery! Aye, with all my heart! [Drinks.] Destruction to steam machinery!

hatfield. Aye, our curse—our ruin!

wilson. Aye, aye; we've been talking about that, and one thing and t'other like, and about what we shall do, you know—

allen. Ah!

sims. I say poaching.

allen. And for a hare, to get sent away, perhaps, for seven long years.

smith. So I said.

sims. But we mayn't be caught, you know, not if we are true to each other. Four or five tightish lads like us can't be easily taken, unless we like, you know!

allen. And if we carry but a stick in our defence, and use it a bit, do you know the law? Hanging!

hatfield. Right! Hanging for a hare!

SIMS. Not so—not hanging. Don't Will Rushton carry on the sport pretty tidishly, and has only been—

ALLEN. In the stocks twice, whipped publicly thrice, and in gaol seven times. And what has he for his pains? Not a coat to his back worth a groat, no home but the hedge's shelter or an outhouse, and himself but to keep. What would he then do had he, as I have, a wife and three young children to support? Besides, isn't he at times wild with thinking of the past—of his lost wife and murdered children? He, poor unhappy wretch, cannot feel more or sink lower—the gaol to him is but a resting-place!

HATFIELD. 'Tis true, indeed. I remember him once a jovial fellow, the pride of all that knew him; but now—

ALLEN [*to* SMITH]. But said you not he would be here?

WILSON. Aye, as by accident.

RUSHTON *partly opens door, when* TAPWELL *stops him.*

ALLEN. Ah, 'tis he!

WILSON [*to* ALLEN]. Be not over anxious.

TAPWELL. No, you can't. You remember the bag you left here the last time, and the scrape it got me into?

RUSHTON. But only a minute or so.

TAPWELL. Not for half a minute.

HATFIELD [*to* ALLEN]. Shall I cleave the dastard down?

ALLEN. Leave it to me. [*Approaches* TAPWELL.] Come, sir landlord, mercy a bit, though you may not like his rags and for bread he snares a hare now and then, he may wear as honest a heart as many who wear a better garment; therefore, let him in. The outcast should sojourn with the outcast. Come, another gallon, and take that.   [*Gives* TAPWELL *money.*

TAPWELL. Oh well, certainly, if you have no objection, gentlemen, and he has no game or snares about him.

HATFIELD. Off!

[*Exit* TAPWELL.

ALLEN. Rushton!

RUSHTON. Allen!

ALLEN. Thy hand.

RUSHTON. 'Tis here, with my heart.

ALLEN. Drink.   [*Gives beer.*

RUSHTON. Thanks. Many's the day since I was welcomed thus.

SIMS. Not since, I dare say, you lost your poor wife.

[RUSHTON *stands transfixed.*

ALLEN. That was foolish to mention his wife.

SIMS. I forgot.

RUSHTON. Who spoke of my wife? Ah, did she call? Ah, she
    did—I hear her screams! They are—are tearing her from me!
    My children, too! I see their mangled forms, bleeding, torn
    piecemeal! My wife—my children! [*Subsides.*] My wife—
    my—[*Looks about.*] Where, where am I? [*Sees* ALLEN.] Allen,
    Allen!

ALLEN. To be sure—George Allen! Don't you know me? Your
    brother, your friend George, who—

RUSHTON. I know. Sent me food while I was in prison! [*Clasps*
    ALLEN's *hand and sobs.*] Heaven, heaven bless you!

ALLEN. Come, come, an end to this! I am now like thyself, an
    outcast—one driven, after years of hard toil, upon the world.
    These the same! [*Pointing to his comrades.*] Come now, say
    honestly, as a man who has seen much and whose hairs are
    gray, what would you advise us to do?

RUSHTON. I know all. You are discharged.

WILSON. Aye, from where we've worked since lads, nearly, if
    not all, and our fathers before us.

HATFIELD. And we are turned beggars on the world, for no
    reason but to make room for that which has ruined hundreds,
    to suit the whims and finery of a thing unworthy the name of
    man!

RUSHTON [*stands absorbed awhile*]. I would, but I dare not
    advise, for my blood now boils, and my flesh is gored with the
    lash of power! Hush! Hither! [*Beckons them round him.*] A
    word. Are you all good here? [*Touching his heart.*] Sound?
    Prime?

HATFIELD. Who dare to doubt?

RUSHTON. Enough. Hush! [*Whispers in their ears, and ends with:*] Dare you?

HATFIELD. I dare!

SMITH. And I!

WILSON. And I!

SIMS. And I!

ALLEN. And I!

RUSHTON. 'Tis well! [*Shakes them by the hand.*] Now then, come lads, the time answers. Hush!

[*Music. Exeunt.*

————

SCENE VI. *A Country Lane. Dark.*

Enter RUSHTON, ALLEN, WILSON, SIMS, SMITH, *and* HATFIELD, *armed variously.*

RUSHTON. Steady—steady, lads, and resolute!

WILSON. 'Tis well no one crosses our path.

HATFIELD. What if they did?

ALLEN. My heart almost begins to sicken; a fear, ever unknown to me, seems to shake me from head to foot.

RUSHTON. Pshaw, fear! Fear is the coward's partner, and the companion of the guilty; not of men who are about to act in their own right, and crush oppression.

WILSON. 'Tis true we are oppressed!

SMITH. We are!

SIMS. Aye, we are!

HATFIELD. And we'll be revenged!

SIMS. Aye, revenged!

ALLEN. But if we meet with resistance—I mean if they attack us?

RUSHTON. Return their attack—blow for blow, if they will have it; aye, and blood for blood. Give in, and you're lost for ever! You'll have no mercy. Look at me, Will Rushton, honest Will

Rushton that was once—hard-working Will Rushton. You know my fate—torture upon torture, the insult of the proud and the pity of the poor have been my lot for years. Trampled on, crushed, and gored to frenzy! My blood boils now I think on't! The pale spectre of my wife, with my slaughtered children now beckons me on! Revenge, revenge! Come, revenge!

[*Takes* ALLEN's *hand and exeunt.*

HATFIELD. Aye, revenge—revenge!

OMNES. Aye, revenge!

[*They follow* RUSHTON *and* ALLEN.

SCENE VII. *Exterior of the Factory. Dark.*

Enter RUSHTON *with a torch, followed by* ALLEN, WILSON, SIMS, SMITH, *and* HATFIELD.

RUSHTON. Now, to the work—to the work! Break, crack, and split into ten thousand pieces these engines of your disgrace, your poverty, and your ruin! Now!

HATFIELD. Aye, now destruction!

WILSON. Aye, spare not a stick! Come, come, Allen!

[RUSHTON, WILSON, SIMS, *and* SMITH *rush into the Factory. The Factory is seen blazing.*

WESTWOOD *rushes in, followed by* CONSTABLES.

WESTWOOD. Ah, villain, stay! It is as I was told; but little did I think they dared. Seize them!

HATFIELD. Ah, surprised!

RUSHTON *comes from the Factory, with firebrand, followed by his comrades.*

WESTWOOD. Submit, I say!

RUSHTON. Ah!

[*Seizes him by the throat, hurls him to the earth, and waves the lighted ember above him in wild triumph.*

ACT II

SCENE I. *Moonlight. Open Country, with View of Factory burning in the distance.*

Enter RUSHTON, *with firebrand.*

RUSHTON. Ha, ha! This has been a glorious night, to see the palace of the tyrant levelled to the ground—to hear his engines of gain cracking—to hear him call for help, and see the red flame laugh in triumph! Ah, many a day have I lain upon the cold damp ground, muttering curses—many a night have I called upon the moon, when she has frenzied my brain, to revenge my wrongs; for days and nights I have never slept—misery and want, and the smart of the lash, with visions of bygone days, have been like scorpions, rousing me to revenge, and the time has come. I have had partners, too, in the deed—men who, like myself, glory in the act. But where can Allen be, and the rest? They must away now. I'll to his cottage, and if the minions of power dare but touch a hair of his head, this brand shall lay them low.

[*Exit.*

———

SCENE II. *Interior, as before, of* ALLEN'S *House. The casement open, and the blaze of the Factory seen in the distance.*

JANE *watching at the window.* MARY *and* MILLY *near her.*

JANE. Oh, horror—horror!

MARY. It's not out yet, mother; it seems as if some other house was on fire.

MILLY. See, mother!

JANE. 'Tis too true, child! Oh, mercy—mercy! The flames have caught the farm next to it. I can no longer look. The worst of thoughts crowd upon my brain. My husband's absence—his wild and distracted look—the factory in flames!

Enter ALLEN, *hurriedly.*

Ah, my husband! Oh say, George, where—where is it you have been?

ALLEN. Jane—my children! [*Embraces them in silent anguish.*] Some ale, water, or something! My throat is parched!

MARY. Some ale, father?

JANE. You've seen the fire?

ALLEN. Yes, yes. Some ale, I said.

MARY. Here it is, father!   [*Gives jug.* ALLEN *drinks.*

ALLEN. Ha, that be sweet! [*To his wife in an undertone.*] Hush! Here—here, take this—[*Gives money.*]—it be all I have, and this, too. [*Gives watch.*] There be, too, a little up-stairs. Take care of thyself, Jane, and of children.

JANE. Oh, George, say not that! You would not leave your Jane, who has ever loved you, and ever will?

MARY. Oh, mother, don't cry!

ALLEN. Mother's not crying. [*Standing before her.*] See to the child; it wakes! [*Fire blazes vividly. To* JANE.] See you that? All be broken and burnt down. Say, if they come, you ha' not seen me, you know. They cannot harm thee.

JANE. Oh, George, say, for mercy's sake, you've had no hand in this!

ALLEN. What be done, Jane, cannot now be altered.

JANE. Oh, George, bad advice has led you to this! I know you would not have done so of yourself.

ALLEN. It matters not now, Jane; it be done, and I must away; but you shall hear from me, Jane, where'er I be. I will send thee all I get.

[*A noise without.*

JANE. Ah, that noise—

ALLEN. It be they come—come to take me.

ALLEN *rushes towards the door, when* WESTWOOD *and* CONSTABLES *appear at the window.*

Ah, 'tis useless!

WESTWOOD. He's here.

Enter WESTWOOD, *followed by* GRIMLEY *and* CONSTABLES.

Seize him! [*They seize* ALLEN.

JANE [*kneels*]. Oh, mercy, mercy! Spare him—spare my husband!

MARY. Oh, spare my father!

MILLY. Don't hurt father!

JANE. He is not guilty, indeed he's not!

WESTWOOD. Not guilty, when I saw him with the rest?

JANE. But he did not set fire the place. I know he did not—he would not.

WESTWOOD. What matters what hand did the deed? Is not all a heap of ashes—all burnt and destroyed?

JANE. Yet mercy!

WESTWOOD. Mercy! What mercy had he to me? Cast thy eye yonder, and petition to the flames.

JANE. Oh, George, George!

WESTWOOD. Away with him! Now for the outcast!

Enter RUSHTON, *frantically, with a piece of burnt machinery in his hand.*

RUSHTON. Who calls for the outcast? Stay! What are you about? Seizing an innocent man? Here stands the incendiary! I, Will Rushton, the outcast, the degraded! Ha, ha! Yes, and the revenged! 'Twas I led them on, and this hand lit the fire brand, and I am satisfied.

WESTWOOD. Seize him! 'Tis the instigator—the ringleader!

[*They attempt to seize him.*

RUSHTON [*in a menacing attitude*]. Approach not, or your grave is at my feet!

[*They retreat, intimidated.*

WESTWOOD. Cowards, do you fear a madman? Surrender, idiot, fiend, wretch, outcast, or this shall tame thee!

[*Presents a pistol.*

ALLEN. Rushton, you escape, I care not.

WESTWOOD. Ah! then stir but one foot, and—

RUSHTON. And what? [*Seizes him by the collar and hurls him to the ground,* WESTWOOD *firing the pistol.*] Away, I say!

JANE. Oh, fly—fly, George!

[WESTWOOD *attempts to rise.* RUSHTON *stands over him and, waving the ember, secures the retreat of* ALLEN. *As he is rushing out, the scene closes.*

SCENE III. *Exterior of an Out-house or Hovel, in Lane. Moonlight.*

Enter ALLEN, *frantic, as if pursued.*

ALLEN. Where shall I fly? My brain is giddy, my legs feeble. I can no further. Oh, my wife—Jane, Jane—my children, too!

[*Falls exhausted.*

WILSON *and* HATFIELD *look out from hovel.*

HATFIELD. It was Allen's voice, I'm sure, yet I see no one.

WILSON. See, who lies there?   [*They come out.*

HATFIELD. Ah, it is he!

WILSON. What is this? Not dead—killed himself! Allen—Allen!

HATFIELD. Allen, lad!

ALLEN [*staring*]. Ah, who calls on Allen? Was't my wife—my children! I'm here! Don't you see me? What—what's—

[*Looks about wildly.*

WILSON. Allen, it's but us, your old friends, Wilson and Hatfield. Don't you know us?

ALLEN. Ah, is it? [*They assist him to rise. He clasps their hands earnestly.*] Have you seen my wife—my children?

HATFIELD. I thought you'd been to see them.

ALLEN. Ah, I remember! Like a wild dream it comes across my brain; but where—where's the rest—Smith and—

[*Voices without cry* 'This way—this way!'

ALLEN. Ah, they come!

HATFIELD. In—in there! Would you be taken?

ALLEN. I care not. Ah, 'tis he—'tis Rushton! Never will I fly. He who would desert his comrade in the hour of peril is worse than coward.

Enter RUSHTON *in haste, followed by* WESTWOOD *and* SOLDIERS.

WESTWOOD. Ah, here are the rest. Seize them all and spare none.

RUSHTON. Hell-hounds, would you murder the poor wretches you have deprived of bread!

WESTWOOD. Villain, have you not deprived me of bread, and set fire to my dwelling, reckless who might perish in the flame?

RUSHTON. That *you had,* then justice had been done and my revenge satisfied!

WESTWOOD. Officer, your duty! Let them not escape.

OFFICER. In the King's name, I desire you to yield!

HATFIELD. Never!

RUSHTON. That's right, my lads—never yield!

[*They stand on the defensive.*

OFFICER. Then at your peril!

[*Presents pistol.* SOLDIERS *advance and a confused combat ensues, ending in the disarming of* HATFIELD *and* WILSON, *and capture of* ALLEN *with a wound across his forehead.*

At that moment JANE ALLEN *enters, distracted.*

JANE [*she screams on seeing her husband wounded and taken*]. Oh, mercy—mercy, my husband! Do not—do not murder him! Oh, George!   [*Kneels and clasps him round the knee.*

ALLEN. Who calls on George Allen?

JANE. It is thy wife! Don't you know me? Thy wife, you know, George. Jane, Jane, thy wife!

ALLEN. Ah, Jane, my doom is fixed! Leave me, and clasp those who are helpless—my little ones!

RUSHTON. There, monster, dost thou see that? Thy doing.

WESTWOOD. 'Tis false! Liar, fiend, reprobate!

RUSHTON. 'Tis true! Liar, fiend, and reprobate again! Didst thou not turn these poor men from their honest employ to beg, steal, starve, or do as they have done—be revenged?

ALLEN. Peace, peace, it is over now! Jane, I feel my life fast ebbing! Home, home!

WESTWOOD. Away with them!

JANE. Oh, pity, mercy! Tear him not away from me.

OFFICER. The law's imperative!

[*The* SOLDIERS *march them off.* JANE *falls fainting.*
JANE *is lying senseless.* MARY *enters.*

MARY. Mother, mother, where are you? Oh, what do I see on the cold ground? It can't be mother? Mother! [*Approaches nearer.*] Mother! Oh, it can't be my mother—she would hear me—yet it looks my mother! Oh, dear, it is, I know it can be no other! Mother, mother! [*Cries and falls on her mother.*] Mother, why don't you speak? Mother!

[*Kneels and kisses her.* JANE, *recovering, looks about her in wild disorder.*

JANE. Where am I?

MARY. Here, mother, on the cold ground!

JANE [*seeing her child*]. Ah, my child, bless you—bless you! But what are we doing here in the open air?

MARY. You came out after father, mother.

JANE. Your father! [*Screams.*] Ah, I now remember all! They are tearing him from me, to take him to a loathsome dungeon! All now crosses me like a wild dream. The factory—the red sky—flames whirling in the air! My eye-balls seem cracked—my brain grows dizzy—I hear chains and screams of death! My husband—they shall not tear him from me!

MARY. Mother, mother, where are you going?

JANE. To thy father—to the gaol—they will not refuse his poor, weak, and broken-hearted wife!

MARY. Nor me either, will they, mother?

JANE [*takes her up*]. Bless you—bless you! Never, never shall they part us!

[*Exeunt.*

SCENE IV. *Interior of a Justice Room.*

The JUSTICE *and* CLERK *discovered seated at table.* GEORGE
ALLEN, SIMS, WILSON, *and* HATFIELD *discovered handcuffed.*
WESTWOOD, CONSTABLES, OFFICER, *and* SOLDIERS, *dragging
in* RUSHTON, *struggling.*

RUSHTON. Why do you drag me thus? Do you think I'm afraid?
   Do you think I fear to own that I was the man who led them
   on? No! I glory in the act—'tis the sweet triumph I've oft
   longed for!

BIAS. Silence, sirrah!

RUSHTON. I speak or am silent as I please! Talking is not
   hanging, is it? What are you more than I am? I remember
   when you were overseer—the man appointed to protect the
   poor.

BIAS. And what has that to do with the present business?

RUSHTON. It has this—to show that an honest man at least
   should sit in that seat, and not one who has crept into it by
   robbery and oppression.

BIAS. Maniac!

RUSHTON. Aye, but I was not so when the cart, laden with
   provisions for the workhouse, by your order stopped at your
   own door to pretend to deliver some articles ordered for
   yourself, but which belonged to the poor famished creatures
   who had no redress but the lash if they dared to complain.

BIAS. It is false!

RUSHTON. Is it false, too, that through your means alone, when
   but seven years of age, I was condemned to six weeks' hard
   labour in a prison for stealing, as you called it, but a handful
   of apples from your orchard?

BIAS. 'Tis false, or why not have made your charge before? Is
   it to be supposed one so vindictive, a common thief, an incendiary, would have concealed this so long? The law is open
   to you, is it not?

RUSHTON. No; I am poor!

BIAS. And what of that? The law is made alike for rich and poor.

RUSHTON. Is it? Why, then, does it so often lock the poor man in a gaol, while the rich one goes free?

BIAS. No more of this. Clerk, draw out the commitment!

RUSHTON. Commitment? Who would you commit? Not these poor men. 'Twas I broke into and destroyed the engines of power. 'Twas I set fire to the mass, and reduced to ashes what has reduced others to beggary. Think you I regret— think you I fear? No, I glory in the act. There! I have confessed, and as in me you see the avenger of the poor man's wrongs, on me, and me alone, heap your vengeance.

BIAS. Clerk, record the prisoner's confession; and Charles George Westwood, proprietor of the factory and buildings adjoining thereunto, lately burnt, stand forth and make your further allegations, and name the prisoners charged in this atrocious act.

WESTWOOD. I charge all the prisoners now standing here as being concerned in the destruction of the factory, dwelling-house, and out-houses. First, their leader there, William, or Will Rushton, as I believe he is called; second, John Hatfield; third, Walter Sims; fourth, Francis Wilson; fifth, Joseph Smith, not here through being wounded; sixth, and last, George Allen.

BIAS. And this you are willing to swear?

WESTWOOD. I am.

BIAS. Prisoners, you have heard the charge, have you aught to say?

HATFIELD. No! If it is to be, let it be; we may as well die on a scaffold as be starved!

WILSON. Don't look down, George; let's bear it up like men.

ALLEN. Yet my wife and children!

BIAS. 'Tis well. This silence shows a proper sense of shame. 'Tis written, they who defy the law must suffer by the law. Prisoners, though it is not my duty to pronounce judgment, still I deem it so to apprize you of the fate likely to await you. To-morrow will commence the assizes at the neighbouring town, where you will be removed and arraigned before a tribunal, which will hear your defence, and give the verdict

according to the evidence produced. Further I have naught to
say. Officer, remove the prisoners.

JANE [*without*]. Unhand me, I will enter!

She enters. ALLEN *conceals himself.*

He is here—must be here! Is it that agony has dimmed my
sight, or that reason has left her seat and madness mocks me?
[*Sees him.*] Ah, he's there! Oh, George, is this the end of all
our former bliss? Torn from me, and for ever? My husband,
he whom I have pressed to my breast—my heart's blood—
the father of my children—oh horror, horror, exposed like
a common felon to the gaze of thousands on a gibbet! Hung?
Oh, my heart sickens! No, no, it cannot be—must not be!
Never shall it be said that my husband, George Allen, died
like a felon, a common robber, a murderer!

BIAS. Seize this frantic woman, and let her be removed.

[*They approach to take her.*

JANE. Oh, touch me not! Off—off, I say! Yet have pity on me,
I know not what I say. A whirlwind rushes through my brain!
[*Falls at* WESTWOOD's *feet clasping his knees.*] Mercy—
mercy, to you I kneel! Pity my poor husband, and I will
pray for thee, work for thee; my children, all—all, shall be
your slaves for ever—ever, but spare him!

WESTWOOD. Cling not to me, justice shall have its due!

[*Spurns her from him.*

RUSHTON. Spurn a helpless and imploring woman, whose heart
is broken—whose mind is crazed? If her *voice* is weak, my
arm is not. Justice shall have its due. Die, tyrant! Quick, to
where water quencheth not!

[*Fires.* WESTWOOD *falls, and the curtain drops on picture of*
RUSHTON *standing in centre, laughing hysterically, pointing
at* WESTWOOD. JANE *in the arms of* ALLEN. HATFIELD,
SIMS, *and* WILSON, *in an attitude of surprise, the* SOLDIERS
with their muskets levelled at RUSHTON.

RICHELIEU

OR THE CONSPIRACY

A PLAY IN FIVE ACTS

BY

EDWARD BULWER-LYTTON (1803–1873)

First performed at Covent Garden Theatre
7 March 1839

CAST

Louis XIII	Mr. Elton
GASTON, DUKE OF ORLEANS, brother to Louis XIII	Mr. Diddear
BARADAS, favourite of the king, first gentleman of the chamber, premier ecuyer, &c.	Mr. Warde
CARDINAL RICHELIEU	Mr. Macready
THE CHEVALIER DE MAUPRAT	Mr. Anderson
THE SIEUR DE BERINGHEN, in attendance on the king, one of the conspirators	Mr. Vining
JOSEPH, a Capuchin, Richelieu's confidant	Mr. Phelps
HUGUET, an officer of Richelieu's household guard, a spy	Mr. G. Bennett
FRANÇOIS, first page to Richelieu	Mr. Howe
CLERMONT	Mr. Roberts
CAPTAIN OF THE ARCHERS	Mr. Matthews
SECRETARIES OF STATE	Mr. Tilbury / Mr. Yarnold / Mr. Payne
GOVERNOR OF THE BASTILLE	Mr. Waldron
GAOLER	Mr. Ayliffe
JULIE DE MORTEMAR, an orphan, ward to Richelieu	Miss Helen Faucit
MARION DE LORME, mistress to Orleans, but in Richelieu's pay	Miss Charles

Courtiers, Pages, Conspirators, Officers, Soldiers, &c.

PREFACE TO *RICHELIEU*

W H E N Edward Bulwer, later Bulwer-Lytton, began work on
Richelieu, he was already a very successful novelist, poet, editor,
and parliamentarian, with a keen interest in theatre and two
plays performed.[1] *The Duchess de la Vallière* (1837), brought
forward by Macready at Covent Garden under Osbaldiston's
management, was a failure. A protracted romantic verse drama
set at the court of Louis XIV, it relates the story of Louise,
mistress of the king and loved by the honourable Marquis de
Bragelone. She finally seeks refuge from wordly intrigues and
passions in a convent. *The Lady of Lyons* (1838) was written
at Macready's request for his own Covent Garden management. Its huge success immediately prompted Bulwer-Lytton
to start a third play, eagerly awaited by his actor. After con-
siderable revision, much difficulty, and constant consultation
with Macready, beginning in September 1838 and stretching
over six months, *Richelieu* was at last put on the stage. Like
The Lady of Lyons its success was immediate, and it was performed thirty-seven times, until the end of the season. Bulwer-
Lytton, who had generously refused any payment for *The Lady
of Lyons*, accepted £600 for *Richelieu*. The next play, a genteel
nautical melodrama, *The Sea-Captain* (1839), was done under
Webster's management at the Haymarket, but in spite of
Macready's help and his acting it was not a success; Webster
ran it for forty nights to scanty houses. However, *The Sea-
Captain* was redeemed by *Money* (1840), given at the Haymarket and performed eighty times in its first season. A satiric
prose comedy sharply observant of Victorian preoccupations
with class and wealth, *Money* none the less has a strong infusion
of domestic sentiment and ideal love. Like *Richelieu* and *The
Lady of Lyons*, it stayed in the repertory for the rest of the
century. Bulwer-Lytton was never able to produce another
commercial success, although he read widely in historical sources
and discarded one theme after another. A comedy, *Not So Bad*

[1] He had been chairman of the parliamentary committee on dramatic literature
in 1832, and introduced a bill to abolish the patent theatre monopoly which passed
the Commons but was defeated in the Lords in 1833.

As We Seem, was written for the Dickens amateurs in 1851; a reworking of *The Sea-Captain* appeared as *The Rightful Heir* in 1868. Another comedy, *The House of Darnley* (adapted by Charles Coghlan), was staged, posthumously, in 1877, and a drama, *Junius Brutus*, performed in 1885.

Bulwer-Lytton is the only example in nineteenth-century England of a man of letters of established reputation turning successfully to the stage, and his success was as much commercial as artistic. It must not be forgotten that his triumphs were achieved in close collaboration with Macready, whose name is linked with so much of the best in the legitimate drama of the first half of the century.[1] As he gained practical experience in the theatre, Bulwer-Lytton's touch became surer. His first three plays are set in France at differing historical periods, and he carefully studied the economical and organized structure of French romantic drama. Bulwer-Lytton believed he was writing an important historical play in *Richelieu*, and was anxious that the reader should not miss nuances of character derived from his own research. Accordingly, the 1839 first edition is liberally sprinkled with footnotes, and he wrote in the Preface:

> The length of the Play necessarily requires curtailments on the Stage. Many of the passages thus omitted, however immaterial to the audience, must obviously be such as the reader would be least inclined to dispense with—viz. those which, without being absolutely essential to the business of the Stage, contain either the subtler strokes of character or the more poetical embellishments of description. . . . To judge the Author's conception of Richelieu fairly, and to estimate how far it is consistent with historical portraiture, the play must be *read*.

Such an ambiguous attitude to the stage was typical of the approach of the literary dramatists and those who put history first and the stage second.[2] Nevertheless, it is a measure of Bulwer-Lytton's talent and adaptability to new conditions that, without ever abandoning the precepts of legitimate drama, in his best plays he compromised successfully with new popular modes and ensured that his work possessed undoubted theatrical

---

[1] The story of Bulwer-Lytton's collaboration with Macready on *Richelieu* and other plays is fully told in Charles H. Shattuck's *Bulwer and Macready* (1958), to which I am indebted for several facts in this preface.

[2] The first draft of *Richelieu* was actually in prose; the author later turned it into poetry—an interesting illustration of the strong hold of the 'legitimate'.

values, something that can be said of few other dramatists of his
school.

The weaknesses of *Richelieu* are obvious today: the cardboard
conspirators, the irrelevant comic relief of Joseph and de
Beringhen, the total dependence on Richelieu himself. Even in
1838 its author admitted in a letter to Macready that a main
weakness was that 'the final triumph is not wrought out by
the pure intellect of Richelieu, but depends on the accidental
success of François—a conception which wants grandeur'.[1] But
Richelieu contains a magnificent central part, one of the great
roles of the nineteenth-century stage, and abounds in first-rate
theatrical effects: the confrontation between Richelieu and his
assassin, Richelieu's reappearance at court, the delivery of the
curse of Rome, Richelieu's sudden revival when the king begs
him to reassume power. Macready staged the play lavishly,
and the production cost £800—before Charles Kean a great
deal of money for a legitimate drama. The spectacular elements
of setting and costume, combined with the actor's rhetoric,
the domestic sentiment, and the melodramatic effects, made
Richelieu the best example of the old literary drama adapted to
new theatrical ways.

After Macready *Richelieu* was frequently performed. Phelps,
the Joseph of Covent Garden, first appeared as the Cardinal at
Sadler's Wells in 1845. Edwin Booth, one of the greatest
Richelieus, played the part in England in 1861, 1880, and 1882.
Irving's *Richelieu* ran for four months at the Lyceum in 1873,
and he revived it three more times, the third in 1892. The last
West End revival was Robert Hilton's, at the Strand in 1910.

Macready made changes in the play for several years after
the first night, cutting down scenes, eliminating lines and
images from individual speeches, and adding linking material
to cover the gaps. Bulwer-Lytton also revised after the first
performance, but the edition he prepared for the publisher is
far longer than the acting version; Richelieu, for instance, opens
Act III with a 115-line disquisition on his past life. It contains
many historical footnotes and is prefaced by an explanation of
his treatment of French history. All this is omitted, since a stage
version has been employed; textually, I have used the Lord
Chamberlain's copy, the 1839 first edition, and the *Dramatic*

[1] *Bulwer and Macready*, p. 108.

Works of 1841, but have relied for stage authenticity on two acting editions, *French*, v. 117, and *Dicks'* no. 317. These two agree on the major omissions and alterations made since the first night; although the former is the earlier edition, the latter is less prone to errors and corruptions. The text that follows probably represents the final form of the play as Macready presented it.

ACT I

FIRST DAY

SCENE I. *A room in the house of* MARION DE LORME. *A table towards the front of the stage with wine, fruits, etc.,* R., *at which are seated* BARADAS, *four* COURTIERS, *splendidly dressed in the costume of 1641–2, the* DUKE OF ORLEANS *reclining on a large fauteuil,* R. MARION DE LORME, *standing at the back of his chair, offers him a goblet and then retires to ottoman* R. *At another table* L., DE BERINGHEN, DE MAUPRAT, *playing at dice.* CLERMONT *and* COURTIERS *of inferior rank to those at the table of the* DUKE *looking on—voices of those at play.*

ORLEANS [*drinking—laughter of* COURTIERS *subdued*]. Here's
   to our enterprise!
BARADAS [*glancing at* MARION *and putting finger on lip*]. Hush,
   sir!   [*Exulting exclamation at table.*
ORLEANS [*aside, having looked round as unconscious of cause of
      alarm*]. Nay, Count,
   You may trust her; she doats on me. No house
   So safe as Marion's.
BARADAS. Still, we have a secret,
   And oil and water—woman and a secret—
   Are hostile properties.
ORLEANS [*she rises and comes to him—murmurs at gaming table*].
   Well, Marion, see
   How the play prospers yonder.
      [MARION *goes to the next table, looks on for a few moments,
      then exit.*
BARADAS [*producing a parchment*]. I have now
   All the conditions drawn; it only needs
   Our signatures: upon receipt of this
   Bouillon will join his army with the Spaniard,
   March on to Paris—there dethrone the King;
   You will be Regent; I and ye, my lords,
   Form the new Council. So much for the core
   Of our great scheme.   [*Voices of gamesters.*

ORLEANS [*rises and comes down disturbed; all at table follow him*].
  But Richelieu is an Argus;
  One of his hundred eyes will light upon us,
  And then—good-bye to life.

BARADAS. To gain the prize
  We must destroy the Argus: ay, my lords,
  The scroll the core, but blood must fill the veins
  Of our design; while this despatched to Bouillon,
  Richelieu despatched to Heaven! The last my charge.
  Meet here to-morrow night. You, sir, as first
  In honour and in hope, meanwhile select
  Some trusty knave to bear the scroll to Bouillon;
  'Midst Richelieu's foes I'll find some desperate hand
  To strike for vengeance, while we stride to power.

ORLEANS. So be it; to-morrow, midnight. [*Voices of gamesters.*]
  Come, my lords.

  [*Through arch* L. *exeunt* ORLEANS *and the* COURTIERS *in his
  train followed by those who were conversing within the arch.*
  BARADAS *detains one* COURTIER *in conversation till* DE
  MAUPRAT *rises, when he dismisses him as if charged with
  some instructions. Those at the other table rise, salute* ORLEANS,
  and re-seat themselves.

DE BERINGHEN. Double the stakes.

DE MAUPRAT. Done.

DE BERINGHEN. Bravo; faith, it shames me
  To bleed a purse at the last gasp already.

DE MAUPRAT. Nay, as you've had the patient to yourself
  So long, no other doctor should despatch it.

                              [DE MAUPRAT *throws and loses.*

OMNES. Lost! Ha, ha—poor de Mauprat!

DE BERINGHEN. One throw more?

DE MAUPRAT. No, I am bankrupt. [*Pushing gold.*] There goes
  all—except
  My honour and my sword.

CLERMONT. Ay, take the sword
  To Cardinal Richelieu—he gives gold for steel
  When worn by brave men.

DE MAUPRAT. Richelieu!

DE BERINGHEN [*to* BARADAS]. At that name
  He changes colour, bites his nether lip.
  Ev'n in his brightest moments whisper 'Richelieu',
  And you cloud all his sunshine.

BARADAS. I have mark'd it,
  And I will learn the wherefore.

DE MAUPRAT. The Egyptian
  Dissolved her richest jewel in a draught;
  Would I could so melt Time and all its treasures,
  And drain it thus. [*Drinking.*]

DE BERINGHEN [*taking his cloak and hat*]. Come, gentlemen,
    what say ye,
  A walk on the Parade?

CLERMONT. Ay; come, de Mauprat.

DE MAUPRAT. Pardon me; we shall meet again ere nightfall.

OMNES. Come, Baradas.

BARADAS. I'll stay and comfort Mauprat.

DE BERINGHEN. Comfort! When
  We gallant fellows have run out a friend
  There's nothing left—except to run him through!
  There's the last act of friendship.

DE MAUPRAT. Let me keep
  That favour in reserve; in all beside
  Your most obedient servant.

                    [*Exeunt* DE BERINGHEN, *etc.*

BARADAS. You have lost—
  Yet are not sad.

DE MAUPRAT [R.]. Sad! Life and gold have wings
  And must fly one day; open, then, their cages
  And wish them merry.

BARADAS. You're a strange enigma:
  Fiery in war, and yet to glory lukewarm;
  All mirth in action—in repose all gloom.
  Confide in me, we have known each other long.
  Fortune of late has sever'd us, and led
  Me to the rank of Courtier, Count, and Favourite—

You to the titles of the wildest gallant
And bravest knight in France; are you content?
No; trust in me—some gloomy secret—

DE MAUPRAT. Ay:
A secret that doth haunt me, as of old
Men were possess'd of fiends! Where'er I turn,
The grave yawns dark before me! I will trust you.
Hating the Cardinal, and beguiled by Orleans,
You know I join'd the Languedoc revolt—
Was captured, sent to the Bastille—

BARADAS. But shared
The general pardon which the Duke of Orleans
Won for himself and all in the revolt
Who but obey'd his orders.

DE MAUPRAT. Note the phrase,
'Obey'd his orders'. Well, when on my way
To join the Duke in Languedoc, I (then
The down upon my lip—less man than boy)
Leading young valours reckless as myself,
Seized on the town of Faviaux, and displaced
The royal banners for the rebel. Orleans,
(Never too daring) when I reach'd the camp,
Blamed me for acting—mark—without his orders.
Upon this quibble Richelieu razed my name
Out of the general pardon.

BARADAS. Yet released you
From the Bastille—

DE MAUPRAT. To call me to his presence,
And thus address me: 'You have seized a town
Of France without the orders of your leader,
And for this treason but one sentence—death.'

BARADAS. Death!

DE MAUPRAT. 'I have pity on your youth and birth,
Nor wish to glut the headsman; join your troop,
Now on the march against the Spaniards; change
The traitor's scaffold for the soldier's grave:
Your memory's stainless—they who shared your crime
Exil'd or dead—your King shall never learn it.'

BARADAS. O tender pity!
  Well?

DE MAUPRAT. You have heard if I fought bravely.
  When the Cardinal
  Review'd the troops his eye met mine; he frown'd,
  Summon'd me forth—'How's this?' quoth he; 'you have
      shunn'd
  The sword—beware the axe; 'twill fall one day!'
  He left me thus—we were recall'd to Paris,
  And—you know all!

BARADAS. And knowing this, why halt you,
  Spell'd by the rattle-snake—while in the breasts
  Of your firm friends beat hearts that vow the death
  Of your grim tyrant? Wake! Be one of us;
  The time invites—the King detests the Cardinal,
  Dares not disgrace, but groans to be deliver'd
  Of that too great a subject—join your friends,
  Free France, and save yourself.

DE MAUPRAT. Hush! Richelieu bears
  A charmed life: to all who have braved his power,
  One common end—the block.
  Better the victim, Count,
  Than the assassin—France requires a Richelieu,
  But does not need a Mauprat. Truce to this;
  All time one midnight where my thoughts are spectres.
  What to me fame? What love?

BARADAS. Yet dost thou love not?

DE MAUPRAT. Love? I am young—

BARADAS. And Julie fair. Ha! [*Aside.*] It is so.
  Upon the margin of the grave his hand
  Would pluck the rose that I would win and wear!

DE MAUPRAT. Since you have one secret keep the other. Never
  Unbury either! Come, while yet we may,
  We'll bask us in the noon of rosy life:
  Lounge through the gardens, flaunt it in the taverns,
  Laugh—game—drink—feast: if so confined my days,
  Faith, I'll enclose the nights. Pshaw! not so grave;
  I'm a true Frenchman. *Vive la bagatelle!*

As they are going out enter HUGUET *and four* ARQUEBUSIERS.

HUGUET. Messire de Mauprat, I arrest you! Follow
  To the Lord Cardinal.

DE MAUPRAT. You see, my friend,
  I'm out of my suspense. The tiger's play'd
  Long enough with his prey. [DE MAUPRAT *gives his sword.*]
    Farewell! Hereafter
  Say when men name me, 'Adrien de Mauprat
  Lived without hope and perished without fear!'

                    [*Exeunt* DE MAUPRAT, HUGUET, *etc.*

BARADAS. Farewell, I trust for ever! I design'd thee
  For Richelieu's murderer—but as well his martyr!
  In childhood you the stronger, and I cursed you;
  In youth the fairer, and I cursed you still;
  And you would rival me with Julie! Loved
  So wildly that my love has grown the bone
  And nerve of my ambition. By the King's
  Aid I will marry Julie, in despite
  Of my Lord Cardinal. By the King's aid
  I will be minister of France, in spite
  Of my Lord Cardinal; and then—what then?
  The King loves Julie—feeble Prince—false master—

          [*Producing and gazing on the parchment.*
  Then, by the aid of Bouillon and the Spaniard,
  I will dethrone the King, and all—ha! ha!
  All, in despite of my Lord Cardinal.

                                  [*Exit.*

———

SCENE II. *A room in the Palais Cardinal, the walls hung with
arras—a large screen in one corner,* R. C.—*a table covered with
books, papers, etc.,* C.—*a rude clock in a recess—busts, statues, book-
cases, weapons of different periods, and banners. Doors* R. *and* L.,
                    and private door L.

          Enter RICHELIEU *leaning on* JOSEPH.

RICHELIEU. And so you think this new conspiracy
  The craftiest trap yet laid for the old fox?

Fox! Well, I like the nickname! What did Plutarch
Say of the Greek Lysander?

JOSEPH. I forget.

RICHELIEU. That where the lion's skin fell short, he eked it
Out with the fox's. A great statesman, Joseph,
That same Lysander.

JOSEPH. Orleans heads the traitors.

RICHELIEU. A very wooden head, then. Well?

JOSEPH. The favourite,
Count Baradas—

RICHELIEU. A weed of hasty growth;
First gentlemen of the chamber—titles, lands,
And the King's ear! It cost me six long winters
To mount as high, as in six little moons
This painted lizard. But I hold the ladder,
And when I shake—he falls! What more?

JOSEPH. A scheme
To make your orphan-ward an instrument
To aid your foes. Your ward has charm'd the King.

RICHELIEU. Out on you!
Have I not, one by one, from such fair shoots
Pluck'd the insidious ivy of his love?
And shall it creep around my blossoming tree
Where innocent thoughts, like happy birds, make music
That spirits in Heaven might hear? The King must have
No mistress but the State: the State—that's Richelieu!

JOSEPH. This is not the worst; Louis, in all decorous,
And deeming you her least compliant guardian,
Would veil his suit by marriage with his minion,
Your prosperous foe, Count Baradas.

RICHELIEU. Ha, ha!
I have another bride for Baradas!

JOSEPH. You, my lord?

RICHELIEU. Ay—more faithful than the love
Of fickle woman: when the head lies lowliest,
Clasping him fondest; sorrow never knew
So sure a soother, and her bed is stainless.

Enter FRANÇOIS.

FRANÇOIS. Mademoiselle de Mortemar.

RICHELIEU. Most opportune—admit her. [*Exit* FRANÇOIS].
 In my closet
 You'll find a rosary, Joseph; ere you tell
 Three hundred beads, I'll summon you. Stay, Joseph,
 I did omit an Ave in my matins—
 A grievous fault; atone it for me, Joseph:
 There is a scourge within; I am weak, you strong,
 It were but charity to take my sin
 On such broad shoulders.

JOSEPH. I! Guilty of such criminal presumption
 As to mistake myself for you. No, never;
 Think it not. [*Aside.*] Troth, a pleasant invitation!
                [*Exit.*

Enter JULIE DE MORTEMAR.

RICHELIEU. That's my sweet Julie!

JULIE [*kneeling at his feet*]. Cardinal, are you gracious?
 May I say 'Father'?

RICHELIEU. Now and ever!

JULIE. Father!
 A sweet word to an orphan.

RICHELIEU. No, not orphan
 While Richelieu lives. Thy father loved me well,
 My friend, ere I had flatterers (now I'm great,
 In other phrase I'm friendless)—he died young
 In years, not service, and bequeath'd thee to me;
 And thou shalt have a dowry, girl, to buy
 Thy mate amidst the mightiest. Drooping? sighs?
 Art thou not happy at the Court?

JULIE. Not often.

RICHELIEU [*aside*]. Can she love Baradas?
 Thou art admired—art young;
 Does not his Majesty commend thy beauty—
 Ask thee to sing to him?

JULIE. He's very tiresome,
 Our worthy King.

RICHELIEU. Fie, kings are never tiresome,
   Save to their ministers. What courtly gallants
   Charm ladies most? De Sourdiac, Longueville or
   The favourite Baradas?

JULIE. A smileless man—
   I fear and shun him.

RICHELIEU. Yet he courts thee?

JULIE. Then
   He is more tiresome than his Majesty.

RICHELIEU. Right, girl, shun Baradas. Yet of these flowers
   Of France, not one, in whose more honied breath
   Thy heart hears summer whisper?

Enter HUGUET.

HUGUET. The Chevalier
   De Mauprat waits below.

JULIE. De Mauprat!

RICHELIEU. Hem!
   He has been tiresome, too. Anon.

                       [*Exit* HUGUET.

JULIE. What doth he—
   I mean—I—does your Eminence—that is—
   Know you Messire de Mauprat?

RICHELIEU. Well! and you—
   Has he address'd you often?

JULIE. Often! No,
   Nine times—nay, ten! the last time by the lattice
   Of the great staircase. [*In a melancholy tone.*] The Court
   Sees him rarely.

RICHELIEU. A bold and forward royster?

JULIE. He? Nay, modest,
   Gentle, and sad, methinks.

RICHELIEU. Wears gold and azure?

JULIE. No, sable.

RICHELIEU. So you note his colours, Julie?
   Shame on you, child, look loftier. By the mass,
   I have business with this modest gentleman.

JULIE. You're angry with poor Julie. There's no cause.

RICHELIEU. No cause—you hate my foes?

JULIE. I do!

RICHELIEU. Hate Mauprat?

JULIE. Not Mauprat. No, not Adrien, father.

RICHELIEU. Adrien!
Familiar! Go, child; no, not that way; wait
In the tapestry chamber. I will join you—go.

JULIE. His brows are knit; I dare not call him father,
But I must speak. Your Eminence—

RICHELIEU [*sternly*]. Well?

JULIE. Come,
Smile on me—one smile more; there, now I'm happy.
Do not rank de Mauprat with your foes; he is not,
I know he is not; he loves France too well.

RICHELIEU. Not rank de Mauprat with my foes? So be it.
I'll blot him from that list.

JULIE [*kisses his hand*]. That's my own father.

[*Exit.*

RICHELIEU [*rings a small bell on the table*]. Huguet!

Enter HUGUET.

De Mauprat struggled not, nor murmur'd?

HUGUET. No; proud and passive.

RICHELIEU. Bid him enter. Hold:
Look that he hide no weapon. Humph, despair
Makes victims sometimes victors. When he has enter'd,
Glide round unseen; place thyself yonder; [*Pointing to the
screen.*] watch him.
If he show violence—(let me see thy carbine;
So, a good weapon)—if he play the lion,
Why, the dog's death.

HUGUET. I never miss my mark.

[*Exit* HUGUET. RICHELIEU *seats himself at the table, and
slowly arranges the papers before him. Enter* DE MAUPRAT,
preceded by HUGUET, *who then retires behind the screen.*

RICHELIEU. Approach, sir. Can you call to mind the hour,
   Now three years since, when in this room, methinks,
   Your presence honour'd me?

DE MAUPRAT. It is, my lord,
   One of my most—

RICHELIEU [*drily*]. Delightful recollections.

DE MAUPRAT [*aside*]. St. Denis! doth he make a jest of axe
   And headsman?

RICHELIEU [*sternly*]. I did then accord you
   A mercy ill requited—you still live.

DE MAUPRAT. To meet death face to face at last.

RICHELIEU. Adrien de Mauprat,
   Doom'd to sure death, how hast thou since consumed
   The time allotted thee for serious thought
   And solemn penitence?

DE MAUPRAT [*embarrassed*]. The time, my lord?

RICHELIEU. Is not the question plain? I'll answer for thee.
   Thou hast sought nor priest nor shrine; no sackcloth chafed
   Thy delicate flesh. The rosary and the death's-head
   Have not, with pious meditation, purged
   Earth from the carnal gaze. What thou hast not done
   Brief told; what done, a volume! Wild debauch,
   Turbulent riot; for the morn the dice-box—
   Noon claim'd the duel, and the night the wassail;
   These, your most holy, pure preparatives
   For death and judgment. Do I wrong you, sir?

DE MAUPRAT. I was not always thus: if chang'd my nature,
   Blame that which chang'd my fate.
   Were you accursed with that which you inflicted—
   By bed and board dogg'd by one ghastly spectre,
   The while within you youth beat high, and life
   Grew lovelier from the neighbouring frown of death—
   Were this your fate, perchance,
   You would have err'd like me!

RICHELIEU. I might, like you,
   Have been a brawler and a reveller; not,
   Like you, a trickster and a thief.

DE MAUPRAT [*advances threateningly*]. Lord Cardinal,
  Unsay those words!

        [HUGUET, *at back, deliberately raises the carbine.*

RICHELIEU [*waving his hand*]. Not quite so quick, friend
  Huguet;
  Messire de Mauprat is a patient man,
  And he can wait. [HUGUET *retires again.*] You have outrun
    your fortune;
  I blame you not, that you would be a beggar—
  Each to his taste! But I do charge you, sir,
  That being beggar'd you would coin false monies
  Out of that crucible, called debt. To live
  On means not yours—be brave in silks and laces,
  Gallant in steeds—splendid in banquets; all
  Not yours, ungiven, unherited, unpaid for;
  This is to be a trickster and to filch
  Men's art and labour, which to them is wealth,
  Life, daily bread—quitting all scores with 'Friend,
  You're troublesome!' Why, this, forgive me,
  Is what, when done with a less dainty grace,
  Plain folks call theft! You owe eight thousand pistoles,
  Minus one crown, two liards.

DE MAUPRAT [*aside*]. The old conjuror!

RICHELIEU. This is scandalous,
  Shaming your birth and blood. I tell you, sir,
  That you must pay your debts.

DE MAUPRAT. With all my heart,
  My lord. Where shall I borrow, then, the money?

RICHELIEU [*aside, and laughing*]. A humorous dare-devil! The
  very man
  To suit my purpose—ready, frank, and bold!
  [*Earnestly.*] Adrien de Mauprat, men have called me cruel;
  I am not; I am just! I found France rent asunder—
  The rich men despots, and the poor banditti,
  Sloth in the mart, and schism within the temple;
  Brawls festering to rebellion, and weak laws
  Rotting away with rust in antique sheaths.
  I have re-created France; and, from the ashes
  Of the old feudal and decrepit carcase,

Civilization on her luminous wings
Soars, phoenix-like, to Jove! What was my art?
Genius, some say—some fortune—witchcraft some.
Not so; my art was justice! Force and fraud
Misname it cruelty—you shall confute them!
My champion you! You met me as your foe;
Depart my friend. [DE MAUPRAT *takes his proffered hand.*]
   You shall not die. France needs you.
You shall wipe off all stains—be rich, be honour'd,
Be great—[DE MAUPRAT *falls on his knee.*] I ask, sir, in
   return this hand,
To gift it with a bride [DE MAUPRAT *rises.*] whose dower shall
   match,
Yet not exceed, her beauty.

DE MAUPRAT [*hesitating*]. I, my lord,
   I have no wish to marry—

RICHELIEU. Surely, sir,
   To die were worse?

DE MAUPRAT. Scarcely; the poorest coward
   Must die, but knowingly to march to marriage—
   My lord, it asks the courage of a lion!

RICHELIEU. Traitor, thou triflest with me! I know all!
   Thou hast dared to love my ward—my charge.

DE MAUPRAT. As rivers
   May love the sunlight—basking in the beams,
   And hurrying on.

RICHELIEU. Thou hast told her of thy love?

DE MAUPRAT. My lord, if I had dared to love a maid
   Lowliest in France, I would not so have wrong'd her
   As bid her link rich life and virgin hope
   With one the deathman's gripe might, from her side,
   Pluck at the nuptial altar.

RICHELIEU. I believe thee;
   Yet since she knows not of thy love, renounce her;
   Take life and fortune with another. Silent?

DE MAUPRAT. Your fate has been one triumph. You know not
   How bless'd a thing it was in my dark hour
   To nurse the one sweet thought you bid me banish.

Love hath no need of words; nor less within
That holiest temple, the heaven-builded soul,
Breathes the recorded vow. Base knight, false lover
Were he who barter'd all, that brighten'd grief
Or sanctified despair, for life and gold.
Revoke your mercy; I prefer the fate
I look'd for!

RICHELIEU. Huguet. To the tapestry chamber
Conduct your prisoner. [*To* DE MAUPRAT.] You will there
behold
The executioner: your doom be private—
And Heaven have mercy on you!

DE MAUPRAT. When I'm dead,
Tell her I loved her.

RICHELIEU. Keep such follies, sir,
For fitter ears. Go.

DE MAUPRAT. Does he mock me?

[*Exeunt* HUGUET *and* DE MAUPRAT.

RICHELIEU. Joseph,
Come, forth.

Enter JOSEPH.

Methinks your cheek hath lost its rubies;
I fear you have been too lavish of the flesh:
The scourge is heavy.

JOSEPH. Pray you, change the subject.

RICHELIEU. You good men are so modest! Well, to business.
Go instantly—deeds—notaries! Bid my stewards
Arrange my house by the Luxembourg—my house
No more! a bridal present to my ward,
Who weds to-morrow.

JOSEPH. Weds, with whom?

RICHELIEU. De Mauprat.

JOSEPH. Penniless husband!

RICHELIEU. Bah! the mate for beauty
Should be a man, and not a money-chest!
When her brave sire lay on his bed of death,
I vow'd to be a father to his Julie;

And so he died—the smile upon his lips.
And when I spared the life of her young lover,
Methought I saw that smile again. Who else,
Look you, in all the court—who else so well
Brave, or supplant the favourite; balk the king—
Baffle their schemes? I have tried him: he has honour
And courage, qualities that eagle-plume
Men's souls and fit them for the fiercest sun
That ever melted the weak waxen minds
That flutter in the beams of gaudy power!
Besides, he has taste, this Mauprat. When my play
Was acted to dull tiers of lifeless gapers,
Who had no soul for poetry, I saw him
Applaud in the proper places: trust me, Joseph,
He is a man of an uncommon promise.

JOSEPH. And yet your foe.

RICHELIEU. Have I not foes enow?
    Great men gain doubly when they make foes friends.
    Remember my grand maxims: first employ
    All methods to conciliate.

JOSEPH. Failing these?

RICHELIEU [*fiercely*]. All means to crush: as with the opening and
    The clenching of this little hand, I will
    Crush the small venom of these stinging courtiers.

JOSEPH. And when
    Check the conspiracy?

RICHELIEU. Check, check? Full way to it.
    Let it bud, ripen, flaunt i' the day, and burst
    To fruit, the Dead Sea's fruit of ashes; ashes
    Which I will scatter to the winds. Go, Joseph;
    When you return I have a feast for you;
    The last great act of my great play.

                [JOSEPH *bows, shrugs his shoulders, and exits.*

Enter JULIE *and* DE MAUPRAT. *They kneel to* RICHELIEU.

DE MAUPRAT. Oh, speak my lord—I dare not think you mock
    me,
    And yet—

JULIE. Are we not both your children?

RICHELIEU. Eh,
How now! Oh, sir—you live!

DE MAUPRAT. Why, no, methinks
Elysium is not life!

JULIE. He smiles! you smile,
My father! From my heart for ever now
I'll blot the name of orphan.

RICHELIEU. Rise, my children,
For ye are mine—mine both; and in your sweet
And young delight—your love (life's first-born glory),
My own lost youth breathes musical.

DE MAUPRAT. I'll seek
Temple and priest henceforward; were it but
To learn Heaven's choicest blessings.

RICHELIEU. Thou shalt seek
Temple and priest right soon; the morrow's sun
Shall see across these barren thresholds pass
The fairest bride in Paris. Go, my children;
Even I loved once. Be lovers while ye may!
How is it with you, sir? You bear it bravely;
You know, it asks the courage of a lion.

[*Exeunt* JULIE *and* DE MAUPRAT.

Oh, godlike power! Woe, rapture, penury, wealth,
Marriage and death, for one infirm old man
Through a great empire to dispense—withhold—
As the will whispers! And shall things like motes
That live in my daylight, lackies of court wages,
Dwarf'd starvelings, mannikins, upon whose shoulders
The burthen of a province were a load
More heavy than the globe on Atlas, cast
Lots for my robes and sceptre? France! I love thee!
All earth shall never pluck thee from my heart!
My mistress France—my wedded wife—sweet France,
Who shall proclaim divorce for thee and me?

[*Exit.*

ACT II

SECOND DAY

SCENE I. *A splendid apartment in* DE MAUPRAT's *new house, opening to the gardens, beyond which the domes of the Luxembourg palace are visible. Door* R. C., *sofa* R.

Enter BARADAS.

BARADAS. Mauprat's new home. What though
 Thou hast 'scaped the fierce caprice of Richelieu;
 Yet art thou farther from the headsman, fool?
 Thy secret I have whisper'd to the King;
 Thy marriage makes the King thy foe. Thou stand'st
 On the abyss—and in the pool below
 I see a ghastly, headless phantom mirror'd,
 Thy likeness ere the marriage moon hath waned.
 Meanwhile—meanwhile—ha, ha, though thou art wedded
 Thou art not wived.

Enter DE MAUPRAT, *splendidly dressed.*

DE MAUPRAT. Was ever fate like mine?
 So blest, and yet so wretched.   [*Throws himself on sofa.*

BARADAS. Joy, de Mauprat!
 Why, what a brow, man, for your wedding day!

DE MAUPRAT. You know what chanced between
 The Cardinal and myself.

BARADAS. This morning brought
 Your letter: a strange account, i' faith!

DE MAUPRAT. We were wed
 At noon. The rite perform'd, came hither; scarce
 Arrived, when—ah!

BARADAS. Well?

DE MAUPRAT. Wide flew the doors and lo,
 Messire de Beringhen and this epistle.

BARADAS. 'Tis the King's hand! The royal seal!

DE MAUPRAT. Read—read!

BARADAS [*reading*]. 'Whereas Adrien de Mauprat, Colonel and Chevalier in our armies, being already guilty of high treason, by the seizure of our town of Faviaux, has presumed without our knowledge, consent, or sanction to connect himself by marriage with Julie de Mortemar, a wealthy orphan attached to the person of Her Majesty, we do hereby proclaim and declare the said marriage contrary to law. On penalty of death, Adrien de Mauprat will not communicate with the said Julie de Mortemar by word or letter, save in the presence of our faithful servant the Sieur de Beringhen, and then with such respect and decorum as are due to a Demoiselle attached to the Court of France, until such time as it may suit our royal pleasure to confer with the Holy Church on the formal annulment of the marriage, and with our Council on the punishment to be awarded to Messire de Mauprat, who is cautioned for his own sake to preserve silence as to our injunction, more especially to Mademoiselle de Mortemar. Given under our hand and seal at the Louvre—Louis.'

BARADAS. Amazement! Did not Richelieu say the King
    Knew not your crime?

DE MAUPRAT. He said so.

BARADAS. Poor de Mauprat!
    See you the snare, the vengeance worse than death
    Of which you are the victim?

DE MAUPRAT. Ha!

BARADAS [*aside*]. It works!

DE MAUPRAT. Snares! Vengeance! Man,
    Be plainer.

BARADAS. What so clear?
    Richelieu has but two passions—

DE MAUPRAT. Richelieu!

BARADAS. Yes!
    Ambition and revenge, in you both blended.
    First for ambition—Julie is his ward,
    Innocent, docile, pliant to his will;

He placed her at the Court—foresaw the rest—
The King loves Julie!

DE MAUPRAT. Merciful Heaven! The King!

BARADAS. Such Cupids lend new plumes to Richelieu's wings:
But the Court etiquette must give such Cupids
The veil of Hymen—(Hymen but in name).
He look'd abroad—found you his foe: thus served
Ambition by the grandeur of his ward,
And vengeance by dishonour to his foe.

DE MAUPRAT. Prove this.

BARADAS. You have the proof. This very letter: [*Returns letter.*]
Your strange exemption from the general pardon,
Known but to me and Richelieu; can you doubt
Your friend to acquit your foe?

DE MAUPRAT. I see it all! Mock pardon—hurried nuptials—
False bounty—all! the serpent of that smile!
Oh, it stings home!

BARADAS. You yet shall crush his malice;
Our plans are sure: Orleans is at our head.
We meet to-night; join us, and with us triumph.

DE MAUPRAT. To-night? Oh, Heaven!
But the King? but Julie?

BARADAS. The King, infirm in health, in mind more feeble,
Is but the plaything of a Minister's will.
Were Richelieu dead his power were mine; and Louis
Soon should forget his passion and your crime.

                   [DE MAUPRAT *is going out.*
But whither now?

DE MAUPRAT. I know not; I scarce hear thee.
A little while for thought: anon I'll join thee;
But now all air seems tainted and I loathe
The face of man.
            [*Exit* DE MAUPRAT *through the gardens.*

BARADAS. Go where thou wilt, the hell hounds of revenge
Pant in thy track and dog thee down.

Enter DE BERINGHEN, *his mouth full, a napkin in his hand.*

DE BERINGHEN. O Chevalier,
    Your cook's a miracle—what, my host gone?
    Faith, Count, my office is a post of danger.
    A fiery fellow, Mauprat! Touch and go—
    Match and saltpetre—pr—r—r—r—!

BARADAS. You
    Will be released ere long. The King resolves
    To call the bride to Court this day,
    And even now the royal carriage waits.

DE BERINGHEN. Poor Mauprat!
    Is Louis still so chafed against the fox
    For snatching yon fair dainty from the lion?

BARADAS. So chafed that Richelieu totters. Yes, the King
    Is half conspirator against the Cardinal.
    Enough of this. I've found the man we wanted,
    The man to head the hands that murder Richelieu,
    The man whose name the synonym for daring.

DE BERINGHEN. He must mean me! You mean—

BARADAS. Whom can I mean
    But Mauprat? Mark, to-night we meet at Marion's,
    There shall we sign: thence send this scroll [*Showing it.*] to
      Bouillon.
    You're in that secret, [*Affectionately.*] one of our new Council.

DE BERINGHEN. But to admit the Spaniard, France's foe,
    Into the heart of France, dethrone the King—
    It looks like treason, and I smell the headsman.

BARADAS. Too late to falter. Of this despatch Mauprat
    Must nothing learn. He only bites at vengeance,
    And he would start from treason. We must post him
    Without the door at Marion's—as a sentry.
    [*Aside.*] So, when his head is on the block his tongue
    Cannot betray our more august designs!

DE BERINGHEN. I'll meet you, if the King can spare me.
      [*Aside.*] No!
    I am too old a goose to play with foxes;
    I'll roost at home. Meanwhile, in the next room
    There's a delicious pâté, let's discuss it.

BARADAS. Pshaw! a man filled with a sublime ambition
  Has no time to discuss your pâtés.

DE BERINGHEN. Pshaw!
  And a man fill'd with as sublime a pâté
  Has no time to discuss ambition. Gad,
  I have the best of it.

Enter CLERMONT.

CLERMONT [*to* DE BERINGHEN]. Messire,
  The royal carriage waits below.

DE BERINGHEN [*hesitating*]. Ohe moment, just to—

CLERMONT. Come, sir.

DE BERINGHEN. I shall not
  Discuss the pâté after all.   [*Exeunt.*

BARADAS. Now will this fire his fever into madness!
  All is made clear: Mauprat must murder Richelieu—
  Die for that crime; I shall console his Julie.
  This will reach Bouillon! From the wrecks of France
  I shall carve out—who knows—perchance a throne!
  All in despite of my Lord Cardinal.

Enter DE MAUPRAT.

DE MAUPRAT. Speak! can it be? Methought that from the
      terrace
  I saw the carriage of the King—and Julie!
  No, no, my frenzy peoples the void air
  With its own phantoms!

BARADAS. Nay, too true. Alas,
  Was ever lightning swifter or more blasting
  Than Richelieu's forked guile?

DE MAUPRAT. I'll to the Louvre—

BARADAS. And lose all hope! The Louvre—the sure gate
  To the Bastille!

DE MAUPRAT. The King—

BARADAS. Is but the wax
  Which Richelieu stamps! Break the malignant seal
  And I will rase the print.

DE MAUPRAT. Ghastly vengeance!
To thee and thine august and solemn sister
The unrelenting death, I dedicate
The blood of Armand Richelieu. When dishonour
Reaches our hearths law dies, and murther takes
The angel shape of justice.

BARADAS. Bravely said!
At midnight—Marion's! Nay, I cannot leave thee
To thoughts that——

DE MAUPRAT. Speak not to me! I am yours!
But speak not. There's a voice within my soul
Whose cry could drown the thunder! Oh, if men
Will play dark sorcery with the heart of man,
Let them who raise the spell beware the fiend!

                                        [*Exeunt.*

SCENE II. *A room in the Palais Cardinal* (*as in the first act*).

Enter FRANÇOIS, *who puts foward the table and chair, then enter*
RICHELIEU *and* JOSEPH.

JOSEPH. Yes, Huguet taking his accustom'd round,
Disguised as some plain burgher, heard these rufflers
Quoting your name: he listen'd. 'Pshaw!' said one,
'We are to seize the Cardinal in his palace
To-morrow.' 'How?' the other ask'd. 'You'll hear
The whole design to-night; the Duke of Orleans
And Baradas have got the map of action
At their fingers' end.' 'So be it,' quoth the other,
'I will be there—Marion de Lorme's—at midnight.'

RICHELIEU. I have them, man, I have them!

JOSEPH. So they say
Of you, my lord: believe me that their plans
Are mightier than you deem. You must employ
Means no less vast to meet them.

RICHELIEU. Bah! in policy
We foil gigantic danger, not by giants,
But dwarfs. The statues of our stately fortune
Are sculptured by the chisel, not the axe!
Ah, were I younger—by the knightly heart
That beats beneath these priestly robes, I would
Have pastime with these cut-throats! Yea, as when
Lured to the ambush of the expecting foe,
I clove my pathway through the plumed sea.
Reach me yon falchion, François—not that bauble
For carpet-warriors—yonder—such a blade
As old Charles Martel might have wielded when
He drove the Saracen from France. [FRANÇOIS *brings him
one, from pile of arms, of the long two-handed swords worn in
the Middle Ages.*] Ah, boy, with this
I at Rochelle did hand to hand engage
The stalwart Englisher—no mongrels, boy,
Those island mastiffs—mark the notch, a deep one,
His casque made here—I shore him to the waist!
A toy—a feather—then! [*Tries to wield, and lets the blade fall.*]
    You see a child could
Slay Richelieu now.

FRANÇOIS [*his hand on his hilt*]. But now, at your command
Are other weapons, my good lord.

RICHELIEU [*about to write, lifts the pen*]. True, this!
Beneath the rule of men entirely great
The pen is mightier than the sword. Behold
The arch-enchanter's wand, itself a nothing,
But taking sorcery from the master-hand
To paralyse the Caesars—and to strike
The loud earth breathless! Take away the sword,
States can be saved without it. [*Looking on the clock.*] 'Tis the
    hour!
Retire, sir.   [*Exit* FRANÇOIS.

[*Three distinct knocks heard—a door concealed in the arras
opens cautiously. Enter* MARION DE LORME.

JOSEPH [*amazed*]. Marion de Lorme!

RICHELIEU. Hist! Joseph,
    Keep guard. [JOSEPH *retires*.] My faithful Marion.

MARION. Good my lord,
    They meet to-night in my poor house. The Duke
    Of Orleans heads them.

RICHELIEU. Yes—go on.

MARION. His Highness
    Much question'd if I knew some brave, discreet,
    And vigilant man, whose tongue could keep a secret,
    And who had those twin qualities for service,
    The love of gold, the hate of Richelieu.

RICHELIEU. You—

MARION. Made answer, 'Yes, my brother—'

RICHELIEU. Your brother.

MARION. 'Bold and trusty,
    Whose faith my faith could pledge.' The Duke then bade me
    Have him equipp'd and arm'd, well mounted, ready
    This night to post for Italy.

RICHELIEU. Aha!
    Has Bouillon too turn'd traitor? So, methought!
    What part of Italy?

MARION. The Piedmont frontier,
    Where Bouillon lies encamp'd.

RICHELIEU. Now there is danger,
    Great danger! If he tamper with the Spaniard,
    And Louis list not to my council, as
    Without sure proof he will not, France is lost.
    What more?

MARION. Dark hints of some design to seize
    Your person in your palace. Nothing clear—
    His Highness trembled, while he spoke; the words
    Did choke each other.

RICHELIEU. So! Who is the brother
    You recommended to the Duke?

MARION. Whoever
  Your Eminence may father.

RICHELIEU. Darling Marion!

      [*Goes to the table and returns with a large bag of gold.*
  There—pshaw—a trifle.
  You will engage to give the Duke's despatch
  To whom I send?

MARION. Aye, marry!

RICHELIEU [*aside*]. Huguet? No,
  He will be wanted elsewhere. Joseph? zealous,
  But too well known—too much the elder brother.
  Mauprat? alas, it is his wedding day!
  François? The man of men! unnoted—young,
  Ambitious. [*Goes to the door.*] François!

              Enter FRANÇOIS.

RICHELIEU. Follow this fair lady:
  (Find him the suiting garments, Marion) take
  My fleetest steed: arm thyself to the teeth;
  A packet will be given you—with orders,
  No matter what! The instant that your hand
  Closes upon it, clutch it, like your honour,
  Which death alone can steal or ravish—set
  Spurs to your steed—be breathless till you stand
  Again before me. Stay, sir! You will find me
  Two short leagues hence, at Ruelle, in my castle.
  Young man, be blithe, for—note me—from the hour
  I grasp that packet think your guardian star
  Rains fortune on you!

FRANÇOIS. If I fail—

RICHELIEU. Fail—fail?
  In the lexicon of youth, which fate reserves
  For a bright manhood, there is no such word
  As fail! (You will instruct him further, Marion)
  Follow her, but at distance; speak not to her,
  Till you are housed. Farewell, boy! Never say
  'Fail' again.

FRANÇOIS. I will not!

RICHELIEU [*patting his locks*]. There's my young hero.

[*Exeunt* FRANÇOIS *and* MARION.

RICHELIEU. So, they would seize my person in this palace?
  I cannot guess their scheme: but my retinue
  Is here too large.

Enter JOSEPH.

  A single traitor could
  Strike impotent the faith of thousands. Joseph,
  Art sure of Huguet? Think—we hang'd his father.

JOSEPH. But you have bought the son; heap'd favours on him.

RICHELIEU. Trash! favours past—that's nothing. In his hours
  Of confidence with you, has he named the favours
  To come he counts on?

JOSEPH. Yes: a colonel's rank,
  And letters of nobility.

Here HUGUET *enters as if to address* RICHELIEU, *who does not
  perceive him.*

RICHELIEU. Colonel and nobleman!
  My bashful Huguet, that can never be!
  We have him not the less—we'll promise it,
  And see the King withholds! Ah, kings are oft
  A great convenience to a minister.
  Yes—we'll count on Huguet.

HUGUET [*aside*]. To thy cost, deceiver.

[*Exit stealthily.*

RICHELIEU. You are right, this treason
  Assumes a fearful aspect; but once crush'd,
  Its very ashes shall manure the soil
  Of power and ripen such full sheaves of greatness
  That all the summer of my fate shall seem
  Fruitless beside the autumn.

Enter HUGUET.

HUGUET. My Lord Cardinal,
  Your Eminence bade me seek you at this hour.

RICHELIEU. Did I? True, Huguet. So, you overheard
  Strange talk amongst these gallants? Snares and traps

For Richelieu? Well, we'll balk them; let me think—
The men-at-arms you head—how many?

HUGUET. Twenty,
My lord.

RICHELIEU. All trusty?

HUGUET. Yes, for ordinary
Occasions—if for great ones, I would change
Three-fourths at least.

RICHELIEU. Ay, what are great occasions?

HUGUET. Great bribes.

RICHELIEU [*to* JOSEPH]. Good lack, he knows some paragons
Superior to great bribes! Well?

HUGUET. True gentlemen
Who have transgress'd the laws—and value life
And lack not gold; your Eminence alone
Can grant them pardon. *Ergo* you can trust them.

RICHELIEU. Logic! So be it—let this honest twenty
Be arm'd and mounted. [*Aside.*] So, they meet at midnight:
The attempt on me to-morrow. Ere the dawn be grey
All could be arm'd, assembled, and at Ruelle
In my old hall?

HUGUET. By one hour after midnight.

RICHELIEU. The castle's strong.
They do not strike till morning,
Yet I will shift the quarter. Bid the grooms
Prepare the litter—I will hence to Ruelle
While daylight lasts—and one hour after midnight
You and your twenty saints shall seek me there.
You're made to rise! you are, sir. Eyes of lynx,
Ears of the stag, a footfall like the snow;
You are a valiant fellow; yea, a trusty,
Religious, exemplary, incorrupt,
And precious jewel of a fellow, Huguet!
If I live long enough—ay, mark my words—
If I live long enough, you'll be a colonel,
Noble, perhaps! One hour, sir, after midnight.

HUGUET. You leave me dumb with gratitude, my lord;
  I'll pick the trustiest [*Aside.*] Marion's house can furnish!

                              [*Exit* HUGUET *after bowing very low.*

RICHELIEU. Good! All favours.
  If François be but bold, and Huguet honest—
  Huguet I half suspect—he bow'd too low—
  'Tis not his way.

JOSEPH. This is the curse, my lord,
  Of your high state—suspicion of all men.

RICHELIEU [*sadly*]. True, true, my leeches bribed to poi-
    soners; pages
  To strangle me in sleep. My very King
  (This brain the unresting loom, from which was woven
  The purple of his greatness) leagued against me.
  Old, childless, friendless, broken—all forsake—
  All, all but—

JOSEPH. What?

RICHELIEU. The indomitable heart
  Of Armand Richelieu!

JOSEPH. And Joseph—

RICHELIEU [*after a pause*]. You—
  Yes, I believe you—yes—for all men fear you,
  And the world loves you not. And I, friend Joseph,
  I am the only man who could, my Joseph,
  Make you a bishop. Come, we'll go to dinner,
  And talk the while of methods to advance
  Our Mother Church. Ah, Joseph—Bishop Joseph!

ACT III

SCENE I. RICHELIEU's *Castle at Ruelle—a Gothic Chamber—moonlight at the window, occasionally obscured.*

RICHELIEU [*discovered seated, reading*]. 'In silence, and at night,
   the conscience feels
  That life should soar to nobler ends than power.'
  So sayest thou, sage and sober moralist!
  Ye safe and formal men,
  Who write the deeds, and with unfeverish hand
  Weigh in nice scales the motives of the great,
  Ye cannot know what ye have never tried!
  History preserves only the fleshless bones
  Of what we are, and by the mocking skull
  The would-be wise pretend to guess the features.
  Still it were sweet—

     Enter FRANÇOIS, *hastily, and in part disguised.*

RICHELIEU [*flinging away the book*]. Philosophy, thou liest!
  Quick—the despatch! Power—empire! Boy—the packet!

FRANÇOIS. Kill me, my lord.   [*Kneels.*

RICHELIEU. They knew thee—they suspected—
  They gave it not—

FRANÇOIS. He gave it—he—the Count
  De Baradas—with his own hand he gave it!

RICHELIEU. Baradas! Joy! Out with it!

FRANÇOIS. Listen,
  And then dismiss me to the headsman.

RICHELIEU. Ha!
  Go on.

FRANÇOIS. They led me to a chamber—there
  Orleans and Baradas, and some half-score,
  Whom I know not, were met—

RICHELIEU. Not more!

FRANÇOIS. But from
  The adjoining chamber broke the din of voices,
  The clattering tread of armed men; at times
  A shriller cry, that yell'd out, 'Death to Richelieu!'

RICHELIEU. Speak not of me: thy country is in danger!
  The adjoining room. So, so—a separate treason!
  The one thy ruin, France; the meaner crime—
  Left to their tools, my murder!

FRANÇOIS. Baradas
  Questioned me close, demurr'd—until at last
  O'erruled by Orleans, gave the packet—told me
  That life and death were in the scroll—this gold—

                                    [*Showing it.*

RICHELIEU. Gold is no proof—

FRANÇOIS. And Orleans promised thousands,
  When Bouillon's trumpets in the streets of Paris
  Rang out shrill answer. Hastening from the house,
  My footstep in the stirrup, Marion stole
  Across the threshold, whispering 'Lose no moment,
  Ere Richelieu have the packet: tell him too—
  Murder is in the winds of night, and Orleans
  Swears ere the dawn the Cardinal shall be clay.'
  She said, and trembling fled within; when, lo!
  A hand of iron griped me; thro' the dark
  Gleam'd the dim shadow of an armed man:
  Ere I could draw the prize was wrested from me,
  And a hoarse voice gasp'd, 'Spy, I spare thee, for
  This steel is virgin to thy lord!' With that
  He vanish'd. Scared and trembling for thy safety,
  I mounted, fled, and kneeling at thy feet
  Implore thee to acquit my faith, but not,
  Like him, to spare my life.

RICHELIEU. Who spake of life?
  I bade thee grasp that treasure as thine honour,
  A jewel worth whole hecatombs of lives!
  Begone—redeem thine honour—back to Marion,
  Or Baradas or Orleans—track the robber—

Regain the packet, or crawl on to age,
Age and grey hairs like mine—and know thou hast lost
That which had made thee great and saved thy country.
See me not till thou'st bought the right to seek me.
Away! [FRANÇOIS *is retiring slowly and drooping—*
    RICHELIEU *looks at him, appears to relent, and pats him*
    kindly on the shoulder and smiles.] Nay, cheer thee—thou
    hast not fail'd yet—
There's no such word as 'fail'!

FRANÇOIS. Bless you, my lord,
    For that one smile!   [*Exit.*

RICHELIEU. He will win it yet.
    François! He's gone. My murder! Marion's warning!
    This bravo's threat! O for the morrow's dawn!
    I'll set my spies to work—I'll make all space
    (As does the sun) an universal eye.
    Huguet shall track, Joseph confess—ha! ha!
    Strange, while I laugh'd I shudder'd, and ev'n now
    Thro' the chill air the beating of my heart
    Sounds like a death-watch by a sick man's pillow.
    If Huguet could deceive me—hoofs without—
    The gates unclose—steps nearer and nearer!

Enter JULIE.

JULIE. Cardinal!
    My father!   [*Falls at his feet.*

RICHELIEU. Julie at this hour! and tears!
    What ails thee?   [*Raises her.*

JULIE. I am safe; and with thee!

RICHELIEU. Safe!

JULIE. Why did I love him, clinging to a breast
    That knows no shelter? Listen—late at noon—
    The marriage day, ev'n then no more a lover,
    He left me coldly. Well, I sought my chamber
    To weep and wonder, but to hope and dream.
    Sudden a mandate from the King—to attend
    Forthwith his pleasure at the Louvre.

RICHELIEU. Ha!
  You did obey the summons; and the King
  Reproach'd your hasty nuptials.

JULIE. Were that all!
  He frown'd and chid; proclaim'd the bond unlawful:
  Bade me not quit my chamber in the palace,
  And there at night—alone—this night—all still—
  He sought my presence—dared—thou read'st the heart,
  Read mine! I cannot speak it!

RICHELIEU. He a king,
  You—woman; well, you yielded!

JULIE. Cardinal,
  Dare you say 'yielded'? Humbled and abash'd,
  He from the chamber crept—this mighty Louis;
  Crept like a baffled felon! Yielded! Ah,
  More royalty in woman's honest heart
  Than dwells within the crowned majesty
  And sceptred anger of a hundred kings!

RICHELIEU. To my breast—close—close!
  The world would never need a Richelieu if
  Men—bearded, mailed men—the lords of earth—
  Resisted flattery, falsehood, avarice, pride,
  As this poor child with the dove's innocent scorn
  Her sex's tempters, vanity and power!
  He left you—well!

JULIE. Then came a sharper trial!
  At the King's suit the Count de Baradas
  Sought me to soothe, to fawn, to flatter; he let fall
  Dark hints of treachery, and stung at last
  By my disdain, the dim and glimmering sense
  Of his cloak'd words broke into bolder light,
  And then—ah, then my haughty spirit fail'd me!
  Then I was weak—wept—oh, such bitter tears!
  For (turn thy face aside, and let me whisper
  The horror to thine ear) then did I learn
  That he—that Adrien—that my husband—knew
  The King's polluting suit, and deemed it honour!
  Then glared upon me all the hideous truth,

Mystery of looks—words—all unravell'd, and
I saw the impostor, where I had loved the god!

RICHELIEU. I think thou wrong'st thy husband.

JULIE. Did you say 'wrong'd' him? Cardinal, my father,
Did you say 'wrong'd'? Prove it, and life shall grow
One prayer for thy reward and his forgiveness.

RICHELIEU. Let me know all.

JULIE. To the despair he caused
The courtier left me; but amid the chaos
Darted one guiding ray—to 'scape—to fly—
Reach Adrien, learn the worst; 'twas then near midnight:
Trembling I left my chamber, sought the queen,
Fell at her feet, reveal'd the unholy peril,
Implored her aid to flee our joint disgrace.
Moved, she embraced and soothed me; nay, preserved;
Her word sufficed to unlock the palace gates:
I hasten'd home, but home was desolate—
No Adrien there! Fearing the worst, I fled
To thee, directed hither. As my wheels
Paused at thy gates, the clang of arms behind—
The ring of hoofs—

RICHELIEU. 'Twas but my guards, fair trembler.
(So Huguet keeps his word, my omens wrong'd him.)
                                    [*Lights a taper.*

JULIE. Oh, in one hour what years of anguish crowd!

RICHELIEU. Nay, there's no danger now. Thou needest rest.
Come, thou shalt lodge beside me. Tush! be cheer'd,
My rosiest Amazon—thou wrong'st thy Theseus.
All will be well—yes, yet all well.
                        [*Exeunt through a side door.*

Enter HUGUET *and* DE MAUPRAT, *in complete armour, his
                    vizor down.*

HUGUET. Not here!   ·

DE MAUPRAT. Oh, I will find him, fear not. Hence, and guard
The galleries where the menials sleep—plant sentries
At every outlet. Chance should throw no shadow
Between the vengeance and the victim. Go!

HUGUET. Will you not
  A second arm?

DE MAUPRAT. To slay one weak old man?
  Away! No lesser wrongs than mine can make
  This murder lawful. Hence!

HUGUET. A short farewell!   [*Exit* HUGUET.

  Re-enter RICHELIEU, *not perceiving* DE MAUPRAT.

RICHELIEU. How heavy is the air!
  The very darkness lends itself to fear,
  To treason—

DE MAUPRAT. And to death!

RICHELIEU. My omens lied not!
  What art thou, wretch?

DE MAUPRAT. Thy doomsman!

RICHELIEU. Ho, my guards!
  Huguet! Montbrassil! Vermont!

DE MAUPRAT. Ay, thy spirits
  Forsake thee, wizard; thy bold men of mail
  Are my confederates. Stir not! but one step,
  And know thy next—thy grave. [*Seizes* RICHELIEU'*s arm.*

RICHELIEU [*shaking him off*]. Thou liest, knave!
  I am old, infirm—most feeble—but thou liest!
  Armand de Richelieu dies not by the hand
  Of man—the stars have said it. Call them all,
  Thy brother butchers! Earth has no such fiend—
  No! as one parricide of his father-land,
  Who dares in Richelieu murder France!

DE MAUPRAT. Thy stars deceive thee, Cardinal.
  In his hot youth a soldier, urged to crime
  Against the State, placed in your hands his life;
  You did not strike the blow—but o'er his head,
  Upon the gossamer thread of your caprice,
  Hovered the axe.
  One day you summoned, mocked him with smooth pardon,
  Showered wealth upon him, bade an angel's face
  Turn earth to paradise—

RICHELIEU. Well!

DE MAUPRAT. Was this mercy?
A Caesar's vengeance? Cardinal, no,
Judas, not Caesar, was the model! You
Saved him from death for shame;
A kind convenience—a Sir Pandarus
To his own bride and the august adulterer!
Then did the first great law of human hearts,
Which with the patriot's, not the rebel's name
Crowned the first Brutus, when the Tarquin fell,
Make misery royal—raise this desperate wretch
Into thy destiny! Expect no mercy.
Behold de Mauprat!   [*Lifts his vizor.*

RICHELIEU. To thy knees, and crawl
For pardon; or, I tell thee, thou shalt live
For such remorse, that, did I hate thee, I
Would bid thee strike, that I might be avenged!
It was to save my Julie from the King,
That in thy valour I forgave thy crime;
It was when thou, the rash and ready tool—
Yea, of that shame thou loath'st—did'st leave thy hearth
To the polluter—in these arms thy bride
Found the protecting shelter thine withheld.
Julie de Mauprat—Julie!

Enter JULIE.

Lo, my witness!

DE MAUPRAT. What marvel's this? I dream. My Julie—thou!

JULIE. Henceforth all bond
Between us twain is broken. Were it not
For this old man, I might in truth have lost
The right—now mine—to scorn thee!

RICHELIEU. So, you hear her?

DE MAUPRAT. Thou with some slander hast her sense infected!

JULIE. No, sir, he did excuse thee in despite
Of all that wears the face of truth. Thy friend,
Thy confidant—familiar—Baradas—
Himself revealed thy baseness.

DE MAUPRAT. Baseness!

RICHELIEU. Ay;
  That thou didst court dishonour.

DE MAUPRAT. Baradas!
  Where is thy thunder, Heaven? Duped! snared! undone!
  Thou—thou could'st not believe him. Thou dost love me.

JULIE [*aside*]. Love you I did: how fondly,
  Woman—if women were my listeners now—
  Alone could tell. For ever fled my dream:
  Farewell—all's over!

RICHELIEU. Nay, my daughter, these
  Are but the blinding mists of day-break love
  Sprung from its very light, and heralding
  A noon of happy summer. Take her hand
  And speak the truth, with which your heart runs over,
  That this Count Judas—this incarnate falsehood—
  Never lied more, than when he told thy Julie
  That Adrien loved her not—except, indeed,
  When he told Adrien Julie could betray him.

JULIE [*embracing* DE MAUPRAT].
  You love me, then—you love me—and they wrong'd you!

DE MAUPRAT. Ah, could'st thou doubt it?

RICHELIEU. Why, the very mole
  Less blind than thou! Baradas loves thy wife;
  Had hoped her hand—aspired to be that cloak
  To the King's will, which to thy bluntness seems
  The Centaur's poisonous robe—hopes even now
  To make thy corpse his footstool to thy bed!
  Where was thy wit, man? Ho, these schemes are glass—
  The very sun shines through them.

DE MAUPRAT. O, my lord,
  Can you forgive me?   [*Kneels.*

RICHELIEU. Ay, and save you!

DE MAUPRAT. Save!
  Terrible word! O save thyself; [*Rises.*] these halls
  Swarm with thy foes; already for thy blood
  Pants thirsty murder!

JULIE. Murder!

PLATE 7

Richelieu. Scharf's drawing of Macready's 1839 production: Richelieu frustrating the assassin. Act Three, scene one.

RICHELIEU. Hush! put by
  The woman. Hush! a shriek, a cry, a breath
  Too loud would startle from its horrent pause
  The swooping death. Go to the door and listen.
  Now for escape!

DE MAUPRAT. None—none! Their blades shall pass
  This heart to thine.

RICHELIEU [*dryly*]. An honourable outwork,
  But much too near the citadel. I think
  That I can trust you now. [*Slowly, and gazing on him.*] Yes,
    I can trust you.
  How many of my troop league with you?

DE MAUPRAT. All!
  We are your troop!

RICHELIEU. And Huguet?

DE MAUPRAT. Is our captain.

RICHELIEU. A retributive Power! This comes of spies!
  All? then the lion's skin too short to-night,
  Now for the fox's!

JULIE. A hoarse, gathering murmur,
  Hurrying and heavy footsteps!

RICHELIEU. Ha, the posterns!

DE MAUPRAT. No egress where no sentry!

RICHELIEU. Follow me—
  I have it—to my chamber—quick! Come, Julie!
  Hush! Mauprat, come!

CONSPIRATORS [*without*]. Death to the Cardinal!

RICHELIEU. Bloodhounds, I laugh at ye! ha! ha! we will
  Baffle them yet. Ha! ha!
                                                        [*Exeunt.*

HUGUET [*without*]. This way—this way!

    Enter HUGUET *and the* CONSPIRATORS *in armour.*

HUGUET. De Mauprat's hand is never slow in battle;
  Strange if it falter now! Ha, gone!

CONSPIRATOR. Perchance
  The fox had crept to rest, and to his lair
  Death, the dark hunter, tracks him.

Enter DE MAUPRAT, *throwing open the doors of the recess, in which is a bed, whereon* RICHELIEU *lies extended.*

DE MAUPRAT. Live the King!
  Richelieu is dead.

HUGUET. You have been long.

DE MAUPRAT. I watch'd him till he slept.
  Heed me. No trace of blood reveals the deed—
  Strangled in sleep. His health hath long been broken—
  Found breathless in his bed. So runs our tale,
  Remember! Back to Paris—Orleans gives
  Five thousand crowns and Baradas a lordship
  To him who first gluts vengeance with the news
  That Richelieu is in heaven! Quick, that all France
  May share your joy.

OMNES. Away, away!

HUGUET. And you?

DE MAUPRAT. Will stay, to crush
  Eager suspicion, to forbid sharp eyes
  To dwell too closely on the clay; prepare
  The rites, and place him on his bier—this my task.
  I leave to you, sirs, the more grateful lot
  Of wealth and honours. Hence!

HUGUET. I shall be noble!

DE MAUPRAT. Away!

CONSPIRATOR. Five thousand crowns!

OMNES. To horse, to horse!

[*Exeunt* CONSPIRATORS.

SCENE II. *Still night. A room in the house of* BARADAS, *lighted, etc.*

Enter ORLEANS, DE BERINGHEN.

DE BERINGHEN. I understand. Mauprat kept guard without;
  Knows nought of the despatch, but heads the troop
  Whom the poor Cardinal fancies his protectors.
  Save us from such protection!

Enter BARADAS.

BARADAS. Julie is fled: the King, whom now I left
  To a most thorny pillow, vows revenge
  On her, on Mauprat and on Richelieu! Well;
  We loyal men anticipate his wish
  Upon the last—and as for Mauprat—[*Showing a writ.*]

DE BERINGHEN. Hum!
  They say the devil invented printing. Faith,
  He has some hand in writing parchment—eh, Count?
  What mischief now?

BARADAS. The King, at Julie's flight
  Enraged, will brook no rival in a subject.
  So on this old offence—the affair of Faviaux—
  Ere Mauprat can tell tales of us, we build
  His bridge between the dungeon and the grave.
  Oh, by the way—I had forgot, your Highness,
  Friend Huguet whisper'd me, 'Beware of Marion:
  I've seen her lurking near the Cardinal's palace.'
  Upon that hint I've found her lodgings elsewhere.

Enter PAGE.

PAGE. My lord, a rude, strange soldier,
  Breathless with haste, demands an audience.

BARADAS. Ay!
  The archers?

PAGE. In the ante-room, my lord,
  As you desired.

BARADAS. 'Tis well—admit the soldier.
                                    [*Exit* PAGE.
  Huguet! I bade him seek me here.

Enter HUGUET.

HUGUET. My lords,
  The deed is done. [*All express delight.*] Now, Count, fulfil
    your word,
  And make me noble!

BARADAS. Richelieu dead? Art sure?
  How died he?

HUGUET. Strangled in his sleep: no blood,
No tell-tale violence.

BARADAS. Strangled? Monstrous villain!
Reward for murder! Ho, there! [*Stamping.*]

Enter CAPTAIN, *with five* ARCHERS.

HUGUET. No, thou durst not!

BARADAS. Seize on the ruffian—bind him—gag him! Off
To the Bastille!

HUGUET. Your word, your plighted faith—

BARADAS. Insolent liar! ho, away!

HUGUET. Nay, Count,
I have that about me which—

BARADAS. Away with him!

[*Exit* HUGUET, *dragged off by* CAPTAIN *and* ARCHERS.

Now then, all's safe; Huguet must die in prison,
So Mauprat: coax or force the meaner crew
To fly the country. Ha, ha! thus, your Highness,
Great men make use of little men.

DE BERINGHEN. My lords,
Since our suspense is ended—you'll excuse me;
'Tis late, and *entre nous* I have not supp'd yet.
I'm one of the new Council now, remember;
I feel the public stirring here already;
A very craving monster. *Au revoir!*

[*Exit* DE BERINGHEN.

ORLEANS. No fear, now Richelieu's dead.

Enter PAGE.

PAGE. A gentleman, my lord, of better mien
Than he who last—

BARADAS. Well, he may enter.

[*Exit* PAGE.

ORLEANS. Who
Can this be?

BARADAS. One of the conspirators:
Mauprat himself, perhaps.

Enter FRANÇOIS.

FRANÇOIS. My lord—

BARADAS. Ha, traitor!
  In Paris still?

FRANÇOIS. The packet—the despatch—
  Some knave play'd spy without, and reft it from me,
  Ere I could draw my sword.

BARADAS. Play'd spy withont!
  Did he wear armour

FRANÇOIS. Ay, from head to heel.

ORLEANS. One of our band. Oh, heavens!

BARADAS. Could it be Mauprat?
  Kept guard at the door—knew nought of the despatch—
  How he—and yet who other?

FRANÇOIS [*aside*]. Ha, de Mauprat!
  The night was dark, his vizor closed.

BARADAS. 'Twas he!
  How could he guess? 'sdeath! if he should betray us.
  His hate to Richelieu dies with Richelieu.
  Find Mauprat; beg, steal, filch, or force it back,
  Or as I live, the halter—

FRANÇOIS. By the morrow
  I will regain it [*Aside.*] and redeem my honour!

                              [*Exit* FRANÇOIS.

ORLEANS. Oh! we are lost—

BARADAS. Not so! But cause on cause
  For Mauprat's seizure—silence—death! Take courage.

ORLEANS. Should it once reach the King, the Cardinal's arm
  Could smite us from the grave.

BARADAS. Sir, think it not!
  I hold de Mauprat in my grasp. To-morrow
  And France is ours!

                              [*Exeunt.*

ACT IV

THIRD DAY

SCENE I. *The Gardens of the Louvre. Iron gates* L.

ORLEANS, DE BERINGHEN, COURTIERS, *etc. meeting* BARADAS.

ORLEANS. How does my brother bear the Cardinal's death?

BARADAS. With grief, when thinking of the toils of State;
With joy, when thinking on the eyes of Julie.
At times he sighs, 'Who now shall govern France?'
Anon exclaims, 'Who now shall baffle Louis?'

Enter LOUIS, CLERMONT, *and* COURTIERS. *They uncover.*

ORLEANS. Now, my liege, now I can embrace a brother.

LOUIS. Dear Gaston, yes. I do believe you love me;
Richelieu denied it—sever'd us too long.
A great man, Gaston! Who shall govern France?

BARADAS. Yourself, my liege. That swart and potent star
Eclipsed your royal orb. He serv'd the country,
But did he serve, or seek to sway the King?

LOUIS. You're right. Then so disloyal in that marriage.
He never loved me!

BARADAS. Oh, most clear! But now
No bar between the lady and your will.
This writ makes all secure: a week or two
In the Bastille will sober Mauprat's love,
And leave him eager to dissolve a Hymen
That brings him such a home.

LOUIS. See to it, Count.

[*Exit* BARADAS.

I'll summon Julie back. Messires, a word with you.
[*Takes aside* 1ST COURTIER *and* DE BERINGHEN, *and
passes, conversing with them, through the gardens,* ORLEANS
and COURTIERS *in the same direction.*

Enter FRANÇOIS.

FRANÇOIS. All search as yet in vain for Mauprat! Not
   At home since yesternoon—a soldier told me
   He saw him pass this way with hasty strides;
   Should he meet Baradas, they'd rend it from him,
   And then—benignant fortune smile upon me;
   I am thy son! if thou desert'st me now,
   Come death and snatch me from disgrace.

Enter DE MAUPRAT.

DE MAUPRAT. Oh, let me——
   Let me but meet him foot to foot—I'll dig
   The Judas from his heart; albeit the King
   Should o'er him cast the purple!

FRANÇOIS. Mauprat! hold:
   Where is the—

DE MAUPRAT. Well! What wouldst thou?

FRANÇOIS. The despatch!
   The packet. Look on me. I serve the Cardinal—
   You know me. Did you not keep guard last night
   By Marion's house?

DE MAUPRAT. I did: no matter now!
   They told me he was here!

FRANÇOIS. O joy! quick—quick—
   The packet thou didst wrest from me?

DE MAUPRAT. The packet?
   What, art thou he I deem'd the Cardinal's spy?

FRANÇOIS. The same—restore it! haste!

DE MAUPRAT. I have it not—

FRANÇOIS. Not!

DE MAUPRAT. Methought it but reveal'd our scheme to
      Richelieu,
   And as we mounted gave it to—

Enter BARADAS.

   Stand back!
   Now, villain, now—I have thee! [*To* FRANÇOIS.] Hence, sir!
      Draw!

FRANÇOIS. Art mad? The King's at hand; leave him to
Richelieu!
Speak—the despatch—to whom—

DE MAUPRAT [*dashing him aside, and rushing to* BARADAS].
Thou triple slanderer!
I'll set my heel upon thy crest!

[*They fight round.*

FRANÇOIS. Fly—fly!
The King!

Enter LOUIS, ORLEANS, DE BERINGHEN, COURTIERS, &c.;
the GUARDS *hastily.*

LOUIS. Swords drawn—before our very palace!
Have our laws died with Richelieu?

BARADAS. Pardon, sire,
My crime but self defence. [*Aside to* LOUIS.] It is de Mauprat.

LOUIS. Dare he thus brave us?

[BARADAS *goes to the* GUARD *and gives the writ.*

DE MAUPRAT. Sire, in the Cardinal's name—

BARADAS. Seize him—disarm—to the Bastille!

[DE MAUPRAT *seized, struggles with the* GUARD, FRANÇOIS
*restlessly endeavouring to pacify and speak to him, when the
gates open.*

Enter four ARQUEBUSSIERS, *three* PAGES, RICHELIEU,
JOSEPH, *six* ARQUEBUSSIERS.

OMNES. The Cardinal!

BARADAS. The dead
Return'd to life!

LOUIS. What, a mock death! This tops
The infinite of insult.

DE MAUPRAT [*breaking from* GUARDS]. Priest and hero,
For you are both—protect the truth!

RICHELIEU [*taking the writ from the* GUARD]. What's this?

DE BERINGHEN. Fact in philosophy. Foxes have got
Nine lives, as well as cats!

BARADAS. Be firm, my liege.

LOUIS. I have assumed the sceptre—I will wield it!

JOSEPH. The tide runs counter—there'll be shipwreck somewhere.

> [BARADAS *and* ORLEANS *keep close to* LOUIS, *whispering and
> prompting him when* RICHELIEU *speaks.*

RICHELIEU. High treason—Faviaux! still that stale pretence!
My liege, bad men (ay, Count, most knavish men)
Abuse your royal goodness. For this soldier,
France hath none braver, and his youth's hot folly,
Misled—(by whom your Highness [*To* ORLEANS.] may
    conjecture)
Is long since cancell'd by a loyal manhood.
I, sire, have pardoned him.

LOUIS. And we do give
Your pardon to the winds. [ORLEANS, BARADAS, *and* COUR-
TIERS *all exult and gather about* LOUIS.] [*To* CAPTAIN.]
Sir, do your duty!

RICHELIEU. What, sire? you do not know—Oh, pardon me
You know not yet that this brave, honest heart
Stood between mine and murder! Sire, for my sake,
For your old servant's sake—undo this wrong.
See, let me rend the sentence.

LOUIS. At your peril!

> [*Takes writ from him and gives it to the* CAPTAIN.

This is too much: Again, sir, do your duty!

> [COURTIERS, *delighted, gather round* LOUIS, *congratulating
> him with eager joy.*

RICHELIEU. Speak not, but go: I would not see young valour
So humbled as grey service!

DE MAUPRAT. Fare you well:
Save Julie, and console her.

FRANÇOIS [*aside to* DE MAUPRAT]. The despatch!
Your fate, foes, life, hang on a word! to whom?

DE MAUPRAT. To Huguet.

FRANÇOIS. Hush!

> [*Exeunt* DE MAUPRAT, CAPTAIN, *and* GUARD.

BARADAS [*aside, going to* FRANÇOIS]. Has he the packet?

FRANÇOIS. He will not reveal. [*Exit* FRANÇOIS.

RICHELIEU [*fiercely*]. Room, my lords, room! The Minister of France
    Can need no intercession with the King.
                                      [*They fall back.*

LOUIS. What means this false report of death, Lord Cardinal?

RICHELIEU. Are you then anger'd, sire, that I live still?

LOUIS. No; but such artifice—

RICHELIEU. Not mine: look elsewhere!
    Louis, my castle swarm'd with the assassins.

BARADAS [*advancing*]. We have punish'd them already. Huguet now
    In the Bastille. Oh, my lord, we were prompt
    To avenge you, we were—

RICHELIEU. We? Ha! ha! you hear,
    My liege! What page, man, in the last Court grammar
    Made you a plural? Count, you have seized the hireling:
    Sire, shall I name the master?

LOUIS. Enough!
    Your Eminence must excuse a longer audience.
    To your own palace: for our conference, this
    Nor place, nor season.

RICHELIEU. Good my liege, for justice
    All place a temple and all season summer!
    Do you deny me justice? [LOUIS *turns from him.*] Saints of Heaven,
    He turns from me! Do you deny me justice?
    For fifteen years, while in these hands dwelt empire,
    The humblest craftsman, the obscurest vassal
    The very leper shrinking from the sun,
    Though loathed by charity, might ask for justice!
    Not with the fawning tone and crawling mien
    Of some I see around you—counts and princes—
    Kneeling for favours; but erect and loud,
    As men who ask man's rights. My liege, my Louis,
    Do you refuse me justice—audience even—
    In the pale presence of the baffled murder?

LOUIS. Lord Cardinal—one by one you have sever'd from me
　　The bonds of human love.
　　You find me now amidst my trustiest friends,
　　My closest kindred; you would tear them from me.
　　They murder you forsooth, since me they love.
　　Enough of plots and treasons for one reign!
　　Home! Home! And sleep away these phantoms!

RICHELIEU. Sire!
　　I—patience, Heaven, sweet Heaven! Sire, from the foot
　　Of that great throne these hands have raised aloft
　　On an Olympus, looking down on mortals
　　And worshipp'd by their awe—before the foot
　　Of that high throne, spurn you the grey-hair'd man
　　Who gave you empire—and now sues for safety?

LOUIS. No: when we see your Eminence in truth
　　At the foot of the throne—we'll listen to you.

　　　　　　　　　　　[*Exit* LOUIS *and* COURTIERS.

ORLEANS. Saved!

BARADAS. For this deep thanks to Julie and to Mauprat!

　　　　　　　　　　　[*Exit* BARADAS *and* ORLEANS.

RICHELIEU. Joseph—did you hear the King?

JOSEPH. I did—there's danger.

RICHELIEU. I will accuse these traitors!
　　François shall witness that de Baradas
　　Gave him the secret missive for de Bouillon,
　　And told him life and death were in the scroll.
　　I will, I will—

JOSEPH. Tush! François is your creature;
　　So they will say, and laugh at you—your witness
　　Must be that same despatch.

RICHELIEU. Away to Marion!

JOSEPH. I have been there; she is seized—removed—imprisoned
　　By the Count's orders.

　　　　　　　　　　Enter JULIE.

JULIE. Heaven, I thank thee!
　　It cannot be, or this all-powerful man
　　Would not stand idly thus.

RICHELIEU. What dost thou here?
  Home!

JULIE. Home! is Adrien there? You're dumb, yet strive
  For words; I see them trembling on your lip,
  But choked by pity. It was truth—all truth!
  Seized—the Bastille, and in your presence too!
  Cardinal, where is Adrien? Think—he saved
  Your life: your name is infamy if wrong
  Should come to his!

RICHELIEU. Be sooth'd, child.

JULIE. Child no more;
  I love, and I am woman!
  Answer me but one word—I am a wife—
  I ask thee for my home, my fate, my all!
  Where is my husband?

RICHELIEU. You ask me for your husband?
  There—where the clouds of heaven look darkest o'er
  The domes of the Bastille!

JULIE. O, mercy, mercy!
  Save him, restore him, father! Art thou not
  The Cardinal-King—the lord of life and death—
  Art thou not Richelieu?

RICHELIEU. Yesterday I was.
  To-day, a very weak old man. To-morrow,
  I know not what.

JULIE [to JOSEPH]. Do you conceive his meaning?
  Alas, I cannot.

JOSEPH. The King is chafed
  Against his servant. Lady, while we speak,
  The lackey of the ante-room is not
  More powerless than the Minister of France.

Enter CLERMONT.

CLERMONT. Pardon, your Eminence—even now I seek
  This lady's home, commanded by the King
  To pray her presence.

JULIE [*clinging to* RICHELIEU]. Think of my dead father!
  Think how, an infant, clinging to your knees,

And looking to your eyes, the wrinkled care
Fled from your brow before the smile of childhood,
Fresh from the dews of heaven! Think of this,
And take me to your breast.

RICHELIEU. To those who sent you!
And say you found the virtue they would slay
Here—couch'd upon this heart, as at an altar,
And shelter'd by the wings of sacred Rome!
Begone!

CLERMONT. My lord, I am your friend and servant—
Misjudge me not; but never yet was Louis
So roused against you: shall I take this answer?
It were to be your foe.

RICHELIEU. All time my foe,
If I, a priest, could cast this holy sorrow
Forth from her last asylum!

CLERMONT. He is lost!   [*Exit* CLERMONT.

RICHELIEU. God help thee, child! She hears not! Look upon
her!

    [JOSEPH *comes down, and receives her in his arms from*
    RICHELIEU.

The storm that rends the oak uproots the flower.
Her father loved me so, and in that age
When friends are brothers! She has been to me
Soother, nurse, plaything, daughter. Are these tears?
Oh, shame, shame! dotage!

JOSEPH. Tears are not for eyes
That rather need the lightning, which can pierce
Through barred gates and triple walls, to smite
Crime where it cowers in secret. The despatch!
Set every spy to work; the morrow's sun
Must see that written treason in your hands,
Or rise upon your ruin.

RICHELIEU. Ay—and close
Upon my corpse! I am not made to live.
Friends, glory, France, all reft from me; my star,
Like some vain holiday mimicry of fire,
Piercing imperial heaven, and falling down

Rayless and blacken'd to the dust—a thing
For all men's feet to trample! Yea, to-morrow
Triumph or death! Look up, child! Lead us, Joseph.

As they are going out, enter BARADAS *and* DE BERINGHEN.

BARADAS. My lord, the King cannot believe your Eminence
    So far forgets your duty and his greatness
    As to resist his mandate! Pray you, madam,
    Obey the King—no cause for fear!

JULIE. My father!

RICHELIEU. She shall not stir!

BARADAS. You are not of her kindred—
    An orphan—

RICHELIEU. And her country is her mother!

BARADAS. The country is the King!

RICHELIEU. Ay, is it so?
    Then wakes the power which in the age of iron
    Burst forth to curb the great, and raise the low.
    Mark, where she stands! Around her form I draw
    The awful circle of our solemn church!
    Set but a foot within that holy ground,
    And on thy head—yea, though it wore a crown—
    I launch the curse of Rome!

BARADAS. I dare not brave you!
    I do but speak the orders of my King.
    The church, your rank, power, very word, my lord,
    Suffice you for resistance: blame yourself
    If it should cost you power!

RICHELIEU. That my stake. Ah,
    Dark gamester, what is thine? Look to it well!
    Lose not a trick. By this same hour to-morrow
    Thou shalt have France, or I thy head!

BARADAS [*aside to* DE BERINGHEN]. He cannot
    Have the despatch?

DE BERINGHEN. No: were it so, your stake
    Were lost already.

JOSEPH [*aside*]. Patience is your game:
    Reflect you have not the despatch.

RICHELIEU. Monk, monk!
  Leave patience to the saints—for I am human!

BARADAS [*aside*]. He wanders!

RICHELIEU. So cling close unto my breast;
  Did not thy father die for France, poor orphan?
  I am very feeble. Of little use it seems to any now.
  Well, well—we will go home.

BARADAS. In sooth, my lord,
  You do need rest—the burthens of the state
  O'ertask your health!

RICHELIEU [*to* JOSEPH]. See, I'm patient.

BARADAS [*aside*]. His mind
  And life are breaking fast!

RICHELIEU [*overhearing him*]. Irreverent ribbald!
  If so, beware the falling ruins! Hark!
  I tell thee, scorner of these whitening hairs,
  When this snow melteth there shall come a flood!
  Avaunt! my name is Richelieu—I defy thee!
  Walk blindfold on; behind thee stalks the headsman.
  Ha, ha, how pale he is!

  [*Falls back in* JOSEPH'*s arms. Tableau.*

ACT V

SCENE I. *The Bastille—a corridor—in the background the door of one of the condemned cells.*

Enter JOSEPH *and* GAOLER, *with lamp.*

GAOLER. Stay, father, I will call the governor.

[*Exit* GAOLER.

JOSEPH. He has it, then—this Huguet; so we learn
  From François. Humph! Now if I can but gain
  One moment's access, all is ours! The Cardinal
  Trembles 'tween life and death. His life is power:
  Smite one—slay both. No Æsculapian drugs,
  By learned quacks baptized with Latin jargon,
  E'er bore the healing which that scrap of parchment
  Will medicine to Ambition's flagging heart.
  France shall be saved—and Joseph be a bishop!

Enter GOVERNOR *and* GAOLER, *with lamp.*

GOVERNOR. Father, you wish to see the prisoners Huguet
  And the young knight de Mauprat?

JOSEPH. So my office,
  And the Lord Cardinal's order warrant, son.

GOVERNOR. Father, it cannot be: Count Baradas
  Has summoned to the Louvre Sieur de Mauprat.

JOSEPH. Well, well! But Huguet—

GOVERNOR. Dies at noon.

JOSEPH. At noon!
  No moment to delay the pious rites
  Which fit the soul for death—quick, quick—admit me!

GOVERNOR. You cannot enter, monk. Such are my orders.

JOSEPH. Orders! vain man, the Cardinal still is Minister.
  His orders crush all others.

GOVERNOR. I'll not be menaced, priest! Besides, the Cardinal
  Is dying and disgraced—all Paris knows it.   [*Bell tolls.*
  You hear the prisoner's knell.

JOSEPH. I do beseech you—
  The Cardinal is not dying. But one moment,
  And—hist, five thousand pistoles!

GOVERNOR. How! a bribe,
  And to a soldier, grey with years of honour?
  Begone!

JOSEPH. Ten thousand—twenty!

GOVERNOR. Gaoler—put
  This monk without our walls.

JOSEPH. By those grey hairs,
  Yea, by this badge [*Touching the Cross of St. Louis worn by the*
      GOVERNOR.] the guerdon of your valour;
  By all your toils, hard days and sleepless nights
  Borne in your country's service,
  Let me but see the prisoner!

GOVERNOR. No!

JOSEPH. He hath
  Secrets of state—papers in which—

GOVERNOR. I know,
  Such was his message to Count Baradas.

JOSEPH. What can be done? Distraction! Richelieu yet
  Must—what? I know not—thought, nerve, strength, forsake
      me.
  Dare you refuse the Church her holiest rights?

GOVERNOR. I refuse nothing—I obey my orders—

JOSEPH. And sell your country to her parricides!
  Oh, tremble yet! Richelieu—

GOVERNOR. Begone!

JOSEPH. Undone!   [*Exit* JOSEPH.

GOVERNOR. A most audacious shaveling, interdicted
  Above all others by the Count—

GAOLER. Oh, by the way, sir, that troublesome young fellow,
    Who calls himself the prisoner Huguet's son,
    Is here again—implores, weeps, raves, to see him.

GOVERNOR. Poor youth, I pity him!

Enter DE BERINGHEN, *followed by* FRANÇOIS, *lighted in by a*
    TURNKEY, *who retires.*

DE BERINGHEN [*to* FRANÇOIS]. Now prithee, friend,
    Let go my cloak; you really discompose me.

FRANÇOIS. No, they will drive me hence: my father! Oh!
    Let me but see him once—but once—one moment!

DE BERINGHEN [*to* GOVERNOR]. Your servant, Messire—
    this poor rascal, Huguet,
    Has sent to see the Count de Baradas
    Upon state secrets that afflict his conscience.
    The Count can't leave His Majesty an instant:
    I am his proxy.

GOVERNOR. The Count's word is law.
    Again, young scapegrace! How com'st thou admitted?

DE BERINGHEN. Oh: a most filial fellow: Huguet's son.
    I found him whimpering in the court below.
    I pray his leave to say good bye to father,
    Before that very long unpleasant journey
    Father's about to take.

GOVERNOR. The Count's
    Commands are strict. No one must visit Huguet
    Without his passport.

DE BERINGHEN. Here it is. Pshaw! Nonsense!
    I'll be your surety. See, my Cerberus,
    He is no Hercules!

    [GOVERNOR *motions* GAOLER, *who unlocks door of cell and*
    gives his lamp to DE BERINGHEN.

GOVERNOR. Well, you're responsible.
    Stand there, friend. If when you come out, my lord,
    The youth slip in, 'tis your fault.

DE BERINGHEN. So it is!

    [*Exit through the door of the cell.*

GOVERNOR. Be calm, my lad. Don't fret so. I had once
    A father too! I'll not be hard upon you,
    And so stand close. I must not see you enter:
    You understand.
    Come, we'll go our rounds;
    I'll give you just one quarter of an hour;
    And if my lord leave first, make my excuse.
    Yet stay, the gallery's long and dark; no sentry
    Until he reach the grate below. He'd best
    Wait till I come. If he should lose the way,
    We may not be in call.

FRANÇOIS. I'll tell him, sir—

                      [Exeunt GOVERNOR and GAOLER.

    He's a wise son that knoweth his own father.
    I've forged a precious one! So far, so well!
    Alas, what then? This wretch has sent to Baradas—
    Will sell the scroll to ransom life. Oh, Heaven!
    On what a thread hangs hope! *[Loud murmurs.]* *[Listens at the
        door.]* Loud words—a cry; *[Struggling behind—looks through
        the key-hole.]*
    They struggle! Ho, the packet! *[Tries to open the door.]* Lost!
    He has it—
    The courtier has it—Huguet, spite his chains,
    Grapples! well done! Now, now! *[Draws back.]* The gallery's
        long,
    And this is left us!

       [Drawing his dagger, and standing behind the door.

    Re-enter DE BERINGHEN, *waving the packet.*

DE BERINGHEN. Victory!

FRANÇOIS. Yield it, robber.
    Yield it—or die!   *[A short struggle.*

DE BERINGHEN. Off! ho, there!

FRANÇOIS *[grappling with him].* Death or honour!

                        [Exeunt, struggling.

SCENE II. *The King's closet at the Louvre. A suite of rooms in perspective,* R. *side. Doors* R. *and* L. *of flat, doors* R. *and* L. *of scene.*

Enter ORLEANS *and* BARADAS.

BARADAS. All smiles! the Cardinal's swoon of yesterday
    Heralds his death to-day.
    All smiles! and yet, should this accurs'd de Mauprat
    Have given our packet to another. 'Sdeath,
    I dare not think of it!

ORLEANS. You've sent to search him?

BARADAS. Sent, sir, to search? That hireling hands may find
    Upon him, naked, with its broken seal,
    That scroll whose every word is death! No—no—
    These hands alone must clutch that awful secret.
    I dare not leave the palace, night or day,
    While Richelieu lives—his minions—creatures—spies—
    Not one must reach the King!

ORLEANS. What hast thou done?

BARADAS. Summon'd de Mauprat hither.

ORLEANS. Could this Huguet,
    Who pray'd thy presence with so fierce a fervour,
    Have thieved the scroll?

BARADAS. Huguet was housed with us,
    The very moment we dismiss'd the courier,
    It cannot be! A stale trick for reprieve.
    But to make sure, I've sent our trustiest friend
    To see and sift him. Hist! here comes the King.

Enter four PAGES, LOUIS, *and* COURTIERS.

How fare you, sire?

LOUIS. In the same mind; I have
    Decided. Yes, he would forbid your presence,
    My brother, yours, my friend, then Julie too;
    Thwarts, braves, defies. [*Suddenly turning to* BARADAS.]
      We make you Minister.
    Gaston, for you—the baton of our armies.
    You love me, do you not?

ORLEANS. Oh, love you, sire?
[*Aside.*] Never so much as now.

BARADAS. May I deserve
Your trust [*Aside.*] until you sign your abdication!
My liege, but one way left to daunt de Mauprat
And Julie to divorce. We must prepare
The death-writ; what though sign'd and seal'd? we can
Withhold the enforcement.

LOUIS. Ah, you may prepare it;
We need not urge it to effect.

BARADAS. Exactly!
No haste, my liege. [*Going to table, aside.*] He may live one
hour longer.

Enter CLERMONT.

CLERMONT. The lady Julie, sire, implores an audience.

LOUIS. Aha, repentant of her folly! Well,
Admit her.

[*Exit* CLERMONT.

BARADAS. Sire, she comes for Mauprat's pardon,
And the conditions—

LOUIS. You are Minister,
We leave to you our answer.

Enter the CAPTAIN *of the* ARCHERS, *and whispers* BARADAS.

CAPTAIN. The Chevalier
De Mauprat waits below.

BARADAS [*aside*]. Now the despatch!   [*Exit with* OFFICER.

Enter JULIE.

JULIE. My liege, you sent for me. I come where grief
Should come when guiltless, while the name of King
Is holy on the earth! Here, at the feet
Of power, I kneel for mercy.

LOUIS. Mercy, Julie,   [*Raises her.*
Is an affair of state. The Cardinal should
In this be your interpreter.

JULIE. Alas!
I know not if that mighty spirit now

Stoops to the things of earth. Nay, while I speak,
Perchance he hears the orphan by the throne
Where kings themselves need pardon. O, my liege,
Be father to the fatherless; in you
Dwells my last hope!

Enter BARADAS.

BARADAS [*aside*]. He has not the despatch;
Smiled, while we search'd, and braves me. Oh!

LOUIS [*gently*]. What would'st thou?

JULIE. A single life. You reign o'er millions. What
Is one man's life to you? And yet to me
'Tis France, 'tis earth, 'tis everything! A life,
A human life—my husband's.   [*Kneels.*

LOUIS [*aside*]. Speak to her.

[LOUIS *walks up stage and joins* COURTIERS.

I am not marble—give her hope or—

BARADAS. Madam,   [*She rises.*
Vex not your King, whose heart, too soft for justice,
Leaves to his ministers that solemn charge.

JULIE. You were his friend.

BARADAS. I was before I loved thee.

JULIE. Loved me!

BARADAS. Hush Julie: could'st thou misinterpret
My acts, thoughts, motives, nay, my very words,
Here—in this palace?

JULIE. Now I know I'm mad,
Even that memory fail'd me.

BARADAS. I am young,
Well-born and brave as Mauprat: for thy sake
I peril what he has not: fortune, power;
All to great souls most dazzling. I alone
Can save thee from yon tyrant, now my puppet!
Be mine: annul the mockery of this marriage,
And on the day I clasp thee to my breast
De Mauprat shall be free.

JULIE. Thou durst not speak
  Thus in his ear. [*Pointing to* LOUIS.] Thou double traitor—
    tremble!
  I will unmask thee.

BARADAS. I will say thou ravest,
  And see this scroll; its letters shall be blood!
  Go to the King, count with me word for word;
  And while you pray the life, I write the sentence!

                    [BARADAS *goes to table, and signs the warrant.*

JULIE. Stay, stay. [*Rushing to* LOUIS, *who comes from the circle.*]
    You have a kind and princely heart,
  Though sometimes it is silent: you were born
  To power—it has not flush'd you into madness,
  As it doth meaner men. Banish my husband,
  Dissolve our marriage, cast me to that grave
  Of human ties, where hearts congeal to ice
  In the dark convent's everlasting winter.
  (Surely enough for justice—hate—revenge)
  But spare this life, thus lonely, scathed, and bloomless;
  And when thou stand'st for judgment on thine own,
  The deed shall shine beside thee as an angel.

LOUIS [*much affected*]. Go, go to Baradas: annul thy marriage,
  And—

JULIE [*anxiously, and watching his countenance*]. Be his bride!

LOUIS. Yes.

      [LOUIS *goes up the stage and passes through the suite of rooms,
      in evident confusion.*

JULIE. O thou sea of shame,
  And not one star!

BARADAS. Well, thy election, Julie,
  This hand—his grave!

JULIE. His grave! and I—

BARADAS. Can save him.
  Swear to be mine.

JULIE. That were a bitterer death!
  Avaunt, thou tempter! I did ask his life,
  A boon, and not the barter of dishonour.

The heart can break, and scorn you: wreak your malice;
Adrien and I will leave you this sad earth,
And pass together hand in hand to Heaven!

BARADAS. You have decided. [*Withdraws for a moment, and
        returns.*] Listen to me, lady;
I am no base intriguer. I adored thee
From the first glance of those inspiring eyes;
With thee entwined ambition, hope, the future.
I will not lose thee! I can place thee nearest—
Ay, to the throne—nay, on the throne, perchance;
My star is at its zenith. Look upon me;
Hast thou decided?

JULIE. No, no; you can see
How weak I am: be human, sir—one moment.

BARADAS [*stamping his foot.* DE MAUPRAT *appears guarded*].
Behold thy husband! Shall he pass to death,
And know thou could'st have saved him?

JULIE. Adrien, speak,
But say you wish to live! if not your wife,
Your slave—do with me as you will.

DE MAUPRAT. Oh, think, my Julie,
Life at the best is short, but love immortal!

BARADAS [*taking* JULIE's *hand*]. Ah, loveliest—

JULIE. Go. That touch has made me iron.
We have decided—death!

BARADAS. Now, say to whom
Thou gavest the packet, and thou yet shalt live.

DE MAUPRAT. I'll tell thee nothing!

BARADAS. Hark—the rack!

DE MAUPRAT. Thy penance
For ever, wretch! What rack is like the conscience?

BARADAS [*giving the writ to the* OFFICER]. Hence, to the
        headsman.

[*The* HUISSIER *announces* 'His Eminence the Cardinal Duke
de Richelieu'. *The doors are thrown open.*

Enter RICHELIEU, *attended by* GENTLEMEN, PAGES, *etc.*, *pale,
feeble, and leaning on* JOSEPH, *followed by three* SECRETARIES
OF STATE, *attended by* SUB-SECRETARIES *with papers, etc.*

JULIE [*rushing to* RICHELIEU]. You live—you live—and
    Adrien shall not die!

RICHELIEU. Not if an old man's prayers, himself near death,
    Can aught avail thee, daughter! Count, you now
    Hold what I held on earth: one boon, my lord,
    This soldier's life.

BARADAS. The stake my head! You said it.
    I cannot lose one trick. Remove your prisoner.

JULIE. No! No!

Enter LOUIS, COURTIERS *and* PAGES, *from the rooms beyond.*

RICHELIEU [*to* OFFICER]. Stay, sir, one moment. My good
    liege,
    Your worn-out servant, willing, sire, to spare you
    Some pain of conscience, would forestall your wishes.
    I do resign my office.   [*All start.*

DE MAUPRAT. You?

JULIE. All's over!

RICHELIEU. My end draws near. These sad ones, sire, I love
    them.
    I do not ask his life; but suffer justice
    To halt, until I can dismiss his soul,
    Charged with an old man's blessing.

LOUIS. Surely!

BARADAS. Sire—

LOUIS. Silence—small favour to a dying servant.

RICHELIEU. You would consign your armies to the baton
    Of your most honour'd brother. Sire, so be it!
    Your Minister, the Count de Baradas;
    A most sagacious choice! Your Secretaries
    Of State attend me, sire, to render up
    The ledgers of a realm. I do beseech you,
    Suffer these noble gentlemen to learn
    The nature of the glorious task that awaits them,
    Here, in my presence.

LOUIS. You say well, my lord.

RICHELIEU. I—I—faint! Air—air—[JOSEPH *and a* GENTLE-
MAN *assist him to a chair.*]
I thank you.
Draw near, my children. Approach, sirs!

BARADAS. He's too weak to question,
Nay, scarce to speak; all's safe.

> [JULIE *kneeling beside the* CARDINAL; *the* OFFICER OF
> THE GUARD *behind* DE MAUPRAT; JOSEPH *near* RICHE-
> LIEU, *watching* LOUIS; LOUIS *seated,* R.C.; BARADAS *at the
> back of* LOUIS' *chair, anxious and disturbed;* ORLEANS *at a
> greater distance, careless and triumphant. As each* SECRETARY
> *advances in his turn, he takes the portfolios from the* SUB-
> SECRETARIES.

FIRST SECRETARY [*kneeling*]. The affairs of Portugal,
Most urgent, sire. [*Gives a paper.*] One short month since the
Duke
Braganza was a rebel.

LOUIS. And is still!

FIRST SECRETARY. No, sire, he has succeeded! He is now
Crown'd King of Portugal—craves instant succour
Against the arms of Spain.

LOUIS. We will not grant it
Against his lawful king. Eh, Count?

BARADAS. No, sire.

FIRST SECRETARY. But Spain's your deadliest foe; whatever
Can weaken Spain must strengthen France. The Cardinal
Would send the succours—[*Solemnly.*] balance, sire, of
Europe! [*Gives another paper.*

LOUIS. The Cardinal! balance! We'll consider—
Eh, Count?

BARADAS. Yes, sire. [*To* FIRST SECRETARY.] Fall back.

FIRST SECRETARY [*rises*]. But—

BARADAS. Oh fall back, sir!

> [FIRST SECRETARY *bows and retires.*

JOSEPH. Humph!

SECOND SECRETARY [*advances and kneels*]. The affairs of
England, sire, most urgent. [*Gives paper.*] Charles
The First has lost a battle that decides
One half his realm—craves moneys, sire, and succour.

LOUIS. He shall have both. Eh, Baradas?

BARADAS. Yes, sire.
[*Aside.*]   Oh, that despatch; my veins are fire!

RICHELIEU [*feebly, but with great distinctness*]. My liege—
Forgive me. Charles's cause is lost. A man
Named Cromwell risen, a great man—your succour
Would fail, your loans be squander'd. Pause—reflect.

LOUIS. Reflect—eh, Baradas?

BARADAS. Reflect, sire.

JOSEPH. Humph!

LOUIS [*aside*]. I half repent! No successor to Richelieu!
Round me thrones totter, dynasties dissolve—
The soil he guards alone escapes the earthquake.

JOSEPH. Our star not yet eclipsed! You mark the King?
Oh, had we the despatch!

Enter GENTLEMAN, *whispers to* JOSEPH, *who exits hastily.*

RICHELIEU. Ah, Joseph! Child!
Would I could help thee!

BARADAS [*to* SECRETARY]. Sir, fall back!

SECOND SECRETARY [*rises*]. But—

BARADAS. Pshaw, sir!

[SECOND SECRETARY *bows and retires.*

THIRD SECRETARY [*mysteriously; kneels*]. The secret Corres-
pondence, sire, most urgent—
Accounts of spies—deserters—heretics—
Assassins—poisoners—schemes against yourself!

[*Offers a number of documents.*

LOUIS. Myself! most urgent!

[*Looking on the documents.*

Re-enter JOSEPH *with* FRANÇOIS, *whose pourpoint is streaked with blood.* FRANÇOIS *passes behind the* CARDINAL'S ATTEN-DANTS, *and, sheltered by them from the sight of* BARADAS, *etc., falls at* RICHELIEU'S *feet.*

FRANÇOIS. My lord!
  I have not fail'd.   [*Gives the packet.*

RICHELIEU. Hush!   [*Looking at the contents.*

THIRD SECRETARY [*to* LOUIS]. Sire, the Spaniards
  Have reinforced their army on the frontiers.
  The Duc de Bouillon—

RICHELIEU. Hold! In this department—
  A paper—here, sire—read yourself, then take
  The Count's advice in't.

Enter DE BERINGHEN *hastily, and draws aside* BARADAS.

BARADAS [*bursting from* DE BERINGHEN]. What, and reft it from thee!
  Ha, hold!

JOSEPH. Fall back, son, it is your turn now!

LOUIS [*reading*]. To
  Bouillon—and sign'd Orleans!
  Baradas, too! League with our foes of Spain!
  Lead our Italian armies—what, to Paris!
  Capture the King—my health require repose—
  Make me subscribe my proper abdication—
  Orleans, my brother, Regent! Saints of Heaven!
  These are the men I loved!   [RICHELIEU *falls back.*

JOSEPH. See to the Cardinal.

BARADAS. He's dying, and I shall yet dupe the King.

LOUIS [*rushing to* RICHELIEU]. Richelieu! Lord Cardinal! 'Tis
  I resign!
  Reign thou!

JOSEPH. Alas, too late! he faints!

LOUIS. Reign, Richelieu!

RICHELIEU [*feebly*]. With absolute power?

LOUIS. Most absolute! Oh, live,
  If not for me—for France!

PLATE 8

Richelieu. Scharf's drawing of Macready's 1839 production: 'There, at my feet!'
Act Five, scene two.

RICHELIEU. France!

LOUIS. Oh, this treason!
The army—Orleans—Bouillon! Heavens, the Spaniard!
Where will they be next week?

RICHELIEU [*starting up, seizing the paper and throwing it on the ground*]. There, at my feet!
[*To* FIRST *and* SECOND SECRETARIES.]
Ere the clock strike the envoys have their answer.

[*Exeunt* SECRETARIES.

[*To* THIRD SECRETARY, *with a ring*.] This to De Chavigny
—he knows the rest.
No need of parchment here. He must not halt
For sleep—for food. In my name—mine—he will
Arrest the Duc de Bouillon at the head
Of his army! [*Exit* THIRD SECRETARY.] Ho, there! Count
de Baradas,
Thou hast lost the stake. Away with him! [BARADAS *passes out guarded*.] Ha, ha!
[*Snatching* DE MAUPRAT's *death-warrant from the* OFFICER *as he passes*.] See here de Mauprat's death-writ, Julie!
Parchment for battledores! Embrace your husband!
At last the old man blesses you!

JULIE. Oh, joy!
You are saved—you live—I hold you in these arms!

DE MAUPRAT. Never to part!

JULIE. No—never, Adrien—never!

LOUIS [*peevishly*]. One moment makes a startling cure, Lord Cardinal.

RICHELIEU. Ay, sire; for in one moment there did pass
Into this wither'd frame the might of France.
My own dear France, I have thee yet—I have saved thee!
I clasp thee still! It was thy voice that called me
Back from the tomb. What mistress like our country?

LOUIS. For Mauprat's pardon—well, but Julie, Richelieu;
  Leave me one thing to love.

RICHELIEU. A subject's luxury!
  Yet, if you must love something, sire—love me!

LOUIS [*smiling in spite of himself*]. Fair proxy for a fresh young
  demoiselle!

RICHELIEU. Your heart speaks for my clients. Kneel, my
    children—
  And thank your King.

> [RICHELIEU *passes up the stage; all the Court bow.*

JULIE. Ah, tears like these, my liege,
  Are dews that mount to Heaven.

LOUIS. Rise—rise—be happy.

RICHELIEU [*beckons to* DE BERINGHEN]. De Beringhen!

DE BERINGHEN [*falteringly*]. My lord—you are—most happily
    —recover'd.

RICHELIEU. But you are pale, dear Beringhen: this air
  Suits not your delicate frame—I long have thought so.
  Sleep not another night in Paris. Go,
  Or else your precious life may be in danger.
  Leave France, dear Beringhen!

DE BERINGHEN. St. Denis travelled without his head:
  I'm luckier than St. Denis.   [*Exit.*

RICHELIEU [*to* ORLEANS]. For you, repentance—absence—
    and confession!

> [*Exit* ORLEANS.

[*To* FRANÇOIS.] Never say fail again. Brave boy! [*To*
  JOSEPH.] He'll be
  A bishop first.

JOSEPH. Ah, Cardinal—

RICHELIEU. Ah, Joseph—
  [*To* LOUIS, *as* DE MAUPRAT *and* JULIE *converse apart.*] See,
    my liege—see through plots and counterplots—
  Through gain and loss—through glory and disgrace—
  Along the plains, where passionate discord rears
  Eternal Babel—still the holy stream
  Of human happiness glides on!

LOUIS. And must we
  Thank for that also—our Prime Minister?

RICHELIEU. No—let us own it—there is one above who
  Sways the harmonious mystery of the world
  Ev'n better than prime ministers!

CURTAIN

APPENDIX

MACREADY'S RICHELIEU

SINCE the effect of *Richelieu* in the theatre was so largely dependent upon the playing of the central character, and since it is helpful to an understanding of nineteenth-century drama to gain some idea of what a great actor like Macready could do with a role like Richelieu, I have thought it useful to append to the play a few contemporary comments on Macready's interpretation of the part, including Westland Marston's extended description of his performance of it.

Macready prepared for Richelieu with his usual thoroughness, reading books on French history sent him by Bulwer-Lytton, studying Alfred de Vigny's historical novel *Cinq Mars* for an understanding of Richelieu's character, and ten days before the first night calling on de Vigny, who was visiting London, for further advice. De Vigny's views turned Macready away from the kind of interpretation Bulwer-Lytton wanted and kept suggesting in letters to his actor: a clever, powerful, high-spirited Cardinal with a streak of broad humour. He never got it from Macready, who apart from de Vigny was temperamentally unsuited to this kind of comic interpretation and saw Richelieu as dignified and intellectual, with a dry rather than a coarse wit. A selection from Macready's diary throws light on some of his difficulties with the part and with the author:

February 20, 1839. Gave my attention to the consideration of the character of Richelieu, which Bulwer has made particularly difficult by its inconsistency; he has made him resort to low jest, which outrages one's notions of the ideal of Cardinal Richelieu, with all his vanity, and suppleness, and craft.

February 22. Gave my attention to the inquiry as to the possibility of reconciling the character which Bulwer has drawn under the name of Cardinal Richelieu with the original, from which it so entirely differs. Was not much cheered by the result of my investigation and experiment. . . . Resumed *Richelieu*, which I must *fabricate*. [On February 21 Macready had called on de Vigny.]

February 25. Bulwer wrote to me about Richelieu, and satisfied me on the justice of his draught of the character from the evidence that history has given us. *Allons donc à la gloire.*

March 7. Acted Cardinal Richelieu very indifferently; lost my self-possession, and was obliged to use too much effort; it did not satisfy me at all, there were no artist-like touches in the play. How can a person get up such a play and do justice at the same time to such a character? It is not possible. Was called for and very enthusiastically received; gave out the play for every night. . . . The success of the play seemed to be unequivocal.

March 8. Went to the theatre, where I cut the play with the performers and expressed myself much obliged by their zeal and industry. When we had separated, Bulwer came and altered all that we had arranged —annoying and disconcerting me very much. I struggled for the omission of several passages, but he was triumphant and therefore no longer *so docile.*

March 11. Attended the rehearsal for the cutting of the play. Acted the part of Richelieu very indifferently; was quite out of temper with myself and everybody else. Was called for and well received—much better than I deserved. Business with Bulwer, making further alterations.

March 13. Two long notes from Bulwer—with more last words and a lengthy criticism on some points of my performance, in which he wishes me to substitute coarse and vulgar attempt at low farcical point in one instance, and melodramatic rant in another for the more delicate shadings of character that I endeavour to give. . . . I am *sure* his taste is not be to depended on.

March 14. Acted the part very fairly. The Queen was in the theatre.[1]

Macready must have been pleased to receive a letter from de Vigny, who had seen *Richelieu* and told him that 'si jamais on perdait en France le portrait du Cardinal de Richelieu, il faudrait passer la mer et venir vous voir, car vous lui ressemblez autant que la nature l'a rendu possible'.[2] As for his performance, Lady Pollock remembered the way he delivered the curse:

While he threatened the offender with the curse of Rome, his attitude assumed a dignity which was that of an immense power; his voice then gave out great peals of thunder. It was no wonder that his enemies shrank away in terror, and that he stood alone in a charmed circle; no wonder that this man should have held the destinies of Europe within his grasp.[3]

A writer for the *Dublin Commercial Journal and Family Herald* compared Macready with Phelps and Calcraft:

Macready brought out boldly much of the attractive heroism of the Cardinal; even in the most ludicrous tricks there was a dignity—the dignity of strong purpose and steady aim—elevating the funniest 'dodge' above the level of farce. Calcraft, our late manager here, was still more 'heroic' than Macready; though, inconsistently, the comedy parts sank too low in burlesque. Phelps presents us chiefly 'the fox', the cunning old Cardinal: one does not reverence him much, but you consistently admire

---

[1] *Diaries,* i. 497–503.
[2] Lady Pollock, *Macready As I Knew Him* (1884), pp. 128–9.
[3] Ibid., pp. 127–8.

his amazing intellectual ability. With Phelps the 'hero' is weakened; the man of *mind*, of intellectual subtlety, comes out characteristically and consistently.[1]

The fullest description of Macready's Richelieu comes from Westland Marston. Marston, the respected author of legitimate tragedies and dramas such as *The Patrician's Daughter, Strathmore,* and *Anne Blake,* also published in 1888 the best account we have of the acting of his time in *Our Recent Actors.* His memory of certain passages spoken on the stage differs slightly from the text in this volume, but since he was primarily recalling the first night of *Richelieu* later changes in the acting version had not yet been made.

In March, 1839, I fought my way with another young enthusiast to the pit door of old Covent Garden, on the first night of Bulwer's 'Richelieu'. What a human sea it was, and how lit up by expectation, that surged and roared for two hours against that grim, all-ignoring barrier! But its stubborn resistance, and the dense pressure which, at last, almost wedged out the breath of every unit in the crowd, gave an almost stern delight, a zest of contest for a prize, of which the lounger in a reserved box or seat has no conception. . . .

Suppose, then, the thronged house hushed, the curtain raised, the gay scene of the conspirators and gamesters going forward beneath the roof of Marion de L'Orme. Even amidst the interest of this opening scene, the thought of the house escapes to Macready. Will he be discovered with all the insignia of his rank and power? Will he be closeted with Louis, or giving audience to a spy? Will his manner have the pride of the churchman, or the smoothness of the diplomatist? The first scene is over, and we have our answer.

Macready, as the Cardinal, enters, followed by the Capuchin Joseph, and the coming revelation—signal, and in some respects new—of the actor's powers, is at once foreshadowed by his appearance. How full of individuality are the whitening hair, the face sharpened to the utmost expression of subtlety and keenness, the gait somewhat loose with age, but now quick and impulsive, now slow or suddenly arrested, which seems to give a rhythm to the workings of his brain—to his swift, contemptuous penetration of the schemes against him, on the one hand, or, on the other, to his suspense, his caution, or his rapid decision. Soon followed one of those 'ultra-colloquialisms' which, when first reading the play, he had thought incompatible with Richelieu's dignity, but which, with the dry, caustic humour he gave them, were not only very telling, but seemed natural reliefs to the strained minds of the statesmen. 'Orleans heads the traitors,' says Father Joseph; 'A very wooden head, then!' exclaims

[1] W. M. Phelps and J. Forbes-Robertson, *The Life and Life Work of Samuel Phelps* (1886), p. 218. In 1858 William Bernard in the *Weekly Dispatch* noted of Phelps's Richelieu that 'he makes him strong—almost robust—and very pleasantly conscious—a man who sees his game clearly, and who enjoys whilst he plays it. . . . He owes much to his humour, which comes out at all points—strong, sharp, and salient—enforced by his massive style and sonorous delivery.' Ibid., p. 229.

Richelieu; and, though the sarcasm was threadbare, it had all the force of novelty and wit. Examples of the actor's unrivalled power in familiar touches abounded through the performance. His manner of exposing the strategy of Baradas to De Mauprat blended with contempt an easy penetration, an amused superiority, which was quite irresistible—

'Where was thy wit, man? Why, these schemes are glass;
The very sun shines through them!'

Early in the play were encountered some of those dazzling, but rather forced metaphors, which the author's better judgement afterwards cancelled. Amongst these, however, was one which, as Macready gave it, drew great applause—

'From rank showers of blood
And the red light of blazing roofs you build
The rainbow, Glory, and to shuddering Conscience
Cry—Lo the Bridge to Heaven!'

Soon after this example of poetic pyrotechnics, Richelieu charges De Mauprat with fraud. The indignant young man advances upon his accuser with an air and tone of menace when, it will be remembered, Huguet, one of Richelieu's guard, who waits armed behind a screen to intercept any possible violence to the Cardinal, raises his carbine to fire. Richelieu, with a wave of his hand, exclaims—

'Not so quick, friend Huguet;
The Sieur de Mauprat is a patient man,
And he can wait.'

The dry, parenthetical utterance of these words, with the careless accompanying gesture, had in them the secret of a terrible humour and the proud assurance of a 'charmed life' that no succeeding impersonator of Richelieu has discovered. The whole of this first act is rich in these contrasts of feeling and character in which Macready delighted. The fervour with which, after finding De Mauprat worthy of his confidence, he asserts the justice of his rule, had in it all the passionate earnestness and dignity of a man who, long scornfully silent under misconception and calumny, at last relieves his heart and vindicates himself to an honourable judge. Soon follow the lines in which, under pretence of dismissing De Mauprat to death, he causes him to be conducted to the presence of the woman for whose sake he has braved it, this act, of course, implying Richelieu's consent to their union. 'Huguet,' says he,

'To the tapestry chamber
Conduct your prisoner. (*To De Mauprat*) You will there behold
Your executioner. Your doom be private,
And Heaven have mercy on you.'

The rapidity and sternness with which these lines were pronounced, as if only by hurry and a forced overdoing of severity he could prevent himself from giving way to the benevolent enjoyment of his device, showed one of the actor's characteristic merits—his just perception of the right note of feeling even to a semi-tone. The look of sly and eager anticipation with which he followed De Mauprat, as he retired, had in it all the *bonhomie* which Bulwer, rather than history, ascribes to the Cardinal, and the zest with which the sceptical mind of a diplomatist may for once taste pure pleasure in bestowing it.

In the second act, the contrast between Richelieu's usual scornful levity in dismissing the schemes of his enemies, and the composed but grave attention which denotes real peril, was strikingly marked. With rapid step and hands carelessly knotted behind him, he had paced to and fro, listening to Father Joseph's rumours of plots, either with incredulity or with smiling confidence in his power to baffle them. But when Marion de L'Orme entered with news of the conspiracy headed by Orleans, every trace of caustic mirth or easy, exulting contempt at once disappeared. Of course, all actors would at this point have made a transition of manner; few, indeed, would have made it with Macready's arresting effect. He questioned Marion in tones the lowness of which expressed the intensity of his interest. His trust in his own resources was still unshaken, but he felt that they might now be taxed to the utmost. The breathless audience listened to the words, 'Now there is danger,' as if each man had his personal stake in the crisis. It was felt that if Richelieu could apprehend danger, there must be danger indeed. The tone of gay flattery to Marion de L'Orme at that moment of peril—

'What an eye you have,
And what a smile, child, . . . 'tis well I'm old,'

and the ringing exhortation to the page François, when sent on his critical mission—'Never say fail again; that's my young hero!''—were brilliant examples of the actor's variety and quick self-adaptation to his instruments. The fascination which illustrious old age has for the young and aspiring could never have been better justified than by Macready's cheery laugh and the look, full of kind encouragement, with which he uttered these words to the page. I have before me a copy of 'Richelieu,' marked from the tragedian's acting copy of 1843 (four years after the production of the play), in which the compliment to Marion de L'Orme is cut out—a mistake, I think, for his delivery of it was certainly one of the brilliant facets which his genius exhibited in this manifold character.

So full of fine variety was his delineation at the close of this second act, as almost to atone for its want of incident. His momentary distrust of Huguet, as he noted 'he bowed too low' (some Richelieus have so over-emphasized this trait of minute observation, that they should, to be consistent, have discharged the guardsman on the spot); his brief lapse into melancholy, as he reflects on the snares that beset his bed and board, and his friendlessness at the height of power; his proud rally from these thoughts to faith in the indomitable heart of Armand Richelieu, and the quaint *bonhomie*, strangely compounded of archness, good-feeling, and dissimulation, with which he addresses Joseph—all received their just proportion. Each trait harmonized with and flowed into its fellow. There was no hard line to divide, or even to distinguish, diplomacy from sentiment, or sentiment from humour, but a living man in whom all these qualities naturally blended.

The third act gave scope for the excellences already noted, and with yet higher development. The Richelieu who awaited, with breathless eagerness, from François the proofs that should convict Baradas; the Richelieu who, minutely observant, even in his excitement, could pause to note the small number of the conspirators—who, learning that the despatch which would have secured his triumph had been wrested from François, one moment sternly warned him to see his face no more till he had regained it, and the next, relented into smiling encouragement— 'Away! Nay, cheer thee; thou hast not failed yet; there's no such word as fail!'—was, in these various aspects, not only the same man, but so happy in expressing them that each new trait seemed to complete and enhance the others.

This third act contains the scene in which De Mauprat, duped into the belief that Richelieu, in causing him to marry, has made him a mere pander to the King, seeks the Cardinal's life in revenge. When Macready, personating the old and feeble man, encountered, without recognizing him, the armed figure whose very vizor was closed, and learned his deadly purpose, nothing could be more intense and life-like, nothing freer from inflation, than the glorious arrogance with which he exclaimed—

> 'Earth has no such fiend—
> No—as one parricide of his fatherland,
> Who dares in Richelieu murder France!'

It should be noticed here that Macready carefully avoided the error into which some of his successors have fallen—that of over-idealizing Richelieu by delivering his patriotic speeches in such tones of exalted devotion as might have befitted Brutus. Macready's apostrophes to France, on the contrary, were given with a self-reference, sometimes fierce in its expression, that showed her triumphs to be part of his own. Her glory was the object of his ambition, for it made him great, while the thought that he laboured for her consciously ennobled his ambition. Thus his haughty boast in the foregoing lines was no expression of abstract and ideal patriotism (of which the Cardinal was incapable), but of passionate and practical sympathy. How fine, again, when De Mauprat, still unrecognized, betrays that the dishonour put upon him has made him an avenger, were the sudden gleam in the eye, and the hushed tones of relief which showed the statesman's sleepless vigilance at that crisis—

> 'I breathe—he is no hireling!'

When, in this scene, De Mauprat reveals himself, and Richelieu arrests his dagger by showing the arts that have deluded him, the actor produced one of those massive effects which make the fortune of a drama. His commanding air, as he motioned the dupe to his knees; his rapid energy, blent with a look of lofty pity, as he proclaimed that, instead of planning dishonour for De Mauprat's wife, he had saved her from it; his indignant look as, with tottering but imperial step, he hurried to the door, and, summoning Julie, confronted De Mauprat with the living proof of his truth,—all this caused an excitement which I have rarely seen equalled. It was surpassed, however, by that supreme moment, in the fourth act, when the might of Rome seemed to pass into the sick man's frame, as he sprang up, dominant and terrible, to shield Julie from the King with the aegis of the Church. At this point the vast pit seemed to rock with enthusiasm, as it volleyed its admiration in rounds of thunder. In the final scene of the fifth act, where the Cardinal, apparently on the verge of death, attends the King to resign, and to 'render up the ledgers of a realm,' words can but faintly hint the excellence of the performance. How touching was the proud humility of the weak old man as he relinquished, seemingly for ever, the splendid cares of State; how arresting the sight of him as, supported in his chair, his face now grew vacant, as if through the feebleness of nature, now resumed a gleam of intelligence, which at times contracted into pain, as he gathered the policy of his rivals—a policy fatal to France! One noted the uneasy movements of the head, the restless play of the wan fingers, though the lips were silent, till at last the mind fairly struggled awhile through its eclipse, as, in a loud whisper, he warned the King his succours would be wasted upon England. Then came the moment when, recovering the despatch which convicted his foes of treason, he caused it to be handed to the King, and sank supine with the effort. Slowly and intermittently consciousness returned, as Louis thrice implored him to resume his sway over France. So naturally marked were the fluctuations between life and death, so subtly graduated (though comprised within a few moments) were the signs of his recovery, that the house utterly forgot its almost incredible quickness when, in answer to the King's apprehensive cry as to the traitors—

'Where will they be next week?'

Richelieu springs up resuscitated, and exclaims—

'There, at my feet!'

But it was not alone by acting, however fine, in this particular situation, that his triumph over probability was obtained. He had from the beginning of the play so seized every opportunity of identifying his fortunes and life with the greatness of his country, that when the King besought him to live for France, it seemed quite in the order of nature such an adjuration should have magical force. Who can forget the electrical rapidity and decision with which Macready, as the revivified minister, cut the Gordian knots of policy? The waiting envoys shall now have their answer. Chavigny, halting not for sleep or food, shall 'arrest the Duc de Bouillon at the head of his armies.' Baradas, who has 'lost the stake,' shall pay it and go out under guard. The barque of the State, but now tossing and plunging, a waif on the bosom of chance, has once more a helmsman, knows a course, and through the sheer waters, bears on. And interests, dear though minor, confess the sudden change. Poor Julie, lately trembling for her husband's life, sees in his death writ but 'parchment for battledores.' The epicure and traitor, De Beringhen, scents danger to his dear health in the air of

Paris. On François, the page who regained the despatch, again falls the smile that cheered and now rewards him. 'He will never say fail again!' Ah, Joseph, trusty Joseph, bishop to be! The minister's policy—prompt action, daring, and retribution—the old man's fondness, the cynic's raillery, the patron's indulgence and humour,—this brilliant *résumé* of Richelieu throughout the play was so given, flash after flash, that its various effects seemed simultaneous rather than successive. Thus it was an audience dazzled, almost bewildered by the brilliancy of the achievement, that, on the instant fall of the curtain, burst into a roar of admiration that, wild, craving, unappeasable, pursued like a sea, the retreating actor, and swept him back to the front. . . .

It may be added that in the foregoing description of 'Richelieu,' he has relied not only on his first youthful impressions, but upon confirmatory ones drawn from many later representations.

I may perhaps here be permitted to observe, for the benefit of younger playgoers, that one of the best 'Richelieus' since Macready's, and the one that most recalls him, is that of Mr. Edwin Booth. He gives the character a more modern air—a greater air of *everyday* realism—than did Macready, though realism of a certain kind was one of the latter's strongest features. That Mr. Booth, however, is not deficient in the more heroic aspects of the character, all who remember his splendid acting at the end of the fourth act can abundantly testify.[1]

[1] *Our Recent Actors,* i. 37–53.

PRINTED IN GREAT BRITAIN
AT THE UNIVERSITY PRESS, OXFORD
BY VIVIAN RIDLER
PRINTER TO THE UNIVERSITY

DATE DUE	